Hair of the Dog

Richard Stivers

Hair of the Dog
Irish Drinking and Its American Stereotype

NEW REVISED EDITION

CONTINUUM

New York   London

2000

The Continuum International Publishing Group Inc
370 Lexington Avenue, New York, NY 10017

The Continuum International Publishing Group Ltd
Wellington House, 125 Strand, London WC2R OBB

Printed in the United States of America

Library of Congress Cataloging-in-Publication Data

Stivers, Richard.
    Hair of the dog: Irish drinking and its American stereotype /
Richard Stivers.— New rev. ed.
        p. cm.
    Includes bibliographical references and index.
    ISBN 0-8264-1218-1 (pbk.)
    1. Drinking of alcoholic beverages--Ireland. 2. Drinking of
alcoholic beverages—United States. 3. Drinking customs—
Ireland. 4. Drinking customs— United States. I. Title.

HV5449.I7 S74 2000
362.292'09415--dc21

                                                    99-055966

CONTENTS

FOREWORD

When I first opened this remarkable book and discovered its patently erroneous thesis, I said to myself, "Stivers will never convince me that he's right." When I finished it, I set the book down gently and said, "He's convinced me: he's right!"

The Irish in Ireland are not heavy drinkers. Indeed, they have the lowest per capital alcohol consumption of any people in Europe. If they appear to be heavy drinkers the reason is that they spend so much time in pubs. However, if one keeps an eye on the "pints" on the table, one notes that not many of them are emptied before the publican announces, with obvious reluctance, "Time!" The Irish like their "jar" and some of them consume too many jars. But most of them do not. As a people they empty a lot less jars than do the French or the Italians or anyone else in Europe.

Where does the stereotype come from? I asked one of my students who had made this discovery on her own. She looked at me in surprise, "Why, from the English, of course. Whom else!"

The Irish reputation for drinking in this country comes in part from the early alcohol research at Yale which compared the Irish with the Jews and Italians in New Haven—and left out people with Slavic and Scandinavian backgrounds who make the Irish look like teetotalers.

However, this research merely seemed to confirm the stereotype which came from the British Isles (and justified the still extant English conviction that the Irish are an uncivilized and inferior people). It is the genius (and I use the word literally) of Richard Stivers's work that he shows how an oppressed people converted a negative stereotype into a positive one, with substantial harm to themselves in the process.

Thus, *Hair of the Dog* is a pioneer work in research on alcohol abuse, stereotyping, and Ireland. It demolishes myths in all three areas, no small feat for a sociological monograph.

It also made my blood boil. It still does.

Andrew M. Greeley
Professor of Social Science
The University of Chicago
May 1999

1

INTRODUCTION

> For Tyrone, as for his sons, so also for the race: drink has been
> their curse. It is the principal fact of Irishness that they have not
> been able to shake. A good deal of competent inquiry has still not
> produced much understanding of the Irish tendency to alcohol
> addiction.
>
> Nathan Glazer and
> Daniel Patrick Moynihan,
> *Beyond the Melting Pot*

Over the years the Irish reputation for drinking, if not the drinking itself, has been prodigious. We all know about St. Patrick's
Day in America, a national drinking celebration matched only by
New Year's Eve. The association between the Irish and alcohol is
indeed firm. The Irish-American sociologist Andrew Greeley writes
"that a weakness for 'The Creature' seems to be one of the few
residues of the Irish heritage that still survives."[1]

In 1944 the distinguished social psychologist Robert Bales completed a study of Jewish and Irish drinking norms as part of a more
general attempt to develop a theory of alcohol addiction. What
caught his attention about Jewish-Americans and Irish-Americans
was the unusually low rate of alcoholism among the former and the
exceedingly high rate among the latter. Bales and other students of
drink have all come to the conclusion that among white American
ethnic groups, no group has given evidence of a greater tendency
toward drunkenness and alcoholism than the Irish.[2] In an exhaus-
tive analysis of comparative ethnic rates of alcoholism around the
turn of the century, Robin Room concludes that "not only Irish bachelors, but also Irish spinsters, wives, and husbands show higher
rates than their equivalent status in other ethnic identifications."[3]
The fact of longstanding differences in alcoholism among ethnic
groups "cannot be adequately explained in terms of characteristics

of a particular sex, marital status, or social level, and suggests that an adequate explanation must take account of characteristics of ethnic groups as wholes, that is, of cultural factors."[4] Excellent advice. It would appear from qualitative observations and quantitative indices of alcoholism that the tendency of Irish-Americans toward alcoholism was present throughout much of the nineteenth century and into the early twentieth century.

Historians have also indicated that the Irish possessed more than a mere reputation for drink; they were stereotyped as drunkards. Could there be a connection, then, between the high rate of alcoholism on the one hand and the stereotype of the Irish-American as drunkard on the other? This possibility will be explored in the following pages.

Definitions and Indices of Drunkenness and Alcoholism

Any attempt to get beyond a mere operational definition of alcoholism is fraught with difficulty. In addition, there are problems centering around the process of being labeled "alcoholic" because the term involves both behavioral and status considerations. However, part of the problem is mitigated by using indices of alcoholism that do not involve the formal label of alcoholism. Thus arrest rates of drunkenness, rates of alcohol consumption, and rates of death from liver cirrhosis are indirect attempts to measure the incidence of alcoholism in a population because the behavior contained in these indicators is not necessarily that of an alcoholic. It is merely asserted that alcoholism varies directly with the extent of these indicators.

Other indicators, such as rates of death from alcoholism (acute or chronic) and rates of first admission to hospitals for alcoholic psychoses, are direct measures. But because these indicators involve physical deterioration, the problem of labeling is less severe than for many other forms of deviant behavior.

With this in mind we might accept with reservation Keller's definition of alcoholism as "a chronic disease manifested by repeated implicative drinking as to cause injury to the drinker's health or to his social or economic functioning."[5] In this definition "implicative" drinking refers to drinking that appears marked or suspicious to the public health worker, social worker, or doctor who must decide in individual cases whether the pattern, circumstances, and frequency of one's drinking warrant the label "alcoholic." Keller prefers implicative to "excessive" (often used in definitions of alcoholism) because excessive implies that a quantitative criterion underlying a conception of alcoholism exists. On the other hand implicative readily admits to subjectivity and hence suggests caution to the investigation of alcoholism.

There are a number of qualifications to be made, however. If we translate implicative to mean "addictive," separate (at least theoretically) addictive drinking from that injurious to health, qualify injury with "serious," and eliminate "social or economic functioning," we have the following definition: Alcoholism is a chronic disease manifested by psychological addition and/or resulting in serious injury to the drinker's health. This definition is much more restrictive than Keller's and, furthermore, draws our attention to the two major forms of alcoholism: alcohol addiction and chronic alcoholism.[7] Alcohol addiction has been defined as

> The inability or failure of the individual to stop drinking, once he has started, until he reaches a state of more or less complete physical exhaustion, or to refrain from starting again after a period of abstinence, in spite of all outer social pressure, apparent considerations of utility, inner guilt feelings and remorse, and in spite of all resolutions or attempts on his part to stop or refrain.[8]

The alcohol addict appears to have a compulsion to drink until a state of extreme intoxication is reached and to continue such behavior.

Chronic alcoholism has been defined as a disease whereby the drinker suffers pronounced physiological deterioration from the continued excessive use of alcohol. The term "chronic alcoholic" refers to patients suffering from polyneuropathy, pellagra, amblyopia,

Korsakoff's disease, delirium tremens, and other diseases and symptoms.[9] From this list, it is evident that the overlap between the designations "alcohol addiction" and "chronic alcoholism" is great indeed. The critical difference between chronic alcoholism and alcohol addiction appears to be that the diagnosis alcohol addiction refers primarily to the subjective psychological condition of the patient, whereas the chronic alcoholism label refers to the objective physical state of the patient. Although chronic alcoholism itself does not constitute a compulsive or rigid habit and uncontrollable craving for alcohol, a person suffering from chronic alcoholism may also be addicted to alcohol. Chronic alcoholism may appear without addiction and vice versa, or they may occur together. However, in the course of diagnosing and treating alcoholism, the distinction between chronic alcoholism and alcohol addiction is difficult to come by.

What we term alcoholism today was often referred to as "habitual drunkenness" in the past. If habitual drunkenness was not addictive, it more often than not led to chronic alcoholism over a long period of time. What we are investigating then is the Irish-American propensity for habitual drunkenness, whether addictive or not. The phrase "hard drinking" will be used to depict drinking in Ireland during the nineteenth and twentieth centuries; today hard drinking is more euphemistically called "habitual social drinking" by social scientists. It does not necessarily imply drunkenness, habitual or otherwise.

Irish-American Rates of Alcoholism

Before the turn of the century, statistical evidence of drinking disorders in Europe and the United States consisted largely of arrests and convictions for drunkenness. From sheriffs' returns of criminal convictions in New York City for the year 1859, Robert Ernst presented data on convictions for drunkenness and disorderly conduct for various ethnic groups.[10] The Irish outranked other nationalities in the rate of this offense: 3,234 arrests per 100,000 population versus 1,548 arrests for those born in Scotland, their nearest competitors.

Contemporary observers and historians unanimously confirm the Irish-American tendency to be arrested and convicted for drunkenness during the second half of the nineteenth and early twentieth centuries. Oscar Handlin, for instance, had this to say about he drinking of Irish immigrants in mid-nineteenth-century Boston:

> In 1846 there were 850 liquor dealers in the city, but by 1849 fully 1,200 groggeries were open for the flourishing trade. A survey by the marshal in November, 1851, showed the great majority of these to be Irish. . . . Frequently drunk and often jailed for inebriety, the Irish "arrested and turned back" the short-lived temperance movement which had made promising progress up to their arrival. Other nationalities, particularly the Germans, were also fond of the glass, but neither their habits nor environment encouraged or even tolerated excessive drinking.[11]

A series of monographs prepared by Robert Woods and his associates at the South End House in Boston around the turn of the century contains some important observations about Irish drinking.[12] In describing the Cambridegport district in Boston, Woods and Kennedy observed:

> This race [the Irish], with one-third of the population, furnishes about one-half of the crime, the major portion of which, however, consists of drunkenness. In unarrested crimes, the Irish again furnish the bulk of the drinking and fighting. . . .[13]

During the same period, in a study of social and economic conditions among various ethnic groups in Boston, Frederick Bushee observed that "not only is there more drunkenness among the Irish than among other nationalities, but drunkenness and crimes resulting directly therefrom constitute a large proportion of the Irish misdemeanors."[14]

Room analyzed vital statistics on alcoholism and liver diseases from the 1890 census. Both Irish men and women have higher rates of alcoholism than other ethnic groups. Quite startling, however, is the Irish women's rate of liver disease, which exceeds that of Irish men.[15] However, as we shall soon discover, all other indices of alcoholism point to a higher rate of alcoholism for Irish men than for Irish women. Yet I do not mean to underestimate the significance of this evidence. Although my study centers mainly on Irish-American male drinking, the problem of female drinking is dealt with briefly in Chapter 7 and more extensively in Chapter 8.

Maurice F. Parmelee presented data about males arrested and indicted for drunkenness in Boston courts in 1909.[16] The sample was chosen within a set time period to minimize the confounding effect of rearrest. The original data included only the proportion of inebriates that each ethnic group had contributed to the total sample of 616, which was then contrasted with the proportion of each ethnic group in the total male population of Boston.

The Irish, Belgian, Scottish, and Canadian groups showed a greater proportion of inebriates than one would expect from their respective contributions to Boston's total population. The Irish, however, showed the outstanding difference in this respect.

As we move further into the twentieth century, a wider range of statistical data on drinking exists. Instead of only arrests for drunkenness, data on alcoholic psychoses, acute alcoholism, and liver cirrhosis become available. Adolph Meyer made a study of admissions to the Worcester (Massachusetts) State Hospital in 1900.[17] He discovered the following percentages of alcoholic cases among the total male admissions for each ethnic group: Irish, 37; German, English, Scotch, 20–25; Massachusetts-born, 14; old Massachusetts stock, 9; Jews, .5. We do not know, however, what the rates of alcoholism were for each group. Taking the total admissions for each group, the Irish showed the highest percentage of alcoholic cases; but whether they also possessed the highest rate of alcoholism is indeterminable from the data Meyer has given.

Subsequently Meyer reported on a 1908 study of admissions to Manhattan State Hospital in New York.[18] His findings included the following percentages of alcoholic cases among the total admissions for each ethnic group: Irish, 27.7; Germans, Native Americans, English, 11.4–11.9; Italians, 7.7; Jews, .3. The picture is more complete in this study because we learn that out of a total of 1,403 admissions, there were 182 diagnoses of alcoholic psychosis and that 62 per cent of these cases were Irish. Yet the Irish accounted for only

29 per cent of all psychoses considered. Meyer also mentioned that Jews were responsible for 22 per cent of all psychoses but that they had less than 2 per cent of the alcoholic psychoses. He concluded that "social habits of the group" brought about this unusual difference between the Irish and the Jews.[19]

World War I military data provide information about ethnic drinking problems. From the millions of those who were drafted or volunteered between 1917 and 1919, almost 70,000 were labeled "neuropsychiatric" and were classified further by type of disorder and ethnic background. Bales noted that for these data alcoholism meant a "chronic intoxication" so serious that the individual was considered completely unfit to serve in the military. He also suggested that such individuals can rightly be designated "chronic alcoholics."[20] Among the total number of Irish neuropsychiatric cases, 11.2 per cent ere diagnosed as alcoholic. This percentage was more than twice as high as that of the next highest ethnic group, the Scotch.

Horatio Pollock has presented statistics on first admissions for alcoholism by ethnic group that cover the entire United States with the exception of Montana.[21] The designation "alcoholic first admissions" refers to alcoholic psychoses such as alcoholic paranoid states and alcoholic hallicinosis. The rate of alcoholism per 100,000 population for each ethnic group has been computed on the total number of that nativity group in America in 1920, but the rates have not been standardized for age. Pollock's statistics include the following rates: Irish, 17.1; Austrian, 14.0; Canadian, 7.6; Polish, 6.3; Scotch, 6.0; all other foreign born, 5.8.

In the same manner, Pollock computed rates of alcoholic first admissions to New York state hospitals in 1930, once again unstandardized for age: Irish, 22.8; Polish, 12.0; Austrian, 9.8; Canadian, 8.8; Hungarian, 8.5; Scandinavian, 7.3; all other foreign born, 5.2.[22]

Benjamin Malzberg formulated standardized rates of alcoholic psychosis (by sex and age) per 100,000 population for New York state mental hospitals in the period 1929–31. For men and women over age 25, the rate of alcoholic psychosis among the Irish was about three times higher than that of the next highest ethnic group.[23]

Donald Glad reported on a study of those rejected in Boston by the military for neuropsychiatric reasons during 1941–42.[24] The rates of rejection for chronic alcoholism as a percentage of total neuro-psychiatric rejections by ethnicity were as follows: Irish, 3.0; Negro, 2.2; Italian, 1.2; Portuguese, .6; Jewish, .2; Chinese, 0. Glad noted that the Chinese and Italian communities proved as dense as those of the Irish and that the Irish and Italian communities were of similar socioeconomic status, thus making comparisons among these groups possible.

Malzberg studied admissions for alcoholic psychoses to mental hospitals in New York state for 1943–44.[25] Malzberg remarked that the Irish-born comprised only 8 per cent of the entire white foreign-born population of the state, yet they accounted for 24 per cent of the alcoholic psychoses among foreign-born groups. The only other ethnic groups to stand out on such comparisons were distinguished in the opposite direction by having a lower percentage of foreign-born alcoholic psychoses than would be expected from their respective contributions to the population.[26]

In the 1950s Robert Straus and Raymond McCarthy reported on a study of 444 "homeless men" in New York's Bowery district.[27] Using subjective criteria, interviewers rated homeless men as "non-drinker," "moderate," "heavy controlled," or "heavy uncontrolled." Seventy-one per cent of all the men were judged to be heavy drinkers, and 43 per cent were regarded as heavy uncontrolled drinkers. Within the category of heavy controlled drinkers, 76 per cent reported difficulties resulting from their drinking, and for heavy uncontrolled drinkers 97 per cent mentioned such problems. In the sample of 444, 119 were black and 325 were white, of whom 44 per cent were first- or second-generation Irish. The implication was that those of Irish descent far outstripped other white ethnic groups in problems of vagrancy and heavy drinking, even though the Irish, Jews, and Italians have all been heavily represented in the population of New York.

Another 1950s study, by Jerome Skolnick, included data on arrests for drunkenness by ethnic groups in New Haven, Connecticut.[28] Irish-Americans had the highest percentage of arrests among ten ethnic groups. But since they were also inordinately represented in the New Haven population, they ended up ranking fifth among the ethnic groups for arrest for drunkenness. However, because of acute methodological problems, the results remain inconclusive.[29]

Several studies of American drinking patterns undertaken in the 1960s indicated that those of Irish national identity ranked high among ethnic groups with respect to heavy drinking.[30] In a study conducted in the late 1970s, Greeley, McCready, and Theisen concluded that "*among drinkers,* the Irish are no more likely to have a serious alcohol problem than are many other groups in U.S. society."[31] But because the Irish are the group least likely to abstain from the use of alcoholic beverages, their overall incidence of drinking problems remained somewhat high. The Irish, however, appear to have lost their preeminent position. Moreover, one begins to wonder how much ethnic identification means today in the United States, the "new ethnicity" notwithstanding, especially among those of the third and fourth generations. Therefore my analysis is restricted to the 100 years from 1850 to 1950—the heyday of Irish-American drinking. (In the afterword I consider what part ethnic consciousness plays in contemporary Irish-American drinking.)

It does not matter all that much if the Irish were the most outstanding ethnic group in respect to alcoholism. Prejudice against the Irish may have inflated somewhat the statistics on their drinking problems. That they stood comparatively high is enough. Further, whether Irish males exceeded Irish females and bachelors outdistanced married men is of much less consequence. Assuredly the most important fact is that the Irish acquired the reputation for drink, yes, were even stereotyped as drunkards. "Irish" and "drunkard" became synonymous in nineteenth-century America.

My contention is that early in the nineteenth century a negative identity of drunkard was foisted upon the Irish by a cultural stereotype and related institutionalized practices. But, later in the nineteenth century, Irish-American culture and the stereotype of the Irishman in the larger American culture converged around a more positive image of the Irish drunk—the "happy drunk," a stage caricature Irishman. What had been a negative identity—drunkard—was transformed into a positive group identity. To develop my thesis, it is necessary to study the sociohistorical setting of drinking in Ireland before analyzing the plight of Irish immigrants in America.

2

Drinking Customs in
Great Britain and Ireland

Small as is the place which this fact [the widespread distillation
and sale of gin] occupies in English history, it was probably, if we
consider all the consequences that have flowed from it, the most
momentous in that of the eighteenth century—incomparably
more so than any event in the purely political or military annals
of the country. The fatal passion for drink was at once, and irrev-
ocably, planted in the nation.

> W.E.H. Lecky, quoted in
> *The Age of the Chartists*

"The consumption of strong drink was connected with every
phase of life from apprenticeship (indeed from birth and baptism) to death and burial," wrote M. Dorothy George in her description
of eighteenth-century London.[1] John Dunlop, the nineteenth-century
Scottish temperance reformer, noted that "on the whole, in Great
Britain, we seem to be behind the more refined nations of modern
Europe, in our progress of getting quit of these barbarisms; and there
appears no parallel elsewhere to the multiplicity and complication of
our drinking usages."[2]

Evidence form several sources indicates a common pattern of
drinking in England, Ireland, and Scotland in the eighteenth and
early nineteenth centuries.[3] Subsequently, from the mid-nineteenth
century through the early twentieth century, there was a significant
differentiation of Irish from English and Scottish drinking practices.
It is only by examining the similarity of their earlier drinking customs, however, that we can fully appreciate later changes in Irish
drinking patterns. Moreover, by comparing drinking customs in the
three countries we can better isolate the crucial variables that
worked to perpetuate hard drinking in Irish society from the mid-
nineteenth century onward.

Communal Drinking Customs

In considering drinking in the three countries, we will rely heavily on Bales's study for Irish usages, comparing them with similar usages in English and Scottish cultures. Bales documented a large number of convivial and utilitarian drinking usages in Irish society. For example, convivial drinking was an integral part of the celebration following the baptism of a child.[4] Dunlop spoke of the custom of drinking to another's health as the foundation of the drinking which followed the English baptism ceremonies.[5] A witness before a British parliamentary committee investigating drunkenness described the rules and etiquette of drinking after baptism in Scotland.[6]

Prominent in Irish culture was a tendency to substitute drinking for eating, which, Bales hypothesized, was the consequence of guilt feelings about eating brought on by poverty, famines, and the Catholic church's encouragement of fasting. Children were socialized into making drink the psychological equivalent to food.[7] In a description of English drinking attitudes and behavior, Harrison observes that "in matter of diet, the most striking apparent irrationality of the Victorian poor was the fact that, when they were forced by poverty to choose between food and alcoholic drink, they tended to choose drink."[8]

Adults also rewarded Irish children for good behavior by giving them hard drink, often in the form of punch. In line with this, Bales discusses "the haphazard discipline of children in the Irish culture" and paternal severity.[9] Children were given tastes of illicitly distilled whiskey frequently enough to make them appear "dull and stupid" to some observers. In the same vein, Engels noted that some "hard-drinking parents" among the English working class gave alcoholic beverages, especially brandy, to their children; moreover, some mothers gave "spirits" to children in arms when frequenting a public house.[10] A visitor to William IV's coronation in 1830 described the celebration afterward, at which not only men and women but also boys and girls appeared "in a condition of beastly drunkenness" and were staggering and passing out.[11] The situation was similar in Scotland. An 1830 newspaper description of a large feast given by a prominent person included scenes in which children became totally confused and passed out from the effects of drink.

Noted too were the tolerance of the Irish clergy for drinking, and heavy drinking at that; the occasional, if not frequent, drunkenness of the clergy; and the inebriety of the laity on pilgrimages.[12] Longmate described the attitudes of English and Scottish Christians toward drink and some related drinking customs:

> When the teetotal movement began no major Christian body regarded alcohol as sinful, although some small sects, and some individual Quakers, abstained from it as a luxury. Drinking customs were common in many churches, especially among the Presbyterian clergy. . . . A Presbyterian minister "sealed the gown" with drink when he graduated, and was "fined" a bottle of wine on moving into a new manse, publishing a sermon, or even, in Edinburgh, preaching in his own pulpit during May. The Presbyterian General Assembly traditionally sent the magistrates two guineas to toast its deliberations, while the beadle who carried the kirk Bible back to the manse after service was automatically rewarded with a glass of spirits.[13]

Harrison remarked that "the drunken clergyman and minister were quite familiar figures in Victorian England." And religious festivals were often the scene of considerable inebriety.[14]

The convivial use of alcohol after a marriage ceremony was widespread in Ireland.[15] this was also common in England and Scotland and, indeed, in many other countries both then and now. This usage is aptly illustrated by the fact that when a member of a British trade was to be married, the rank and file would surround the house of the bridegroom on the day of the wedding and create an awful din with "old pots, kettles, and horns" until the bridegroom gave them "socket money" for drink or until they were routed by the police.[16]

Convivial drinking in Ireland was also the context for the expression of political aggression against the English, whose rule the Irish detested. As Bales has noted:

> It was always comparatively easy for an Irish patriot, sincere or otherwise, to gain an audience at the gatherings of the boys, or men, at some hidden "shibbeen" and stir up a minor rebellion.[17]

While whiskey drinking served as a primary means of political resistance against England and the political integration of all Irishmen, the English situation was not too dissimilar:

> Beer was an evocative drink which aroused plenty of patriotic sentiments—John Bull with his foaming tankard, agricultural prosperity, contempt for the wine-drinking, frog-eating French and so on. . . . Pubs were the natural focus for late-Victorian imperialism; a lot of them helped to recruit the armed services, and one Thamesside publican in London gained a great deal of favour with government during the Crimean War by going about in a small steamer with music playing and streamers flying, recruiting sailors for the Fleet. Sydney Smith asked rhetorically in 1823: "What two ideas are more inseparable than Beer and Britannia!"[18]

The economic sphere of life was not free from the influence of drink either. Many bargains and transactions were agreed on over a few drinks, especially at fairs and markets. Farmers sometimes repaid their neighbors' assistance at harvest time in whiskey. Irish fairs were often the scene of drunkenness in which friendships were renewed over several drinks. Friends "treating" friends was part of a system of compulsory drinking usages.[19] And England and Scotland were not exempt from such usages. Drinking at fairs was common as was drinking to cement an economic transaction. As Harrison observed, "for many goods and services, drink was actually part of the payment."[20] In the opinion of many observers, the proliferation of pubs and the ease with which one could become a publican (licensee of a public house) at fair time led to the widespread inebriety that accompanied the selling and buying of stock and agricultural products.[21]

Medicinal uses of alcohol in Ireland have been long-standing and widespread. Whiskey was taken as a palliative for the effects of Ireland's dank climate. At other times it was used to revive someone from unconsciousness and to cure cholera and other diseases. Workers drank whiskey to strengthen themselves and dispel fatigue. The particular medicinal usage—"hair of the dog that bit you"—stood out. This involved the consumption of alcoholic beverages the morning after to cure a hangover. Bales felt that that usage was most directly related to the evolution of alcohol addiction because it (hair of the dog) brought the full involvement of the individual into the process of addiction. Drinking to relieve the effects of past drinking episodes places the individual in a vicious circle of alcohol use. A drink upon rising to set the day off right and a drink before bed to cure insomnia were also quite popular. Bales summarily asserted that "it is hard to think of a medicinal use of alcohol which has not been current, at one time or another, in the Irish culture."[22]

Once again, however, the drinking of the English and the Scots appeared quite similar. Harrison noted:

> Alcoholic drinks were important as painkillers, too. Criminals about to be flogged, patients being prepared for an operation or for tooth-extraction, pregnant women entering upon labour, babies unable to sleep—alcohol kept them all quiet. Doctors even administered alcoholic drinks as medicines: the zealous Dr. Todd prescribed six pints of brandy in 72 hours for Charles Hindley, MP for Ashton; Hindley did not recover. No wonder the goutrest formed part of the furniture of every West End club till the end of the century.[23]

And again:

> Alcoholic drinks were thought to strengthen you for any kind of hard work. Fat redfaced men were considered models of good health. . . . Farmers thought they'd never get the harvest in if they didn't first fortify their labourers with "harvest beer." Soldiers and sailors prized their rum-rations as a way of keeping out the cold. Rum also helped banish fear. . . .[24]

A nineteenth-century Scottish psychiatrist mentioned that the "hair of the dog that bit you" was a generalized custom in the British Isles, as were other medicinal uses.[25] Dunlop described the custom among English joiners and carpenters of being drunk the day following a trade celebration so that "the parties may enjoy a "hair of the dog that bit them."[26] Indeed, taking a drink the day after the night before is still a generalized usage. Related to this practice was that of taking a drink upon rising, common among Englishmen and

Scotsmen and even Scotswomen, who often took a drink of whiskey in the morning and called it bitters.

Irish drinking patterns at wakes, which immediately preceded funerals, were widely known. Wakes were a form of entertainment. Games were quite popular and were frequently punctuated with drinking, as were storytelling, singing, and smoking. The drinking episodes at wakes sometimes proved to be endurance tests. Harrison related a macabre anecdote about an English wake:

> There was lavish drinking at funerals: Lord Ashley, as a schoolboy at Harrow, was inspired to undertake his life's work as defender of the poor by seeing some drunken bearers drop a pauper's coffin and expose the contents.[27]

With respect to the funeral customs in a region of Scotland, it was noted that:

> In Skye old on their death-beds said "they could not be happy unless men were drunk and fought at their funerals" and one saw "the distressed widow . . . going without shoes or dead-dress with six, seven, or eight, ragged and starving children; while perhaps her only cow must be disposed of to procure whiskey to make her neighbours drink."[28]

In both English and Scottish circles, a "decent funeral" often necessitated that 10–15 pounds be spent on drink for those in attendance.[29]

There was also another type of Irish wake—one held for a long departed Christian saint. The occasion eventually became something akin to a fair at which various modes of merrymaking became the principal concern of all present. The English counterpart to this custom has been sketched:

> Thus it was reported in 1817 from Shropshire that "during a certain week in every year there takes place in most parishes in this county a kind of rural revelling generally known by the name of wake. . . ." On these occasions it is not unusual (in villages where there is no public house) for unlicensed persons to brew a certain quantity of beer to be sold during the wake, at all hours. . . .[30]

Interestingly enough, there were drinking customs in English
and Scottish history that did not exist in Ireland (or perhaps did
exist but were not uncovered by Bales's research). Among them was
the English custom of serving free drinks at general elections. Each
tavern in an area would be taken over for the day by one party or its
opposition, and local voters drank wherever and whenever at the
expense of some political group.[31]

Drinking by inmates of English prisons was prevalent in eigh-
teenth- and early nineteenth-century London. New prisoners were
assessed "garnish," or money for drink, by other inmates.[32] Prisons
were infamous for their orgies, in which heavy drinking played a
large part. There was a tavern in many prisons because jailers were
legally allowed to serve draft beer and sometimes even gin to supplement their incomes. In addition, many publicans were also constables and jailers. George has observed:

Smaller prisons were sometimes even situated in public-houses;
there was the old White Lyon in Southwark, and toward the end of
the eighteenth century White Chapel prison was also a public-
house to which outsiders resorted to play skittles and drink; if the
prisoners did not join them it was because they had no money. The
gaol of the Tower Royalty was in a public-house in Well Close
Square. It was the custom for the debtors in Newgate to send out
invitations to club meetings and convivial gatherings in their
rooms at which drink was sold. Cards were sent to invite people
(who were not prisoners) to "Mr. Such a one's Public,—Free and
Easy Society at No.—Mrs. So and So's Route.—A dance at No."
These, Neild says, took place generally twice and sometimes three
times a week, though by 1807 the practice had been checked by
"the bar newly made by which the quantity of liquor daily consumed is ascertained." In the King's Bench there were at one time
no less than thirty gin shops, and in 1776, 120 gallons of gin were
sold weekly besides other spirits and eight butts of beer a week; in
the Fleet, though there was much more order and decency than in
the King's Bench, there were still "few hours in the night without
riots and drunkenness." The parish watch-house, or round house
where night-charges were confined till they could be brought

before a justice in the morning, or till they squared the constable of the night, was a place where drink was sold and where the treatment of the prisoner depended upon his consumption of liquor.[33]

There were still other usages that apparently did not exist in Ireland. For example, liquor licenses were easy to come by in England, and the resulting overabundance of publicans promoted competition. Thus clients were frequently offered new attractions at the public houses, such as organized prostitution and gambling. To demonstrate their open-mindedness, however, some publicans successfully completed with organized religion by offering hymn singing on Sunday night.[34]

Dunlop described several drinking practices in Scotland that centered around the man-woman relationship. It was a courtship custom during the eighteenth and early nineteenth centuries for the man to ask his prospective wife to drink with him in a public house, and she was required to accept the offer. Related to this was the nostalgic practice of husbands and wives drinking together in their old courtship "hangouts" (public houses) as a way of renewing their marriage vows after the birth of a child. Less romantic and more in keeping with realistic husband-wife relationships was the custom of a husband offering his wife a taste of his drink when she came to fetch him from the pub; if she refused to drink, he could refuse to come home.[35]

In summary, then, the pervasiveness of drinking customs in the eighteenth- and nineteenth-century United Kingdom can hardly be exaggerated. Drinking customs extended even to the English judiciary in that new appointees were fined "colt money" to be spent on drink for their fellow judges.[36] Indeed, every new state or stage of life was celebrated through the extensive use of alcohol as part of what appeared to be an initiation rite.

But to appreciate just how totally drink was integrated into the daily routine, one must take into account occupational drinking customs. And these have to be seen against the economic backdrop of the British drink trade and in relation to the roles of the public house and the publican in the life of the town.

Social and Economic Aspects of the Drink Trade

> . . . as much of the history of England has been brought about in public-houses as in the House of Commons.
>
> Sir William Harcourt

The eighteenth and nineteenth centuries witnessed the growth of urban slums in England as an outgrowth of rapid industrialization.[37] But, contrary to what Engels thought, slum existence did not always drive men to drink.[38] Rather, it was often their jobs—not because they were alienated from their work (although this undoubtedly was the case), but because the rules of their various occupations required hard drinking. In his 1839 masterpiece of sociological analysis, *A Philosophy of Artificial and Compulsory Drinking Usages in Great Britain and Ireland,* John Dunlop documented over 300 drinking usages in 98 different occupations. This is not really as remarkable as it might first appear when one remembers that work and recreation then were not rationalized and segregated to the extent they are today. Drinking on the job was not an occasion for dismissal; but refusing to pay one's share of occupational fines, which often went toward drinking at work, was. It is appropriate here to describe English pubs and publicans and the contribution of alcohol to the English economy. Ireland and Scotland were under the political and economic control of England, and many changes—occupational included—flowed outward from England, the hub of commercial activity. The following two sections apply equally well to the urban areas of Ireland and Scotland.

The Pub and the Publican

First and foremost, we must remember that the pub was almost the only meeting place for recreational and occupational purposes. It was only later, in the mid-nineteenth century, that temperance halls and temperance reading rooms were opened and the number of museums, public libraries, and tea and coffee shops increased.

The public house was an essential cog in the transportation system of Great Britain. It served as a hiring hall and hotel for members of trade unions who were in search of work. Inns, whether owned by the trade unions or not, accommodated travelers with food, drink, and lodging.

Shop meetings, union meetings, and political meetings and rallies were all held in public houses; sometimes they were held in workingmen's debating halls adjacent to public houses. Even military recruiting was carried out in pubs.

It was not unusual, because of the scarcity of public meeting places, for the pub to function as a center for commerce or even as a coin exchange. Public auctions were held, and such commodities as farmers' grains were bartered or sold in pubs.

As mentioned earlier, a public house was sometimes the backdrop for a small jail or was contained within a larger jail or prison.

And, of real import to the local community, the pub served as town crier and newsstand for the dissemination of oral and written news.

Business aside, the pub was the community recreation center. It was sometimes a restaurant that featured entertainment, such as circuses and acting companies or music for dancing. Some pubs were houses of prostitution, a type of entertainment many patrons favored. For those with simpler tastes, it was the backdrop for good talk and tall stories. Harrison provided an interesting description of the well-endowed public house:

> Pubs offered communally many comforts which working men could never afford to buy for themselves—light, heat, cooking facilities, furniture, newspapers, and companionship. Drink-sellers even remembered the need for public lavatories at a time when jerrybuilders and parsimonious local authorities often forgot them. The lavish baroque facade of the Victorian pub, its brilliant blaze of light, its extravagant fittings, gained effectiveness from the drabness of its slummy surroundings.[39]

The social role of the publican reflected the position of the pub in the social and economic life of the community. He was the overseer of both orders—business and pleasure. He was sometimes both employer and paymaster for numerous trades. If the public house was owned by a particular trade, the publican was often a retired member of that trade. "Local friendly societies," such as benefit clubs or savings clubs, often utilized a publican as their treasurer; sometimes it was the publican who promoted the society in the beginning.

Because the pub was the center of the news network, the publican could to some degree control the channel of communication in a community, It was reported in 1800 that many English publicans were members of the Radical party and frequently displayed "newspapers of a pernicious tendency."[40] Of course "radical" then often meant "bourgeois."

The publican, then, was provider and procurer of entertainment, a vital link in the dissemination of community news and gossip, and a not unimportant economic influence. But he did not flaunt his authority, partly because he was dependent on the consumer for his trade and the brewer for his ale. Often the beer brewer owned the pub the publican tended. Harrison offers a description of the publican:

> The drink-seller was never the parasitic villain portrayed in the temperance tract; he was a popular and respected provider of recreation to a world which would have been intolerably dull without him. In a poor climate, and in cities which hadn't many open spaces, the tavern was a vital source of fun.[41]

Alcohol and the British Economy

In order to take the most general view of occupational drinking, we must ascertain the place of drink in the English economy. From the end of the seventeenth century through the early twentieth century, England was the stage for a vast political conflict over drink. There were attempts to encourage the making, selling, and drinking of beer or spirits on the one hand and to suppress or regulate the kind of number of public houses, gin shops, and beer shops on the other. Even before the rise of the great temperance movements, politicians and the interest groups they represented debated the drink question.

At the end of the seventeenth century, commercial competition with France gave some politicians the occasion to encourage the distillation and sale of English corn-made spirits. The result was the mass consumption of gin at a prodigious rate. "Ginshops, with straw-strewn cellars for the drunk and disabled, sprang up everywhere; 'drunk for 1d., dead drunk for 2d., straw for nothing,' was a common sign."[42]

The eighteenth century witnessed repeated and partially successful attempts to control the spirit trade through a series of duties and liquor licenses. Near the end of the century magistrates, whose domain included the issuance of liquor licenses, began—with the force of new laws behind them—a systematic effort to regulate and suppress the orgylike atmosphere of public houses. The Webbs called this "the most remarkable episode in the whole history of public-house licensing in England."[43] It was short-lived, however.

After 1825 the power of the magistrates was reduced, partly because they had made themselves unpopular by some rather arbitrary decisions. A far-reaching decision was made by Parliament when it passed the Beer Act of 1830. In a move to control the evils associated with spirit drinking and to assist the sagging interests of the farmer, whose intake from the sale of barley and hops had been diminished by the reduced consumption of beer, the retail of beer was opened to anyone who could afford a beer license. One of the rationalizations behind the Beer Act was that spirit drinking was responsible for the social problem of drunkenness; moreover, almost every type of crime was seen to be the direct result of excessive drinking. Eighteenth-century gin drinking had cut the national consumption of beer from one barrel to half a barrel per capita. Everything would be all right if only the lower classes could be induced to adopt beer as the national drink once again.

Not unexpectedly, beer houses appeared overnight in every grocery store and building having a spare room. In 1829 there were no beer houses separate from the previously licensed public houses; in 1830 there were 24,342 separate and distinct beer houses, but in only six years the figure jumped to 44,134.[44] Beer houses were subject to the same abuses as public houses, and some contractors bullied their workers into spending part of their wages there at the risk of being dismissed. Publicans, acting as employers and paymasters for contractors and master craftsmen sometimes forced workers to spend a large share of their paychecks in drink in order to insure full employment.

Duties and taxes on alcoholic beverages provided the government with one-third or more of its total revenue. The large beer brewers increasingly came to own public houses and to complete successfully with the beer houses; however, they stood to win either way. Publicans provided essential economic services for tradesmen and acted as mediators between workers and their work. Agricultural interests were best served by a heavy rate of consumption nationally. Thus the state, big business in the form of breweries, work contractors, master craftsmen, farmers, and publicans all stood to gain from the extensive network of occupational drinking usages that coerced workers. But this was actually only the semblance of coercion and exploitation. If the apprentice was occasional taken advantage of by his master and his publican, his recreational needs were still being met quite inexpensively. The main reason the worker did not feel exploited and coerced, at least with regard to his drinking, was that nearly everyone was coerced to varying degrees by the extensive drinking customs. Compulsory drinking usages also accrued to such upper-class positions as judge and clergyman. To drink heavily in most situations was as natural as eating heartily after a hard day's work. Summing up the relationship between drink and recreation, Dorothy George noted:

> The eighteen-century attitude toward popular amusements was almost exactly the opposite of the modern one. It was assumed that they were necessarily connected with drinking to excess, and that they led to breaches of the peace and many social evils."[45]

What George said about the relationship between popular amusements and excessive drinking might just as well have been said about the alignment of work with drink. Occupational drinking was often excessive.

Occupational Drinking Customs

Occupational drinking was centered about a system of fines that members of a trade levied on each other and on their clients. Fines were spend for drink. There were fines on becoming an apprentice (called an "entry" or a "footing"), on getting married, and on the birth of a child. There were numerous fines for mistakes made on the job. Change of job or place of work and completion of a job all entailed fines. Shop and union meetings, national holidays, and paydays involved fines for drink. The pressure on individuals to both pay their fines and drink with the work group was immense. Failure to do so led to dismissal from work, and oftentimes deviant individuals found their tools or clothes stolen and were even physically abused.

John Dunlop described occupational drinking among Irish carpenters:

> There is much drinking on the pay-night. Some masters or foremen keep a public-house, where they excite the men to take drink upon credit (tick), and strike it off the week's wages. . . . There is a union in this trade; the men meet at a public-house rent free, because the drink taken pays the room. . . . Footings are quite general for apprentices at entry to their business, and for journeymen on shifting from one workshop to another. . . . . The apprentice's footing is state to be what will give the whole workshop a "decent drink." It may average from 10's to 20's. At expiration of apprenticeship, another drink is claimed. If the apprentice be dilatory in coming forward with the footing, the men will show him nothing of the business; if he ask a question, they will "shy the answer"; they will cease to teach, and the master not being always present, the boy will remain untaught. . . .
>
> A variety of measures of severity are resorted to with a view to ensure the regular payment of the apprentice and journeymen's footings, and drink fines; as the last resort, the master would be applied to for the regulation amount, that it might be stopped out of the wages; and the consequence of his refusal, I was assured, would be a strike and turn out. . . .
>
> When a carpenter does a job, the proprietor frequently gives him a dram to attempt to soften him, and thereby avert a heavy charge. When one workman recommends another to a job or place, a treat of whiskey is expected for this exercise of patronage. Those dealers that supply a workshop with articles necessary in the trade, find it absolutely requisite to treat or "mug" the men, otherwise they will complain of the items supplied; thus in the trade of nails, wood, putty, and other articles, lovers of drink have it in

their power in various ways to deprive sober-men of their place or job, by false complaints; and oblique hints.[46]

In Scotland the occupational drinking customs and fines were no less coercive or widespread. Among Scottish joiners or cabinetmakers:

> The custom of the shop is to pay a sum as *an entry,* or footing, to be disposed of in drink by the workmen. He receives charge of the fine in a small sum, to be expended in whiskey: failure in putting out candles at the proper time, or in watching the work at meal-hours, and a number of other petty offenses, are met by small amercements for the same purpose. . . .
>
> If one leaves the shop, his station at a particular bench is *rouped,* i.e. auctioned by the men who remain, and the price spent in drink: sometimes six shillings are thus obtained. When furniture is carried to a customer's house, at moving, packing, the employer generally bestows a glass or two . . . and whenever the smallest sum is raised by a fine, the men greedily add to it, and thus a nucleus is easily formed and drinking perpetuated. The penalties for nonconformity to the usages are so various, inge-nious, and severe, that it is nearly impossible . . . for an operative to stand out against them, and be able to continue in his business. On refusal to comply, men are sent to Coventry; refused assis-tance and cooperation, which is sometimes essential to carry on work; ridiculed, affronted, maltreated in a variety of ways.[47]

Dunlop observed that although Scotland's network of family, or "domestic," drinking usages was more extensive than that of England, occupational usages were more highly developed in England, occupa-tional usages were more highly developed in England than in Scotland.[48] The deviant who failed to pay drinking fines was handled in much the same manner in the different trades:

> A coal porter who failed to pay the ten shillings due when he first used a cart would find the wheels removed. A nonpaying tailor would have the point of his scissors broken off and a triangular hole cut in the rim of his hat. Among printers the offender was identified by filling the sleeves of his coat with printer's ink, so that his shirt-sleeves were indelibly stained, and "preparations of gunpowder

with burning matches attached to them" might be hung from his coat buttons. A man might find the pockets into which he had been slow to dip his hand glued together, or discover a pawn ticket in place of his coat, pawned to buy his workmates the missing drink.[49]

And it could become more physical than that. Paddlings were not uncommon, and a recalcitrant member might even be beaten.

These drinking usages cut across class boundaries. Although the upper classes often thought that the lower classes were not subject to the same compulsory drinking usages, and each of the various trades felt its drinking customs unique, the truth is that such customs were almost universal in the three countries. George mentions that "drinking customs were also the rule for the initiation of the well-to-do youth into a trade or business."[50] Lawyers, physicians, and merchants often completed business deals over a few drinks in an inn or pub. Judges and clergymen were subject to occupational usages. In Scotland clergymen were fined a bottle of wine on receiving a new manse, on publishing a sermon, on becoming married, or on the birth of a child. As was the custom in most other trades, ministers who did not achieve one of the aforementioned (i.e., did not have a sermon published or did not have a child) were also fined. It was a most equal system. One was fined if he did and fined if he did not.

Much of the occupational drinking took place on the job because most public houses or beer houses had "potboys" who attended to the needs of workers. Apprentices also took this part in the context of their initiation into a trade.

In short, all occupations required apprentices to pay a "footing," or "entry," which was used for drink. At the conclusion of apprenticeship another fine was levied. There were numerous other occasions for the imposition of fines. Any violation of an occupational rule—coming to work unshaven or with a dirty shirt, not cleaning up one's bench or leaving one's tool in the wrong place—brought a fine. Both vertical occupational movement, as in a promotion, and horizontal movement, as in a shift to a different work site, were occasions for a fine to be levied. Entry into a shop or union meeting entailed drink fines. The completion of an occupational task or job was a drinking situation, and the money for it was to come from the workers or employer or both. Certain occasions for fining a workman implied that the others would contribute to a drink fund to facilitate a drinking spree. Thus at the initiation of an individual into a trade, besides the footing or entry the apprentice paid, other workers were expected to contribute to the celebration that followed.

Drink fines at payday also occurred; however, the role of the publican as paymaster meant that these fines were often assessed indirectly. Because some public houses and beer houses were owned by a trade (or the foreman or master had an arrangement with the publican), wages were often paid at a public house, usually after the men had been drinking for several hours on credit. The publican allowed men to drink on credit even when they were unemployed, which thus obligated them to drink there in the future. The publican as employer for a trade could demand that men drink a certain amount in order to be eligible for work. Payday, then, became the time to give the publican his due, acknowledging one's dependence on him as employer and paymaster. It was a not too subtle form of extortion.

It was worse among some trades. The coal-heavers were especially tied to the publican. A parliamentary investigation into drunkenness uncovered the following:

> There is one class of individuals in the coal-trade called "undertakers" and another "coal-whippers," or coal-heavers." The coal ships from the north are consigned to the former by the owners, factors, or captains to "deliver" or unload, and they employ the latter for that purpose, in "gangs" of nine men each; one gang being appointed to each ship. The great evil in this arrangement is that almost all of these "undertakers" are publicans, or connected with publicans; and no coal-heaver, with the exception of a very small number, can be employed but through them. The understood conditions of employment are, that the men shall spend, in ardent spirits and malt liquor, a considerable portion of their earnings. The "score" at the end of the week always amounts to one-third, and frequently one-half, and sometimes more than half of their wages.[51]

Unskilled workers were much more subject to abuses than were skilled craftsmen. Skilled workers had powerful trade unions and were not as dependent on intermediaries, such as publicans, for employment. Most important of all, the position of master craftsman, to which status most apprentices could realistically aspire, was at least as powerful as that of publican.

Occupational usages also permeated one's private life. Weddings, funerals, baptisms—indeed all the rites of passage and all holy days—were occasions for levying occupational drinking fines. It was not so much the invasion of the private sector by the public as it was the fact that work and play were not rationally distinct segments of life. Changing one's place of residence or taking one's first pleasure cruise elicited a drink fine in some trades. It appears that almost any event could become the occasion for a drink fine or a drinking spree.

Socialization of the Hard Drinker

Apprenticeship was the immediate occasion of hard drinking among the young. Dunlop has provided us with a brief resume of the process:

> Boys at first are shy of taking drink, and seem to dislike it, but before they are half out of their time they generally acquire the usual relish for stimulation, and are eager to subject new comers to the same exercise which was so disagreeable to themselves.[52]

What exactly did occupational drinking usages symbolize to the participants? A witness before the 1834 British parliamentary investigation into drunkenness shed much light on this question in his description of drinking among coal-heavers:

> There are two sets of coal-heavers employed, the "constant" and the "extra men"; and it is a common practice for the former, in consideration of their being constantly employed, to pay the "undertaker" [publican] 2s. 6d. a week for "lodging money," while they always lodge at home with their families. One qualification is indispensable for being put on the list of "constant" men, viz. "hard drinking. The hardest drinker is the best man."[53]

It was not just from the publican's perspective that the hardest drinker was the best man. An individual's work group held the same belief. The hard drinker demonstrated loyalty to other members of his trade. Hard drinking was a primary means of gaining and maintaining status within one's work group; it was a sign of commitment to one's occupational code. This interpretation of hard drinking is supported by a drinking usage in the tailoring trade: "When two tailors were caught drinking only a modest amount together they had to buy a similar drink for every man in the shop, sometimes amounting to sixty half-pints."[54]

Whether one stresses the workers' normative commitment to occupational drinking rules or the threat of reprisals from other members of the work group in explaining the hard drinking of workers, the fact remains that young men were socialized into a pattern of hard drinking as apprentices in a trade. Occupation proved the structural context in which most drinking usages and attitudes were embedded. Rules that specified the occasions and amounts of drinking were means of occupational social control. Young men were initiated into a trade, gained status within it, and maintained their standing, if not their employment, by conforming to a vast network of drinking usages. The sanctions accompanying the drink rules were reprisals from co-workers, which could be mild (e.g., ridicule), more serious (e.g. loss of clothing or tools), severe (e.g., a beating), or final (e.g., murder or loss of job). Drinking fines delimited the amount of money or drink owed by each individual. Dunlop obtained a list of rules for Scottish cotton spinners from a worker in a cotton factory; this list is given in Table 1.

A specific drinking rule included a definition of both the occasion for the assessment of a fine and the amount of fine incurred. Often but not always the collection of a drink fine was a sufficient condition for the immediate consumption of alcohol. The sanctions that accompanied such drinking rules have already been discussed. But prevailing over the numerous concrete drinking rules was the most general drinking norm: treating. This norm of reciprocity made all men equal and bound them to each other. A man was obligated to buy drinks for his friends, as they were for him. The norm of treating cut across class boundaries and occupational lines and permeated both the public and private sectors of life. It was a symbol of group integration and an affirmation of male identity.

TABLE 1 Compulsory Drinking Usages among Scottish Spinners

Occasion for Drink	Fines		
	£.	s.	d.
On getting the first wheels, entry-money for drink	1	1	0
All other workmen who attend such entry, each	0	2	0
When changing from one mill to another (in some places it is only 5s).	0	10	0
When changing from one pair of wheels to another, even in the same mill, from 2s. 6d. to	0	5	0
All who attend such meeting, each	0	0	6
If changing from one flat or room to another	0	10	0
When a man is turned off, and taken back, although it were the same day that the difference took place, he must there and then pay over again	0	10	0
At all marriages, the bridegroom	0	5	0
At all births	0	5	0
If a young man spin a pair of wheels in the same shop for one year, and be so unfortunate as not to get married, he pays	0	10	0
And every nine months that he remains single, and in the same shop (this, however, is not insisted on in some shops)	0	10	0
At every shop-meeting—these being held every two months—from every spinner in the mill, whether present or not	0	0	6
At the pay table which is every regular pay-day	0	0	6
A country spinner coming to town	1	1	0

Thus the young man was socialized into occupational drinking patterns as an apprentice, and he quickly learned that the best man—whether through the eyes of his employer, co-workers, or friends—was the hard drinker, the constant man who never let down his friends. The young man's father, often a hard drinker himself, sometimes admonished his son about the evils of a public house while concomitantly paying for his entry, or footing, in a trade. The dangers were seen in advance by parents, but the necessity of getting a son established in an occupation was an overriding concern.[55]

Occupational drinking customs, reflective of an extensive division of labor, were more an urban than a rural phenomenon; hence they were much more central to English than to Irish life. At the same time, however, occasions for drinking were omnipresent whether in urban or rural areas. Drinking was associated with literally every significant (and many an insignificant) social occasion and social change. In Ireland from the mid-nineteenth century onward the context of drinking was often the all-male group, whose genesis is depicted in Chapter 5.

With the increasing rationalization of work through industrialization and with the rise of temperance in the early nineteenth century, the hold of occupational drinking usages would eventually be broken. But is was to be such an intense struggle that early temperance reformers sometimes feared for their personal safety. Ireland's temperance movement, under the direction of Fr. Theobald Mathew, met with almost immediate success. The movements in England and Scotland took much longer to incubate, but their eventual success proved more long-standing than that of Father Mathew's movement.

3

Temperance
and the Redefinition
of Drinking

There is no such thing as a moderate use of intoxicating drinks,
or at least there are very few, if any, who will persevere in using
them but moderately.

James Brimingham,
A Memoir of the
Very Rev. Theobald Mathew

This statement, made by a disciple and biographer of Fr. Theobald
Mathew, the great Irish temperance reformer, expresses quite
well an underlying assumption of those who advocate total abstinence
as opposed to the selective and restrained use of alcohol. An intemperate statement by today's standards, in the light of the widespread
inebriety in western Europe, it seemed a fitting conclusion about
human nature then.

In general, temperance movements and organizations should be
studied to understand societal drinking patterns, just as drinking
patterns should be studied if one's primary concern is temperance.
Each partly defines itself in opposition to the other. Temperance
movements in nineteenth-century Ireland, England, and Scotland
played a significant part in the eventual decline of occupational
drinking usages. They also led to a redefinition of the role of the
drinker and eventually to a redefinition of masculinity itself. Only
Ireland among the three countries preserved a culturally demanded
link between drinking and male identity. That industrialism missed
Ireland helps explain why the Irish variant of middle class morality
encouraged hard drinking.

The Irish Temperance Movement:
Father Mathew's Crusade

Skibbereen, Ireland, was the site of the first total abstinence society in Europe. Composed of about 500 artisans and tradesmen, it was founded in 1817 by Jeffrey Sedwards, a nail maker.[1] Its influence never reached beyond the local community, however, and its existence was brief.[2]

Twelve years later Dr. John Edgar, professor of divinity at the Royal College of Belfast, founded the Ulster Temperance Society, which attained considerable success in the north of Ireland. There were reportedly 25 such societies in Ireland by 1830. Membership entailed abstinence from spirits, but beer and wine were allowed. Thus some observers claimed that temperance societies favored the wine-drinking upper classes. It was argued that the lower classes were more dependent on spirits than the upper classes, which exhibited a preference for wine. In any case, Protestants and Catholics alike founded and were active members of temperance societies, although the former were more involved at the early stage of the movement.

Although those who advocated total abstinence and those who supported moderation were sometimes at odds with one another, their mutual opponents often classified them together. Total abstinence was regarded as a special form of temperance. In this chapter total abstinence societies are viewed as part of a vaster temperance enterprise which spread over western Europe in the nineteenth century.

The influence of the British Association for the Promotion of Temperance by Total Abstinence led some reformers to doubt the efficacy of the moderate use of alcohol, so once again total abstinence came to the fore. In 1836 the Dublin Total Abstinence Society was formed, and other groups soon shifted from advocating temperance to advocating total abstinence. One of these was the Old George's Street Society, located in the city of Cork and directed by William Martin, a Quaker. After attending a general temperance meeting in Dublin in 1836, Martin and several compatriots attempted to coordinate the

work of the six temperance societies in Cork and decided to simultaneously adopt total abstinence as their policy.

Since Cork was predominantly Catholic, Martin and his associates realized that their work would flourish only if a Catholic priest
could be persuaded to lead their movement. The man they chose
was Fr. Theobald Mathew, a Capuchin priest and moderate drinker.
A pledge drawn up by Martin and signed by Father Mathew in
April 1838 read:

> I promise to abstain from all intoxicating drinks, except used med-
> icinally and by order of a medical man, and to discountenance the
> cause and practice of intemperance.[3]

The new organization was named the Cork Total Abstinence
Society, and its president was Father Mathew. The news that Father
Mathew was associated with temperance as received with disbelief
in some quarters because the advocates of both temperance and
abstinence were regarded as a queer lot by most. Father Mathew,
however, was immensely popular among members of all classes of
Cork, and his outstanding relief work during the cholera outbreak
of 1832 was well remembered. Also, he had established numerous
charitable and education organizations for the poor.[4]

At first many people came to listen to Father Mathew simply out
of curiosity. But the crowds began to swell, and the movement flour-
ished because of the great influence Father Mathew had on the people. The fact of his charismatic appeal is indisputable. Although he
was not an outstanding public speaker in terms of technique, his sin-
cerity was obvious to those in attendance. The judgments of his contemporaries were almost unanimously favorable to him and his
movement. One of them saw him in the following light:

> No man can hesitate to believe that Father Mathew has been
> stimulated by pure benevolence to the work he has undertaken.
> The expression of his countenance is peculiarly mild and gracious.
> His manner is persuasive to a degree, simple and easy and humble
> without a shadow of affectation, and his voice is low and musical
> such as moves men. A man more naturally fitted to obtain influence
> over a people easily led and proverbially swayed by the affectations

we have never encountered. No man has borne his honours more meekly encountered opposition with greater gentleness or forbearance or disarmed hostility by weapons better suited to a Christian.[5]

Father Mathew's earnestness, humility, and intensity of emotion, the record of his work in the past, and the increasing conviction with which he spoke all combined to produce a remarkable effect on his followers. But if his personality had a part to play in his great appeal, his alleged ability to work miracles created a veritable state of frenzy among his enthusiasts. As the Reverend James Birmingham, Father Mathew's first biographer, observed:

> The chief causes of Mr. Mathew's success . . . are the well-known zeal and sanctity of his former life, his devotion to the general good, and an almost universal impression that he possesses great virtue and power to cure not only the mental disorders, but even the corporal maladies of his race.[6]

The following incident was related by a man coming late upon the scene of a supposed miracle:

> Last Sunday as I was going into Donegal I heard that Father Mathew, who has been the means of turning thousands of our poor people from whiskey, had been in the town on Friday, induced many to take the total abstinence pledge, and had healed a cripple. On the pump in the midst of the marketplace I saw his crutches exhibited.[7]

One of the Father Mathew's biographers described the excitement his followers exhibited:

> The news sank like wildfire through the slums that Father Mathew had a gift to cure drunkenness; some said he had been told in a vision to found his Society; anyone who took the pledge from him was safe. This was all that was needed to wake a contagion of enthusiasm in such an excitable race.[8]

Father Mathew claimed he had had a vision in which a former chaplain of his church and close friend, who had been dead for a few years, told him to preach total abstinence. This episode occurred some time before Father Mathew became a teetotaler, and all his life he believed he had spoken with a dead man. But he denied that he possessed the ability to cure the sick. His first biographer, James Birmingham, noted:

> The acts of the simple and of the superstitious are not the acts of Fr. Mathew, and should not be made to reflect upon him or his laudable undertaking. He cures from drunkenness by receiving those who would come forth from its degrading captivity—and so far he is a worker of miracles; but he professes not to heal the lame, the blind, the dumb, or the decrepit. Of this, he assures the numerous applicants for the exercise of his supposed supernatural power; and if he touch the prostrate cripple, or the man who has been blind from his youth, it is merely to gratify him, and to be free from his importunities.[9]

Personally, however, Father Mathew did not feel that any lasting damage would result from the peasants' belief in his power to heal people. This superstition was better than addiction to alcohol.

Whether he effected cures is not our concern; but the people, especially the peasants, believed it, and this was a vital source of his magnetism. The peasants' belief in his ability to heal might lead one to think that his appeal lay only with Catholics. But this was not the case. Father Mathew's previous charitable enterprises had been nonpartisan, and from the very beginnings of the temperance movement he had striven to keep his work from political or religious sectarianism. Thackeray, in *The Irish Sketch-Book,* commented on Father Mathew's universal appeal:

> He is almost the only man, too, that I have met in Ireland, who, in speaking of public matters, did not talk as a partisan. With the state of the country, of landlord, tenant, and peasantry, he seemed to be most curiously and intimately acquainted; speaking of their wants, differences, and the means of bettering them, with the minutest practical knowledge. And it was impossible in hearing him to know, but from previous acquaintance with his character, whether he was Whig or Tory, Catholic or Protestant.[10]

His contemporaries lauded the nonpartisan approach of his movement. This was especially true of the upper classes and the British, who wished to see a diminution of sectarian strife between Protestant and Catholic, Irishman and Englishman. They were also fearful of certain revolutionary elements beginning to stir in the country, one of which was the Young Ireland Movement.

The ideology of Father Mathew's movement was relatively simple. His insistence that teetotalism assisted one's relationship to God is underscored by the following:

> Father Mathew stressed the importance of total abstinence in the spiritual life of the people. Teetotalism was not religion, he reminded his hearers, but the foundation on which religion must securely rest. By taking the pledge a person removed the greatest obstacle to the performance of his religious duties, and this was the end which should always be kept in mind.[11]

Father Mathew believed that drunkenness was Ireland's greatest social problem, the cause of almost all crimes, and the course of disorder at all levels of society. The following passage from John Maguire's biography was a public statement by Father Mathew on the effects of drink:

> I had long reflected on the degradation to which my country was reduced—a country, I will say, second to none in the universe for every element that constitutes a nations' greatness, with a people whose generous nature is the world's admiration. I mourned in secret over the miseries of this country; I endeavoured to find out the cause of those miseries, and, if that were possible, to apply a remedy. I saw that those miseries were chiefly owing to the crimes of the people, and that those crimes again had their origin in the use that was made of intoxicating drinks. I discovered that if the cause were removed, the effects could cease.[12]

And again:

> Father Mathew often gave them straightforward rebukes; he told them their wretched state was caused not only by English misrule, but also by their own folly, their own drunkenness, quarrel-

someness, idleness, and unthriftiness. Their worst faults were caused by their drunkenness; this was the head and front of their offending. Let them forswear drink, the other faults would soon disappear.[13]

Not only was total abstinence supposed to reduce crime and political conflict, but also, in Father Mathew's words:

> The pledge I ask you to take does not enslave, it makes free. The fewer passions that rule us the freer we are, and no man is so free as the man who places himself beyond and out of the reach of temptation, for "those who court danger shall perish therein." The freedom I advocate is one you can obtain without any sacrifice of health, of pleasure, of money, or of comfort. On the contrary, it will add to your health, your wealth, your pleasure, and your comfort. Temperance brings blessing for eternity.[14]

The reason why only the teetotaler was free from the temptations of drink was that, as Birmingham, Father Mathew's associate, asserted: "There is no such thing as a moderate use of intoxicating drinks, or at least there are very few, if any, who will persevere in using them but moderately."[15] In the ideology of the movement, moderation led to excess. The conception of man underlying this tenet was the corrupted man who, after the Fall from Grace, was absolutely unable, without God's help, to control his passions and save himself from a life of sin and an eternity of damnation. In its extreme forms this conception of man was more akin to Protestant than Catholic theology of the time. Father Mathew was careful not to condemn moderate drinkers or moderate drinking. But in public statements made by him and his associates, grave suspicion was cast on an individual's ability to continue using drink moderately; excessive use of alcohol lay just around the corner.

A corollary was Father Mathew's insistence on the security, peace of mind, and certitude of being one of the "elect." He was reported by Maguire to have exclaimed:

> I never knew what true happiness was till I became a teetotaler; for until I became so, I could never feel that I was free or out of

danger, or could say to myself, with confidence, that I would not at
one time or another be that most degraded thing, a drunkard.[16]

If teetotalism were the foundation upon which religion was
built and if it were the only possible means by which to be completely free from the danger of drunkenness, then teetotalism would
become a prerequisite for certitude about one's religious salvation.
This doctrine was a carefully disguised form of predestination, and
teetotalism became a sign of salvation.

In summary, the ideology of the movement might be articulated
as follows: The country's immense political and social problems are
the result of crime, the principal cause of which is drunkenness.
Behind drunkenness stands the inability that most of us share to
drink only in moderation. Drunkenness has been on the increase for
several decades (much as a contagious disease), tempting and infect-
ing more and more people. Only teetotalism, as the foundation upon
which religion builds, can free an individual from the temptation of
drunkenness. Therefore teetotalism leads to the amelioration of social
problems, individual health, and ultimately individual salvation. And
insofar as teetotalism eliminates social problems, it will allow Ireland
to solve its political problems and become a great nation.

Father Mathew's charismatic appeal, his alleged ability to heal
the sick, and the utopian goals of the movement all contrived to produce a contagion that swept the country.[17] The movement was decidedly Father Mathew's.[18] He did all the work himself—administering
the pledge, passing out temperance medals, blessing the people. What
organization he did bring to the movement was the result of his
establishment of temperance reading rooms and adult industrial
and literary education programs in many of the towns he visited. This
philanthropy left him to constant financial trouble; he also insisted on
giving rather expensive temperance medals to new recruits whether
they paid for them or not. Usually they did not. McKenna mentioned
the lack of organization in Mathew's movement:

> ... the movement was not sufficiently organized. When Father
> Mathew had come to a parish, and had gone again having distrib-
> uted his cards, he left no machinery behind him to bring his

pledge-bearers to act on each other by mutual example, aid, exhortation and reproach. When an individual had broken his pledge, there was no influence to shame him or to lift him up again. That the work was wanting in permanence Father Mathew was himself anxiously conscious.[19]

What he failed to leave behind was an organization of local societies or chapters with officers, members, dues, and regular meetings. Partly because it generated fantastic enthusiasm and unrealistic expectations, but principally because it was too much identified with Father Mathew, the movement was short-lived. Though transient the effect of the movement, its immediate impact was remarkable.

The movement grew from a few hundred true believers in April 1838 to well over 100,000 members by September of that year. By January 1839 the estimate was 200,000; and by June 1840 the ranks had swollen to 2,000,000.[20] It was thought that 5,000,000 men, women, and children had taken the pledge by 1842.[21] The zenith of the movement occurred in 1843, when Father Mathew had enrolled nearly 6,000,000 people out of a population of approximately 8,000,000.[22] The movement began its decline in the following year, but there were still more than 3,000,000 faithful followers in 1844.[23]

Not only did millions change their drinking habits, but they also exhibited a great deal of restraint in other areas. In a description of the social effects of the Irish temperance movement, Longmate observed: "Brewers and distilleries went out of business and publicans deserted their trade. In many areas drunkenness virtually disappeared and everywhere serious crime dropped sharply. . . ."[24] In 1838 12,300,000 gallons of spirits had been consumed; by 1840 this had been reduced to 7,400,000 gallons, and in 1842 only 5,300,000 gallons were reported to have been consumed.[25] The consumption figures were slightly higher for 1843 and 1844 owing in part to a reduction of the duty on spirits but more still to a loss in the hold the movement exerted on its members.[26]

The rates of the various categories of crime were reduced: Homicides, 247 in 1838, dropped to 105 in 1841; robberies were reduced from 725 in 1837 to 257 in 1841; faction fights were cut from

20 cases to 8 between 1839 and 1841.[27] Table 2 indicates that the overall reduction in crime was nothing short of amazing.

Of course one must be wary of criminal statistics, but the evidence of a downward trend, supported by the observation of many individuals, was reported by Maguire. The following testimony concerns the manifold benefits of the temperance movement:

> In our village of Edgeworthstown the whiskey-selling has diminished since the pledge has been taken within the last two years, so as to leave public houses empty, and to oblige the landlords to lower house-rent considerably. . . .
>
> The appearance of the people, their quiet demeanour at markets and fairs, has wonderfully improved in general; and to the knowledge of this family many notorious drinkers, and some, as it was thought, confirmed drunkards, have been completely reformed. . . .[28]

Others noted the self-discipline of the teetotalers, not only at temperance rallies but also at political meetings, which many teetotalers attended. The diminution of crime in Ireland at the height of the temperance movement is not surprising in the light of what is known about social movements. The Irish masses had been given a utopian cause to believe in, and for a short period such collective motivation can produce unusual changes in behavior.

TABLE 2   Criminal Convictions In Ireland

Year	Individuals Committed to Prison	Individuals Sentenced to Death
1839	12,049	66
1840	11,194	43
1841	9,287	40
1842	9,875	25
1843	8,620	16
1844	8,042	20
1845	7,101	13
1846	——	14

What were the consequences of the temperance movement for publicans, brewers, distillers, and public houses? Many public houses, especially beer houses, were forced to close and publicans were out of work. However, for the most part publicans were not embittered by this. Many, in fact, became teetotalers. The following is a letter from a publican to Father Mathew:

Newbawn, New Ross: May 16, 1840

Rev. Sir,—I beg leave to inform you that about a year ago, I commenced public business, in a house which cost me upwards of 100£. I gave credit to respectable farmers' sons to a considerable amount but in consequence of they having taken the Temperance Pledge, they say that you would not allow them to pay for any kind of intoxicating liquor. I therefore humbly request that you will write a few lines to my parish priest, the Rev. Mr. Ryan, on the subject, as it will be the means of keeping myself and family from begging. *I do hereby pledge myself to resign this business the moment Mr. Ryan shall have received your letter, and that I will take the Temperance pledge myself, as my son has done.*

Awaiting with anxiety your favourable reply, I have the honour to be,

Rev. Sir, your most
obedient servent,
Michl. Cannon[29]

There were publicans, brewers, and distillers opposed to Father Mathew's work, but most were a least tolerant of it. Some even commended him. A most influential Dublin distiller, George Roe, remarked, " 'No man . . . had done me more injury than you have, Father Mathew; but I forget all in the great good you have done my country.' "[30] A relative of Father Mathew who was involved in the distillation of spirits wrote to him that his business had fallen off considerably since the rise of temperance and that his financial ruin was imminent. Father Mathew responded by advising him to "turn his premises into factories for flour."[31] Thus the brewing and distilling interests were not given special consideration by Father Mathew even when in his own family.

Irish Nationalism: The Alignment of Temperance with Repeal

Initially Father Mathew's movement proved functional for the maintenance of the existing political union with England. This is the reason most Englishmen backed his efforts up to the time when they thought he was supporting Daniel O'Connell's attempt to repeal the union between Ireland and England. There is little doubt about Father Mathew's political orientation:

> . . . he was strongly conservative by nature. He never forgot that he was a gentleman born, one of the Mathews of Thomastown, a representative of law and order, and by nature opposed to violent upheavals and reversions of the proper order of precedence.[32]

From the very beginning Father Mathew had spoken out vociferously against political and religious partisanship. The temperance movement would not become pro-Catholic and anti-English if he had his way because the movement was to encompass all men, whatever their social affiliations. Next to abstaining from drink, the rule enforced with the greatest diligence was that forbidding political and religious discussion at temperance meetings and rallies.[33] Father Mathew was well received in Protestant England and Scotland because of his temperance endeavors, and even some of those most devoted to the political cause of Great Britain praised him. Testimony in the House of Lords was favorable to his work, especially because his movement was associated with a diminishing rate of crime and greater discipline among the lower classes (something the English had long felt to be impossible). Moreover, Father Mathew stood forthrightly against secret societies and all forms of violence, even the Young Ireland Movement of the 1840s. Middle- and upper-class leaders of both countries praised his efforts, at least initially. But the freedom from sectarian strife that his movement enjoyed was to be short-lived.

Ireland had long been under the political domination of England, and concurrent with the Irish temperance movement was a movement for repeal of the formal political ties between the countries. The Repeal party was a political party and had been in existence during the 1830s. Daniel O'Connell, foremost leader of the party, had earlier succeeded in obtaining state recognition of Catholicism. The Catholic Emancipation Act of 1829 granted to Catholics, their clergy, and their church a measure of religious freedom.

In 1840 O'Connell founded the Loyal National Repeal Association, which he hoped would enlist millions of Irish. O'Connell became known as "the Liberator," and his repeal association held numerous political rallies across the country in an attempt to mobilize public opinion.

While Father Mathew was blaming drink for the social ills of the country, O'Connell attributed the problems to England. At temperance meetings, Father Mathew criticized the people for their drunkenness and the resultant crime, idleness, and lack of thrift, and he general bemoaned the fallen state of Ireland. At repeal meetings, in contrast, O'Connell praised the people and blamed English misrule for the many problems besetting Ireland. Praise and criticism were different techniques, but both helped arouse the people. The two men were immensely popular and commanded large followings.

O'Connell publicly praised Father Mathew and privately hoped to unite the two movements. Maguire recorded this speech of O'Connell's:

> Whatever our politics may be—whatever our creeds may be—whatever our condition or avocation in life may be, we are all here of one mind, and that is how Ireland should express her sense of the merits and virtues of Father Mathew. . . .[34]

O'Connell told the crowd that Father Mathew had "performed a mighty moral miracle," in his transformation of Ireland.[35] O'Connell himself became a teetotaler in 1840, although he later resigned membership on doctor's orders that he stood in need of liquor for medicinal purposes.[36] Fully aware of the immense enthusiasm the temperance movement had generated and the large following it possessed, O'Connell realized that together the movements would be a sign of Ireland's unity on the repeal question. This would place pressure on England to acquiesce to the demands of a united, recalcitrant Ireland.

The matter of separate movements was complicated by the fact that both O'Connell and Mathew drew their followers from the lower classes. Indeed, there was anywhere from a three-fourths to a nine-tenths overlap in membership between the movements.[37] A contemporary observer recalled that

> . . . nearly the nine-tenths of those who had taken the pledge at his hands were Repealers, more or less advanced in their opinions, and that there was another man in Ireland who divided their admiration and affection with himself [Fr. Mathew]—and that man was Daniel O'Connell.[38]

Teetotal bands played at repeal meetings, and teetotalers sometimes marched in procession to hear O'Connell.

O'Connell, like Mathew, was opposed to violent revolution; but he rather hoped to bluff England into acceding to the demand for repeal by the size, intensity, and discipline of his movement. He held forth the threat of revolution without the intent to follow through. Temperance played no small part in O'Connell's ploy. The temperance movement had been the training grounds for his army of repealers.

In spite of Father Mathew's nonsectarian intentions for temperance, the two movements became symbolically linked on Easter Monday in 1842. On that day Daniel O'Connell, as Lord Mayor of Dublin, walked with Father Mathew at the head of a temperance procession. A newspaper reported the event:

> When it [the procession] had proceeded as far as the Country Club House, it was met by the Lord Mayor of Dublin, who came to join Father Mathew. Their greeting was warm and affectionate. . . . Who could tell of the wild joyous shout that rent the very air as the two great men of Ireland, the political and the moral emancipators of her people met together. The eagerness—the exclamations of delight—the rushings forward to snatch a look at both—the rapture and enthusiasm of that moment—are beyond our poor powers of description.[39]

Among the 10,000 or so in attendance that day were 57 temperance societies and 41 temperance bands.

Although Father Mathew warmly received O'Connell, he had not desired the other's presence at the procession. Father Mathew realized that O'Connell's participation would lead many to doubt the nonsectarian claims of the temperance movement.[40] Shortly thereafter the public meeting of Father Mathew and O'Connell became grist for the mill of Protestant and English propaganda. It was claimed that Father Mathew now supported repeal of the union; moreover, he was accused of being anti-Protestant. His critics grew in number, and their criticism became vitriolic.

But the people, especially those in the working classes, had been given the promise of a better life. Their excited and enthusiastic condition was inspired by the future utopia Father Mathew and O'Connell had articulated for them. O'Connell had told the people that freedom from the tyranny of English rule, to be gained through repeal of the union between the two countries, would put an end to most of their social problems. Father Mathew, although calling on the people individually to renounce their vices, fell prey to an idealism as well. Abstention from drink would bring about the same utopia O'Connell described. That freedom from English misrule or freedom from intoxicating beverages would bring beneficial results was not illusory; rather, it was the offer to the people that social problems could be eliminated and the good life realized by accomplishing a single act (repeal of the union) or by abstaining from a single activity (drinking) that was illusory. In the end Fr. Mathew became a victim of the rhetoric of his own movement.

The two movements were linked inexorably under a mantle of nationalism. With the failure of the repeal movement, temperance dramatically declined; but it lingered on until Father Mathew's death in 1856. For two years, 1842 and 1843, the two nationalistic movements swept the country. However, in May 1844 Daniel O'Connell was imprisoned for his political agitation. When released a few months later he was physically and spiritually exhausted, and this signaled the end of the repeal movement:

> The exaltation of the people was followed by a reaction of despair. Those who did not lie down under despondency believed that the only hope now lay in conspiracy and revolt. With the new spirit in

the country, a spirit which was being led by the young men of the *Nation,* Father Mathew was out of touch. He had openly opposed conspiracy and rebellion, and in so far the people must have felt that he was against them. After all, he was an old-fashioned country gentleman, naturally as much out of touch with the revolution as a French abbé or curé might have been with the spirit of '93. He saw the danger of the Temperance movement losing its hold on the people. The glorious days were over.[41]

During 1844 relatively few new members were enrolled in local temperance organizations, and many of those previously enrolled drifted away.[42] The temperance movement had begun to wane. As long as Father Mathew lived there would always be groups of loyal followers, but the disillusionment of the people had set in. The temperance and repeal movements—with their large overlap in membership, their symbolic connection in 1842, and their similar promises to the populace—were destined to fall together. The failure of the repeal movement hastened the decline of temperance.

Several other factors weakened the efficacy of the temperance movement. The Great Famine was beginning its reign of devastation in 1846. Father Mathew spent most of his time during the famine years administering to the needs of its victims, legion in number. In addition he had accumulated a large debt as a result of his temperance work, something his critics never forgot. And finally, his poor health limited his ability to travel great distances to see members of the movement. The Great Famine must have driven home to the people the point that teetotalism could not solve their social problems. The disillusionment and the despair were great indeed. Father Mathew was not spared these reactions either; he often expressed anxiety and sorrow over the state of the movement.

The Irish versus the English Temperance Movement

That Irish temperance was decidedly a nationalistic and only secondarily a class movement is of great import. When to this are added the facts that the Irish were overwhelmingly lower class and that industrialization had made no inroads in Ireland, we can begin to understand the differences in temperance between Ireland and England.

Superficially the most striking difference between temperance enterprises in the two countries was the brevity of the Irish movement and the longevity of the English movement. By 1845 Father Mathew's movement was in retreat, and his death in 1856 brought its activities to a standstill. He had passed on an organization without "organization." Father Mathew had done so much of the work himself and his personality had shaped the movement to such a degree that no one could really replace him. Local temperance chapters had long been in a state of disarray. McKenna described the aftermath of his movement: "when the wave of popular enthusiasm had passed—nay, even before the great apostle himself had died—the old habits of drunkenness had reconquered much of their former sway."[43]

The situation in England was remarkably different. Here temperance was most decidedly not the work of one man, nor was it aligned with a nationalistic political movement (albeit it was politically well connected). The English temperance movement developed more gradually and was vital even up to the time of World War I. Although the English temperance movement was torn apart on occasion by the conflicting interests of competing religious denominations, it slowly helped to eliminate many drinking usages, occupational and otherwise. Eventually public drinking was discredited.

To account for the loss of respectability of public drinking, Harrison mentions the values of independence, sobriety, and respectability that formed the ideological foundation of the temperance movement.[44] The association of one with the other (i.e., sobriety with respectability) was a common feature of Victorian life.

But other factors accompanied industrialization. The old patterns of occupational drinking proved incongruent with the increasing rationalization of economic life. Modern industrial techniques demanded a well-disciplined and regular work force. Also, the roles of the publican and public house in the occupational life of the worker were critically diminished. Public houses no longer functioned as hiring halls, and publicans seldom acted as employers.

The development of libraries, coffee houses, temperance halls, amusement centers, and other public meeting areas diminished the previously unique position of the public house as the hub of communication in the community. Meetings could now be held in a variety of locations, and recreation was enjoyed outside the pub. Temperance agitation brought about stricter drinking hours for public houses, a tightening of liquor license proceedings, and increased police vigilance about drinking disorders.

The contrast with Ireland is illuminating. During the nineteenth century and into the twentieth century, Ireland remained largely unindustrialized. In addition widespread poverty precluded the proliferation of amusement centers to compete with pubs. Then, too, temperance in Ireland all but died in the late 1840, while in the rest of Great Britain it was only beginning to develop. (Isolated temperance groups emerged in Ireland after Father Mathew's death, but nothing substantial developed until the Pioneer Total Abstinence Society was formed in the early twentieth century.) But the greatest difference lay in the integrative nature of the Irish movement in contrast to the sectarian character of the English and Scottish movements. In Ireland the nationalistic aspirations which overlay repeal and temperance causes unified the Irish, the great majority of whom were Catholic and lower class, against the English and their few representatives in Ireland. The English were mostly Protestant and were in a collective sense and with respect to the Irish a ruling class, yet the consciousness directed against England was not a class consciousness at all but rather a fused religious-nationalistic consciousness. But even here the nationalistic aspect was the stronger for a number of Protestants joined in the struggle to emancipate Ireland from English tyranny.

Throughout much of the nineteenth century, the English temperance movement was essentially a middle-class movement opposed to the irresponsibility of the upper class and the "dangerous classes" (the disreputable poor). Thus a union existed between the middle class and the "respectable" working class.[45] Harrison detailed the attitudes and behavior of the respectable workingman, who was

. . . distinguishable from other working men by his relatively smart personal appearance. He also shared many middle-class attitudes: a distaste for mobs, and a repudiation of the whole complex of behaviour associated with racecourses, fairs, wakes, brothels, beer-houses and brutal sports. He was more likely than his inferiors to vote Liberal, if only because his working situation frequently fostered individualism, self-education and social ambition. If he drank at all, he drank soberly, without neglecting his wife and family; he often took his recreation with them, and believed that the family should keep to itself. He was probably interested in religious matters—often a chapelgoer or a secularist. He was strongly attracted by the ideology of thrift, with its stress on individual self-respect, personal moral and physical effort, and prudence.[46]

In no way should members of the respectable working class be seen as lackeys of the middle class; the two classes had their differences. However, their joint adherence to a middle-class morality and their common opposition to the upper leisured class (the aristocracy) and the lower leisured class (the permanently unemployed "dangerous classes") brought them together in temperance work.[47]

It should not be thought that Father Mathew's temperance movement and nationalist movements in general did not share to some extent this middle class morality. Remember that Father Mathew's movement was also one of self-improvement—but one for the improvement of the entire country. He stressed the individualistic virtues of sobriety, thrift, prudence, and industry that were so much a part of middle class morality. He felt that individual improvement led to national improvement. On the other hand O'Connell, himself very much middle class, reflected the liberal notion that the reform of institutions (in this care the repeal of the union between Ireland and Great Britain) would result in individual happiness and security. Rather than being contradictory, these seemingly diverse views were complementary. There were the opposite sides of the liberal doctrine of collective individualism.

By the mid-nineteenth century, middle-class reform movements, the rationalization of work, industrialization, and the proliferation of public meeting places and recreational areas had combined to all but eliminate compulsory occupational drinking customs and to make drinking, at least hard drinking, less than respectable in England. Drinking in Ireland, especially after the demise of Father Mathew's temperance movement, remained respectable—although compulsory occupational drinking usages were largely eliminated there as well.

Compulsory hard drinking did continue to some extent in both countries. In England it was more restricted to upper-class drinking societies and lower-class gangs. In Ireland compulsory hard drinking became embedded in another institutional setting—the all-male group—which tended to cut across class divisions. Actually the male group and its ethic of hard drinking provided to be essential for the maintenance of a new family system and for the social order of the rural community.

4

The Irish Family and the
Reemergence of the Avunculate

> The history of a nation is not in parliaments and battlefields, but
> in what the people say to each other on fair-days and high days,
> and in how they farm, and quarrel, and go on pilgrimage.
>
> W. B. Yeats, introduction to
> *Stories from Carlton*

In the nineteenth century, dramatic changes occurred in the Irish
farm economy and in the Irish family. The following aspects of the
structure of the Irish family were affected: inheritance pattern, age at
marriage, rate of marriage, husband-wife relationship, brother-sister
relationship, father-son relationship, and maternal uncle-nephew
relationship (the avunculate).

Inheritance and Marriage

In the late eighteenth century, the potato as an instrument of familism and capitalism appears to have been behind the Irish tendency to
marry early. The introduction of the potato markedly increased agricultural output, thereby allowing English landlords to subdivide their
property even further than previously and thus increase their rent
income from Irish tenants. The Irish families who rented the land
actually did the subdividing. They permitted, even encouraged, their
young sons to have a small plot of land to support a wife and family
on. K. H. Connell described the conditions and consequences of the
extensive subdivision of land prior to the Great Famine of 1845–48:

> In the two or three generations following the 1780's peasant chil-
> dren, by and large, married whom they pleased. The opportunity

to marry in their society was the occupation of land that promised
a family's subsistence. Dependence on the potato, ever more
extreme, on varieties ever more prolific, reduced the area needed
for food. At the same time, rising corn prices and the conversion of
pasture to tillage, allowed a given rent to be earned on less land.
There appeared, in consequence, a margin of land needed neither
to sustain the customary population nor to pay the customary
rent. An exigent landlordism tended to annex it for rent. But, with
the maximization of rent resting now on the maximization of
small tillage farms, landlords allowed sons to settle on holdings
carved from their parents'. More holdings meant more and earlier
marriage, more and larger families: but in the event they under-
lay not just the extra labour tillage needed, but so sharp a growth
of population that subsistence land tended to encroach on rent
land. Landlords were alarmed, the more so after 1815 as corn
prices slumped; as the small man's endless corn and potatoes
exhausted the soil; as there was talk of a poor-law financed by the
landlords' rates. "Consolidate and clear" became their cry. But
they had lost the power to do what they would with their own.
Their shortlived encouragement of subdivision had shown the
peasants how easily and (it seemed) painlessly second sons might
be established; and as these married young, soon there were yet
more second, and third, sons. Only a minority was drawn or pushed
to the Irish towns, to Britain or America. For most, the landlord
notwithstanding, provision was made by continued division, facili-
tated by the potato's bolder trespassing on rent land, by its reach-
ing higher up the mountain and farther into the bog.[1]

Michael Drake has disagreed with Connell about how early men
married in the period preceding the Great Famine. On the basis of
the 1841 census, Drake maintained that between 1831 and 1840 the
median age of bridegrooms never dipped below 25; however, this
finding conflicts with results of the Poor Inquiry commission of
1836, which indicated a substantially earlier median age at marriage.[2] Literary evidence and the reports of contemporary observers
for the period 1780–1840 also point to an early marriage age for
men; moreover, the pattern of early age at marriage had already
begun to change gradually before 1830 in the direction of one of later
age at marriage.[3]

As the subdivision of land became less frequent, later marriage became necessary. The Great Famine imprinted on the Irish the lesson of unwise subdivision, the consequences of which they had begun to understand even earlier. Continued subdivision meant a smaller and smaller plot of land for everyone. Subsistence was being threatened, for the small plot could maintain a family only under perfect climatic conditions and if the soil was not exhausted.[4]

In addition to the economic ruination that continued subdivision of the land would surely bring, reasons for postponed marriage included a desire for a higher standard of living (partly the result of a "contrast in the way of life between the United States and Ireland") and the dashing of hopes for national improvement with the failure of the repeal movement.[5] Also, improved agricultural techniques, especially horse-drawn implements, necessitated a large area of land to prove efficient. Emigration increased for the same reasons. Kennedy argues that "emigration from Ireland or remaining single in Ireland were alternative solutions to the same basic problem of obtaining a respectable adult status."[6]

The dramatic shift in the size of agricultural holdings bears witness to the new reluctance to subdivide one's property, as illustrated in Table 3. As one can readily see, between 1841 and 1861—20 brief years—a remarkable shift in the patterns of agricultural holding took place, especially in the one-to-five acres category. Such an economic upheaval was not without its effects on the institution of marriage.

For a long time in Ireland, and in most parts of Europe for that matter, marriage was intimately bound up with the inheritance of property. Marriage signified the transfer of land from father to son

TABLE 3   Distribution by Size of Agricultural Holdings in Ireland (Number of Holdings in Thousands)

Year	1–5 Acres		5–15 Acres		15–30 Acres		Above 30 Acres		Total
	No.	%	No.	%	No.	%	No.	%	
1841	310	43.6	253	36.6	79	11.5	49	7.0	691
1861	85	15.0	184	32.3	141	24.8	158	27.8	568
1891	56	11.8	139	29.7	120	25.7	153	32.7	469

and the attainment of full economic status for the inheritor. Marriages were arranged through the process of matchmaking, which was at the discretion of the fathers of the prospective bride and groom. The period 1780–1840, however, had witnessed a relaxation of this custom in Ireland. Connell has called the marriages of this time "spontaneous"; sometimes the young man and woman married without parental approval.[7] Since land was easily obtained, a son felt less dependent on his father. Also, a young man could on occasion obtain a small plot of land to rent from someone other than his father.

But the famine and the decrease in subdividing changed all this. Matchmaking once again fell within the domain of the father's authority because now land was hard to come by. Since the father's retirement was implied by his son's marriage, the father held off as long as he realistically could the transfer of land, authority, and status. Conrad Arensberg enlisted the aid of an Irish farmer to detail the process of matchmaking:

"When a young man is on the lookout for a young lady . . . it is put through his friends for to get a suitable woman for him for his wife. It all goes by friendship and friends and meeting at public-houses. . . . Getting married is no carefree, personal matter; one's whole kindred help, even to suggesting candidates.

"The young man," the farmer goes on, "sends a 'speaker' to the young lady and the speaker will sound a note to know what fortune she has, will she suit, and will she marry this Shrove? She and her friends will inquire what kind of man he is, is he nice and steady. And if he suits, they tell the speaker to go ahead and 'draw it down.' So then he goes back to the young man's house and arranges for them to meet in such a place, on such a night and we will see about it.

". . . The speaker goes with the young man and his father that night and they meet the father of the girl and his friends or maybe his son and son-in-law. The first drink is called by the young man; the second by the young lady's father. . . . The young lady's father asks the speaker what for fortune do he want. . . .

"Well, . . . if it is a nice place, near the road, and the place of eight cows, they are sure to ask 350 fortune. Then the young lady's father offers 250. Then maybe the boy's father throws off 50. If the young lady's father still has 250 in it, the speaker divides the 50 between them. So now it's 275. Then the young man says he is not willing to marry without 300—but if she's a nice girl and a good housekeeper, he'll think of it. . . .

". . . After this they appoint a place for the young people to see one another and be introduced. The young lady takes along her friends. . . . The young man takes along his friends and the speaker.

"If they suit one another, then they will appoint a day to come and see the land. . . . If the girl's father likes the land he returns, and there will be eating and drinking until the night comes on them. Then they go to an attorney next day and get the writings between the two parties and get the father of the boy to sign over the land. With the writings, the match is made, and the wedding can go forward."[8]

Quite different from the "spontaneous" marriage of previous decades was the new, arranged marriage. The famine had taught the Irish peasant not to subdivide injudiciously; but land shortage, land reform (consolidation of holdings), increased living standards and higher aspirations, and improved agricultural techniques had persuaded him not to subdivide at all. His land (even though he was rarely the owner) was in the family and part of the family; and the only way to insure that this would continue to be so in the future was to transfer the land intact to one son, ideally the eldest son. But in reality it was often the youngest son, thereby affording the father a longer stay in power.[9]

Even so, there was great difficulty in finding a suitable spouse, even when the prospective groom was in possession of inherited property. The ideal marriage would involve a bride whose dowry included a sizable plot of land that could help support both families (the groom's parents and siblings and his wife and children). But the prospective bride faced several obstacles: her brothers stood closer in line to inherit property and she had to wait until her father relinquished the land. Thus there were relatively few women of child-bearing age who had no brothers at home and whose father had died or retired early with whom a marriage might be arranged.[10]

But this ideal often had to be compromised in practice. With the arranged marriage, the groom's parents moved to the "west room" of the house to retire; also, the groom's brothers and sisters were expected to leave the land either to migrate to a town or emigrate to another country to secure employment. The Irish "stem family system" (i.e., an extended family with several generations living together under the same roof, although only one child, usually a son, inherited the land) was consequently pared down to a son, his parents, his wife, and his offspring.

Connell described the consequences of arranged marriage:

> . . . peasant children married little and late. They married late because a "boy" not needing a wife until his mother could no more milk the cows, was not entitled to one until his father, at last, made over the land. . . . They married little because, though the normal family was large, only one of its boys and one of its girls married like their parents into peasant society: for the other (save in emigration) there was small chance of wife or husband.[11]

In the decades following the famine, the rate of marriage declined considerably and late marriage became institutionalized, as illustrated in Tables 4 and 5. The increase in age at marriage is reflected in the percentage single for the age categories 20–24 and 25–34; the increase in permanent celibacy is indicated by the rise in

TABLE 4   Marriages and Marriage Rates, 1864–1950 (Representative Decades)

	Number of Marriages	Crude Marriage Rate (Marriages per 1,000 Population)
Average for 1864–1870	21,150	5.10
Average for 1871–1880	18,014	4.54
Average for 1881–1890	14,692	4.02
Average for 1901–1910	15,325	4.84
Average for 1921–1930	14,245	4.76
Average for 1941–1950	16,585	5.59

TABLE 5   Percentage Single in Certain age Groups
(Representative Decades)

	20–24 Years	25–34 Years	35-34 Years	45–54 Years	55–64 Years
Males					
1841	___[a]	43.3[b]	15.4[b]	10.0[b]	___[a]
1851	___[a]	60.7	20.9	11.6	___[a]
1871	92.6	57.3	25.5	16.4	12.7
1891	95.8	67.3	33.0	19.7	15.6
1911	96.6	74.5	44.5	28.6	22.7
1936	96.2	73.8	44.2	33.5	28.2
1951	94.9	67.4	40.5	31.0	28.8
Females					
1841	___[a]	28.0[b]	14.7[b]	11.7[b]	___[a]
1851	___[a]	39.1	15.2	11.4	___[a]
1871	77.7	38.2	19.8	15.2	13.4
1891	86.0	48.1	23.1	16.6	15.8
1911	88.4	55.5	31.0	24.0	20.8
1936	86.4	54.8	30.2	25.1	23.7
1951	82.3	45.6	27.6	25.7	24.7

[a] Not available.
[b] Age groups for 1841 were 26–35, 36–45, 46–55, and 56 and over.

the percentage single in the age categories 45–54 and 55–64 (Table 5). These data point to a pattern of few marriages, late age at marriage, and a large number of permanent celibates.

In regard to marriage, the family, and inheritance, the patterns just described were most pronounced in rural areas, where most of the Irish population lived in the nineteenth century. However, these patterns also held sway in the towns and cities. Kennedy explained the convergence of rural and urban marriage patterns by the following factors:

> ... the acceptance by parents of the responsibility for helping to establish their offspring in socially accepted positions in life; and awareness of the persona link between one's own decisions about marriage and one's changes of realizing a certain material standard

of living; a belief that an unmarried status for an adult did not reflect individual deviance in sexual matters (for example, being single was not taken to mean [that one] was sexually frigid, homosexual, or perverted); and a willingness to postpone marriage until one had achieved a certain social status for oneself even if this meant the possibility of permanent celibacy.[12]

The dearth of tillable land, the need to consolidate holdings because of land reform, and a stem family system worked to produce a high rate of emigration and a pattern of few and late marriages in the rural areas. In the urban areas, the lack of opportunity for decent employment together with rising social and economic aspirations had much the same effect.

Between the 1870s and 1930s advances in agricultural technology and the consolidation of agricultural holdings were relatively insignificant; but the average age at marriage increased, the marriage rate decreased, and the percentage who remained permanently celibate increased. The tendency for females to migrate from rural areas to towns at a greater rate than males eventually created an imbalance in the sex ratio in rural Ireland, leaving men with a diminishing pool of marriage prospects. In addition, changes in Irish land laws after 1870, which permitted Catholics to own land, were more important in a subjective than in a purely objective way; that is, few were able to avail themselves of the opportunity. Nonetheless it served to titillate the acquisitive instinct of those who desired to better themselves. Kennedy has interpreted the oblique influence of sexual puritanism in the Irish reluctance to marry in a similar vein. He suggests that sexual puritanism was a by-product of, rather than the stimulus for, remaining celibate. Of paramount import was the readiness of the young to postpone or even abandon their hopes for marriage in order to realize their ambition of improved economic and social standing. In the desire to avoid romantic involvements, the young almost enthusiastically embraced a strict morality whose preoccupation was sex. The Irish clergy, themselves of peasant stock, encouraged the intense segregation of the sexes. If the young would not marry young, as one variant of Catholic teaching desired, then at the very least they must be kept at arm's length in the interest of chastity.

Irish Puritanism: The Virtue of Chastity

The 1782 Catholic Relief Act provided Catholics with a modicum of religious freedom: Catholic churches could be built within towns, Catholic bishops and order priests could live in Ireland, and Catholic teachers could teach in public schools. The influence of the clergy in secular matters was enhanced by the passage of the act.[13] The Catholic Emancipation Act of 1829 further increased the power of the clergy. Before these measures of religious freedom were enacted, the Catholic clergy had been less than a dominant force in the social life of the people. But one must not place undue emphasis on this legislation; even more important were two interrelated phenomena: the demise of the traditional Gaelic culture and the rise of a devotional/ puritanical Catholicism.

The Gaelic culture was a mixture of folk custom and belief not unlike those of other folk cultures. This culture was concerned with man's total relation to and place within nature. There existed in the literature and oral tradition "a sense of the harmony and mystery of man's place in nature." Included was a pagan yearning for communion with all of nature. As Evans succinctly put it, in this tradition, "the gods dwelt among the hills, and the living spirits of the land were ever present."[14] Thus animistic and pantheistic orientations were prevalent.

The traditional culture was able to exist side by side with Christianity because the Celts never formalized their beliefs into a religion.[15] The folk culture appealed to the imagination and emotions rather than the intellect. Yeats noted that "everyone is a visionary if you scratch him deep enough," but "the Celt is a visionary without scratching."[16] The intellectual and legalistic bent of Roman Christianity was a complement to, not in competition with, the visceral orientation of the Gaelic culture. Yet in another sense Christianity was in conflict with the folk culture because Christian thought turned man away from nature and toward God.[17] If Gaelic culture emphasized man's relation to nature, Christianity stressed man's relation to God.

The Gaelic culture had been declining at least since the eighteenth century[18] in part because industrialization and the rationalization of agriculture in England affected Ireland as well. The decline was so rapid in the nineteenth century that the formation of the Gaelic League in 1893, which was an attempt to preserve Irish as the native language and to encourage the study of and creation of Irish literature, was not the regeneration of this folk culture but actually its death knell.[19] Self-conscious cultural revitalization movements invariably believe the fact that the culture has already died.

Concomitant with the decline of Gaelic culture was the spectacular rise of a devotional Catholicism. In pre-famine Ireland, church was attended by less than half of the Catholic population, partly due to the dearth of priests. Over the next fifty years this situation was reversed so that by the 1880s over 90 per cent of the population attended mass every Sunday, the ratio of laity to nuns and priests declined sharply, and the number and variety of devotional practices, all well-attended, burgeoned.[20]

Behind the drive to institutionalize Catholicism in Ireland was Paul Cullen. Appointed rector of the Irish College in Rome in 1831 at a young age, later to become a Cardinal while Archbishop of Armagh, Cullen "retained throughout life the character of the headmaster of the Irish Church."[21] He regarded himself as the Pope's right-hand man, and at the synod of Thurles in 1850 was instrumental in effecting great discipline among the clergy and greater uniformity in religious practices. Cullen believed in the separation of Church and state and in clerical specialization in spiritual matters; both policies were later to be violated in practice.

Cullen pressed hard on the clergy, whom he envisioned as models for the laity, to encourage the more frequent reception of Holy Eucharist and confession of sins in penance. Related devotional practices such as the rosary, forty hours, perpetual adoration, novenas, the way of the cross, benediction, shrines, and retreats became immensely popular.[22]

Larkin has argued that devotional Catholicism filled a void in Irish society—that of identity—brought about by decline of the traditional culture.[23] In that sense devotional Catholicism represented a new culture. Likewise he maintains that Irish Catholicism merged with Irish nationalism so that to be a good Catholic was to be a good Irishman. Undoubtedly this is correct. However, several observations are in order.

First, these devotional practices should be seen in part as substitutes for the magical rites and practices of the traditional culture. Magic and superstition were integral to Gaelic culture.[24] Insofar as devotional practices were used by the laity principally to grant requests or to obtain favors and in general to control their world, they functioned as magical rites which always are an attempt to make the gods do man's will. Ostensibly these devotional practices were to give God glory, but then so were magical rites manifestly intended to appease the gods.

The devotional aspect of Irish Catholicism is only one side of a complex phenomenon; the other is puritanism. Devotionalism and puritanism should not be seen as antithetical but as complementary to one another. Devotionalism and puritanism were the positive and negative poles of an amalgam of religious rites and moral standards. Devotional practices were simultaneously a set of purification rites and prescriptions depicting the life of a virtuous Christian; puritan prohibitions were both rites of avoidance and proscriptions circumscribing the role of sinner. But devotional and puritanical Catholicism alike were necessitated by the demands of a single-inheritance agrarian economy.

Initially Irish Puritanism was influenced by French Puritanism or what Noonan calls French Augustinianism. Prior to the nineteenth century, Irish priests attended seminaries in France for the most part; their religious training reflected strict Augustinian teachings with regard to marriage, procreation, and the family. Noonan pointed out that "the theory expounded by these books and by these professors condemned any premarital sexual activity, restricted sexual initiatives in marriage to the procreative act, and viewed the whole sexual area of human life as peculiarly prone to concupiscence and actual sin."[25] Women were regarded as inferior beings and the source of many of men's temptations. Celibacy was elevated over the married state, and sins of the sexual variety were viewed as the most frequent and serious transgressions of God's law.

By 1850 the national Catholic seminary, Saint Patrick's College at Maynooth, was producing over half of the priests in Ireland.[26] Added to the former French influence on Irish pastoral work was the fact that many priests were by now of peasant backgrounds. And the priest's parents taught that the purpose of marriage was to provide "labour for the land and an heir for the family" and not to satisfy romantic instincts.[27] Moreover, the parents admonished their children that a marriage without parental consent meant disaster for everyone.

A condition of few and late marriages could be highly explosive if chaste celibacy was not expected and demanded of many, sometimes for life. Parents, out of economic and social considerations, warned their children against marriage, while the clergy did the same for religious reasons. The course of study at Maynooth included, in the seminarian's last year, instruction in counseling the laity about sins against chastity:

> They were instructed, as confessors, "never to omit pointing out . . . the means of overcoming temptation; such as, avoiding the external occasions of sin, averting the mind instantly from the object of temptation and fixing it on some other object." The young should be "special objects of a most paternal solicitude: if, in early youth, the heart be preserved from the taint of corruption; if the virtue of chastity be firmly planted therein resistance to temptation grows into a habit and becomes easy, and virtue strengthens with advancing years." Priests, accordingly, must impress on parents the importance of watching over their children, "of seeing the sorts of books they read; the sports they engage in; the places they frequent; and, above all, the companions with whom they associate." A former student of *De Matrimonio*, asked if his class had treated the subject lightly or with ribaldry, said that, on the contrary, "it was a dirty or a dreadful matter—a horrible matter. They . . . seriously thought it was filthy stuff altogether."[28]

The clergy saw a danger—premarital intercourse—in the recent demand that many remain celibate for long periods. To prevent the laity from engaging in such immorality, priests emphasized sins of the flesh in their sermons and homilies. The temptations inherent in courting were stressed. Connell described the chastity-enforcement activities of the clergy this way:

> There were priests who dissuaded their parishioners from marriage, not merely by creating the impression that it was "a secondary and often imperfect state of life," but by imposing rules of conduct that made courtship less likely. "The bare thought of company-keeping or courtship filled them with horror." After several changes theologians had fixed the number of Deadly Sins as seven; Irish parish priests in practice made courtship an eighth. For lovers to walk the roadside in rural Ireland when the average priest was abroad was a perilous adventure. . . . "It was considered a disgrace to be seen walking with one of the opposite sex in broad daylight." . . . The clergy in a western county "used to arm themselves with sticks long ago, and go out at night and anywhere they'd meet a courting couple they'd work the stick on them."[29]

The net result of this remarkable emphasis on chastity, the severe restrictions on courtship, and a disparagement of the married state was to promote, especially among women, a real fear of sex—even in marriage. This "ferocious" chastity among peasant girls became less a virtue and more a detriment to harmonious marriage. They often entered marriage leery of the sins they might commit against the Sixth Commandment instead of anticipating the love that might be given to their spouses. It was said that nuns did not regard marriage as a vocation from God, as they did the religious state, and omitted any discussion of it in their instruction of girls. The implication was clearly that marriage was a necessary evil, something about which one felt ashamed.

Nothing less than the complete segregation of the sexes was effected. Young boys and girls were taught in separate schools; men and boys did not intermingle with women and girls in church, but worshiped separate and apart. As the children matured into adolescence, the restrictions grew tighter. Young men and women were expected to walk on opposite sides of the road and refrain from talking to each other. Dancing, so popular before the mid-nineteenth century, was declining under clerical pressure. Integrated games, amateur theatricals, and parties were all discouraged.

The religious life was regarded as the highest calling; therefore each peasant family hoped for a vocation to the priesthood and sometimes one to the sisterhood. Peasant family life, in turn, reinforced religious teachings regarding marriage. And many priests came from this background.

Clerical influence on courtship and marriage patterns cannot be fully understood without reference to the social role of the priest. As mentioned previously, the influence of the priest in secular affairs increased with the passage of British laws granting Catholics a greater measure of religious freedom. The priest, in addition to his spiritual duties, often served as matchmaker, arbiter of family disputes, economic adviser, political adviser,[30] and psychological counselor. In brief, he played the role of the expert on most aspects of life. The priest was not adequately prepared for this role because his background and education had been almost entirely devoted to religious matters. But why then did the people not only acquiesce to this definition of the priest's role but also encourage it?

The reasons are many and complex. The long history of English domination had left Ireland with little control over its political and economic destiny. The conflict between the two countries had been more than political and economic. It had also been religious—protestant England suppressing Catholic Ireland—and Catholicism and the priesthood had become intertwined with political sentiments. To be a good Catholic was to be a patriot and vice versa. As England slowly loosened her grip on Irish institutions, the priest was the natural man to look to for leadership. Few besides priests were educated. The only other class from which leaders might be conscripted was that of Catholic landowners; however, they were hardly better regarded than the alien landowning class because of their complicity in much of the suppression of Irish self-determination. Doctors, lawyers, and teachers were not as yet professionally organized forces and did not possess the confidence of the people.

The priest was thought by some to have magical powers and therefore was capable of solving material as well as spiritual problems. Ultimately the reason why the role of expert or man of knowledge was thrust upon the priest was the faith of the people, which was more steadfast than that in any other Catholic country.[31] Through centuries in which political, economic, and educational institutions were stifled by British rule, religion and kinship provided the basis for social order in Ireland. Moreover, religion assumed a great import in the daily lives of the peasantry.

Religion would have to be this important to explain the wholesale acceptance of chastity among the peasantry, many of whom were destined to remain celibate permanently. Where the Irish actually as chaste as their religion demanded? Comparative statistics on illegitimacy would seem to indicate a small incidence of premarital relations in Ireland.[32] This statistic is even more convincing when one realizes that birth control devices could not be obtained legally in Ireland.[33]

Yet coeval with the sexual puritanism was a ribald attitude toward sex, especially among married men. Arensberg and Kimball resolve what is only an apparent contradiction:

> In any event the laughter and hearty guffaws with which references of nearly any kind to sexual intercourse, sexual attraction, and childbearing are greeted, and the evident interest they evoke, are very much part of the everyday behavior of the small farmers. They do not imply in any sense an approval or acceptance of the deeds described. They are rather expressions of a very definite judgment. They are in the nature of a condemnation in which laughter is itself a sanction upon the forbidden.
>
> The "earthiness" and the ribaldry of the country people is not an antithesis to their strict moral code. Rather it reinforces it. It gives its pietistic and too-respectable, churchly and town-bourgeois aspects an authentic indigenous touch. Even more important, it makes for a modification of the conventional attitudes which fit them for the country people's social life.
>
> In this ambivalence of attitude one can see the identification between status in human relations and norms about sexual behavior more clearly. The one view, that "holiness" denies sex, can be reserved to suit the nonprocreant statuses of family life. The other, the heart and open view embodying animal analogy, frank interest, overt desire, can be reserved for the persons whose roles in social life allow free rein to the amatory and procreative urges.[34]

However, a ribald, "raunchy" attitude toward sex often only covers up and obscures a deep-seated sexual puritanism. Those who piously speak about the adhere to this sexual code and those who openly joke about its violations both take seriously the sexual code and accept its moral legitimacy.

Irish sexual puritanism is of course legendary. And as such it has been used to explain too many aspects of Irish life. Some have used puritanism to explain the Irish reluctance to marry. Kennedy, on the other hand, maintains that "the Irish Catholic emphasis on the sinfulness of pre-marital sex . . . is a result rather than a cause of the high proportion of single persons in the Irish population."[35] In support of this thesis is the fact that Catholic teaching encouraged adults to marry and to marry young at that; moreover, marriage was regarded as a sacrament. It was only after Irish social structure had conspired to make marriage unfeasible for many that the Catholic church settled for second best: the prevention of sexual indiscretion among the unmarried. Therefore, Kennedy skillfully argues, the pattern of little and late marriage was not the result of sexual puritanism, but both were a consequence of economic desire and economic necessity.

But perhaps it is not necessary to choose between conflicting explanations. Is it possible that sexual puritanism and individual socioeconomic aspiration are actually complementary aspects of a still more general phenomenon that itself worked in diverse ways? Sexual puritanism appears to have been a widespread phenomenon in western Europe, affecting protestant and Catholic country alike, as was the sharp increase in the desire for goods and services. These related phenomena are best understood in the context of the spectacular rise of the middle class, its ideology, and its morality.[36] Secular puritanism provided a justification for avoiding romantic involvements that, if they ended in marriage, threatened one's desire for an increased standard of living. Thus middle-class morality stressed delayed gratification by focusing on the "restraining" virtues of thrift, abstinence, prudence, and, most of all, hard work. It was the practice of these virtues that would insure success. In the same spirit the Irish man was expected to delay marriage until he could well afford it. Sexual puritanism and the resultant segregation of the sexes were but a means to economic success. Middle class morality, which at times bifurcated the public from the private sphere, still stressed the older Christian virtues of charity, humility, and purity for the edification of one's family. Sexual purity as one of the traditional Christian virtues needed only be exaggerated and overemphasized to become sexual puritanism. Therefore the sexual puritanism advocated in the home was not only privately virtuous but also publicly advantageous in helping one succeed.

Irish Puritanism like all "lived morality" had its roots in collective necessity and the ideal image the Irish had of themselves.[37] It was necessitated by the lack of land, consolidation of holdings, the stem family system, a desire to improve one's standard of living, and the Irish image of themselves as good Catholics. This last point assumes then that there were traditional Catholic prohibitions against unfettered sexual activity. Without such an already extant morality, free love or sex with love—whose consequences could have been checked by infanticide and birth control—might have been preached instead of sexual puritanism. Thus sexual puritanism deriving from both Irish and French sources on the one hand and economic aspirations and necessities on the other were interactive, not one the cause of the other.

Irish social and economic conditions worked to intensify and exaggerate already existing prohibitions against premarital sex until this sin became paramount, necessitating the segregation of the sexes. At the same time a general sexual puritanism was emergent in Europe for much the same reasons as in Ireland. As transmitted through French seminaries, it served to exacerbate Irish sexual morality when economic considerations necessitated changes in the pattern of courtship and marriage. In a certain sense Irish parents more than Irish priests were responsible for sexual puritanism as a means of maintaining a stem family system. And the Irish priests, who by the nineteenth century were of peasant origins, received from both home upbringing and their religious training a sense of the necessity of sexual puritanism.

Many things suffered as a result of changes in the structure of the family after the Great Famine, not least of all the status of marriage. At times the clergy demeaned the matrimonial state, especially in comparison with its own. Chastity was elevated to the plateau of supreme virtue; therefore marriage eliminated one's chance to be supremely virtuous and in this sense constituted a failure or fault. Also, marriage lost much of its former stature within the community. In one Irish community study focusing on the 1950s and early 1960s, attitudes toward marriage (which have their origin in post-famine society) were analyzed:

> The consensus of opinion seems to be that in the course of time one marries, just as in the course of time one grows old, and that as old age is a limitation of life, a narrowing of one's sphere of activity, so marriage is also an inevitable limitation. The community is not opposed to marriage . . . but each individual avoids it as long as possible, just as one tries to avoid old age. Where such an attitude to marriage reigns, the institution has low status. It may be a personal necessity but it is not a social ideal nor is it a positive goal for the majority of the community.[38]

A low status for marriage is functional to a system in which relatively few marry and chastity is expected of the unmarried. If sex is allowable only in marriage, the undesirable aspects of married life have to be stressed to offset its natural attraction. And stressed they were in Ireland until the point was reached where the son who married and inherited the land sometimes wished he, too, had been allowed to emigrate. If the status of marriage was low, that of bachelorhood was high.

This generalization must be qualified and explained, however. If marriage naturally followed the realization of economic security—in the rural areas this meant the inheritance of land—then must not marriage be highly valued? But this is precisely the point: It was the economic transaction which made marriage possible that was the overwhelming concern. Marriage was contingent on the assumption of economic status and was the obligation that accompanied it. Marriage offered economic and sexual gratification; nevertheless its romantic attraction was dimmed by the realistic economic planning and haggling that always preceded it. Furthermore, the segregation of the sexes that followed as well as preceded marriage made the psychological relationship between spouses less than satisfactory.

Ultimately then the Irish were ambivalent about marriage: The Catholic church promoted it for lay people but held celibacy to be a holier state. The Irish family, which saw its economic future in the consolidation of agricultural holdings, needed to arrange the marriage of one of its sons in order to keep the land within its control; at the same time parents had to urge most of their children to remain celibate. Since full economic status preceded marriage, marriage itself had to be devalued to mollify those who would never marry and thus never attain full socioeconomic standing in the community.

Family Relationships before the Great Famine

Apparently, during the period of early marriage (late eighteenth and early nineteenth centuries) father-son and husband-wife relationships were markedly different from what they were after the Great Famine (1845–48). About this Connell noted:

> In a community which lacked so largely institutional provision for sickness, widowhood, and old age, common prudence pointed to the virtues of early marriage. By its means, too, the peasant father in Ireland, more fortunate than many of his kind elsewhere, was spared the anxieties associated with the establishment of his children. His sons, on their own initiative and whenever they pleased, could marry and secure their customary standard of living on land which their father or a neighbour did not miss, or on land newly won from mountain or bog. We should, perhaps, be chary of believing that Irish-peasant life ever glistened with the gaity and contentment reflected in the novels of a Carleton or a Love. But, such is human resourcefulness, we are not required to believe that all was drab, even in the half-century which Ireland used to demonstrate how European life might most frugally be maintained and multiplied. Some relief, some contentment, there was; and when its source was neither religion nor the potato-pot, ever filled with its strikingly adequate diet, most probably it was to be found in an institution of marriage entered virtually by all, of their own choice at an uncommonly youthful age.[39]

And again:

> Before the Famine, then, it was not unreasonable for peasant sons
> and daughters, while still young adults, to feel that they could, at
> will, transform themselves into husbands or wives: the first move
> towards marriage was their own. But during the Famine and in
> the following years, children commonly lost this initiative to their
> father. A marriage came to be heralded by commercial rather than
> biological advances; and until the two fathers concerned had com-
> pleted their negotiations their children remained unmarried. Any
> clash of will between fathers and sons was incidental to this shift
> of the source of decision.[40]

Thus it may be inferred that father-son and husband-wife relationships were more intimate and mutually satisfying before the
Great Famine than afterwards. Sons were less subject to the arbitrary authority of their fathers, and marriages took place at the discretion of the young because a small plot of land with which to form
a homestead was easily obtained. Courtship was not restricted;
rather, it was encouraged. That marriage was eagerly anticipated
and provided some measure of relief in an otherwise austere environment suggests that the husband-wife relationship was then more
romantic and friendly. Certainly the husband-wife relationship was
far more than the largely economic transaction it subsequently
became. This being so, the Irish kinship system was less dependent
on the brother-sister and maternal uncle-nephew relationships as
sources of mutuality and emotional support for the generations
prior to the Great Famine than it was afterward.

Family Relationships after
the Great Famine

Not only the pattern of marriage but also the pattern of relationships
among family members were affected by the single-inheritance system. Irish kinship underwent profound change.

Claude Levi-Strauss has provided us with a method for studying kinship that he calls "structural analysis." Taking a cue from structural linguistics, he views kinship metaphorically, that is, as language—a means of communication. As Levi-Strauss noted:

> Like phonemes, kinship terms are elements of meaning; like phonemes, they acquire meaning only if they are integrated into systems. "Kinship systems," like "phonemic systems are built by the mind on the level of unconscious thought. Finally, the recurrence of kinship patterns, marriage rules, similar prescribed attitudes between certain types of relatives, and so forth, in scattered regions of the globe and in fundamentally different societies, leads us to believe that, in the case of kinship as well as linguistics, the observable phenomena result from the action of laws which are general but implicit. The problem can therefore be formulated as follows: Although they belong to *another order of reality,* kinship phenomena are *of the same type* as linguistic phenomena.[41]

Just as structural linguistics has focused on the "unconscious infrastructures" of phonemes, the "relations" between terms of a language and "systems" of phonemes, structural anthropology emphasizes the unconscious infrastructures of kinship, the relations between kinship terms, and systems of kinship terminology and kinship attitudes.

In the past the social sciences have stressed the content of terms instead of the relations between terms. For instance, A. R. Radcliffe-Brown theorized that the basic unit of kinship is the "elementary family," which consists of a husband (father), a wife (mother), and their children. Three fundamental relationships are subsumed in the unit: between parent and child, between children of the same parents, and between husband and wife. Ultimately human kinship is formed of the relations among these elementary families, which bind family to family in a community. Levi-Strauss objected to Radcliffe-Brown's formulation of kinship, remarking that "it is not the families (isolated terms) which are truly 'elementary,' but, rather, the relations between those terms."[42] The terms Levi-Strauss refers to are "brother," "sister," "father," and "son." These terms are related in a manner by which, for both generations, both a positive and a negative relationship exist. Within this structure the relationship between father and son is to the relationship between husband and wife as the relationship between brother and sister is to the relationship between maternal uncle and nephew. In other words, if the father-son relationship is cold and formal (negative), the maternal uncle-nephew one will be warm and sympathetic (positive). Likewise, if the husband-wife relationship is negative, the brother-sister one will be positive. Knowledge of one relationship enables the observer to predict the other relationships.

In Radcliffe-Brown's formulation, the maternal uncle-nephew relationship was a secondary relationship, not part of the elementary family. In objecting to this, Levi-Strauss noted that the avunculate is the cornerstone of the kinship system. He explained the origin of the avunculate thus:

> The primitive and irreducible character of the basic unit of kinship, as we have defined it, is actually a direct result of the universal presence of an incest taboo. This is really saying that in human society a man must obtain a woman from another man who gives him a daughter or a sister. Thus we do not need to explain how the maternal uncle emerged in the kinship structure: he does not emerge—he is present initially. Indeed, the presence of the maternal uncle is a necessary precondition for the structure to exist. The error of traditional anthropology, like that of traditional linguistics, was to consider the terms, and not the relations between the terms.[43]

Let us apply Levi-Strauss's theory to Irish kinship. Arensberg and Kimball described the father-son relationship in early twentieth-century Ireland:

> ... the father exercises his control over the whole activity of the "boy." It is by no means confined to their work together. Indeed, the father is the court of last resort, which dispenses punishment for deviations from the norm of conduct in all spheres. Within the bounds of custom and law he has full power to exercise discipline. Corporal punishment is not a thing of the past in Ireland, and, especially in the intermediate stages of the child's development, from seven to puberty, it gets full play.[44]

And again:

> There is none of the close companionship and intimate sympathy
> which characterizes, at least ideally, the relationship in other
> groups. . . . Coupled with this is the lifelong subordination the
> retention of the name "boy" implies, which is never relaxed even
> in the one sphere in which farmer father and son can develop and
> intense community of interest—farm work . . . everything within
> the behavior developed in the relationship militates against the
> growth of close mutual sympathy. As a result, the antagonisms
> inherent in such a situation often break through very strongly
> when conflicts arise.[44]

Thus the primary relationship between father and son was one of
strictness and latent hostility. The son owed the father labor,
respect, and subordination; the father owed one of the sons his land.

The relationship between husband and wife was also one of
estrangement. Arland Usser observed:

> If married, he seldom thinks of bringing home presents or giving
> his house any grace of decoration. He does not go out walking
> with his wife or often take her to amusements; in the summer he
> does not generally take his family with him on tours, even when
> he can afford it. Frequent days at the races with male "buddies"
> are more to his taste. . . . The Irish wife, at grips with a numer-
> ous family in a rather comfortless home, with a not-too-generous
> housekeeping allowance, comes off less well. . . . Irishmen do not
> treat women coarsely or brutally. They simply try to ignore and
> forget them.[46]

As another observer put it:

> In relation to the mother, the role of the father is neither that of
> companion nor lover. This is not to say that there is a bad rela-
> tionship between them. The husband is in most cases consider-
> ate, but the relationship is markedly unsentimental. . . . There is
> . . . a certain amount of conflict in the wife's attitude to her hus-
> band's role; she would like him to play a more intimate role but,
> at the same time, fears that he may become a nuisance. Since the

mother's role is strong and she has no compensatory roles outside
the family, she fears that any change in her husband's role would
weaken her own.[47]

And further:

Because her role and that of the father does not allow for the
development of companionship between them, and that if it were
not for the work she has to do and a fairly large family, she would
lead a lonely life, the mother compensates by seeking that companionship with at least one son which is missing in her relations
with her husband.[48]

The husband's primary obligation to his wife was to provide economically for a household wherein she would wield immense power.
Their relationship was neither intimate nor especially friendly. Just
as their childhood and adolescent social activities had been segregated along male-female lines in the interest of chastity, so now husband and wife often enjoyed their leisure separately. But it was the
man who did most of the enjoying because his wife was tied to the
household. Irish courtship was above all an economic transaction
between two families; romance and friendship were secondary considerations.

On the other hand the brother-sister relationship was one of
mutuality and tenderness. Arensberg and Kimball observed:

. . . there is a good deal of the boy's regard for his mother in his
attitude toward his sister. Likewise for the sister, especially in the
years when both are fully adult, the brother comes to have much
of the position of the father. . . .[49]

But there was a debtor-creditor aspect to their relationship in that
the sister was dependent on her brother for a dowry if she married
after his inheritance of the farm. Moreover, if the sister did not
marry and remained at home, she was placed indefinitely under his
auspices.

The avuncular relationship in Ireland was so covert that, as
Arensberg and Kimball noted, "The country people marvel that a

young child may often like its mother's brother better than 'its own uncles.'"[50] However, Levi-Strauss has pointed out that the avunculate is not manifest at all times and in all societies. Furthermore, the importance of kinship varies from culture to culture so that in certain modern societies other institutions have assumed the function of kinship in the regulation of social relationships. Moreover, in more complex societies, the avuncular relationship may become "submerged with a differentiated context," and be "obliterated or may merge with other relationships."[51] It is not surprising then that the remnants of the avunculate in rural Ireland were not always recognized for what they were. Important to this analysis is the fact that the maternal uncle-nephew relationship in Ireland was one of affection and intimacy.

The unit of kinship—the relationships between the terms "father," "son," "brother," and "sister"—has been described for Ireland in the mid-to-late nineteenth and early twentieth centuries. Its structure is represented in Figure 1. In each generation there is a positive and a negative relationship. Consequently the relationship between father and son is to the relationship between husband and wife as the relationship between brother and sister is to that between maternal uncle and nephew.

Let us return to the avunculate for a moment. During a crisis within a culture or between cultures the avuncular relationship often reasserts itself because it is part of the elementary structure of the family.[52]

Until the advent of the Great Famine in Ireland, the lesson of a minute subdivision of land had only slowly been learned—even in the wake of overworked land and potato shortages. In addition, land legislation and Catholic emancipation provided a few Irish with the

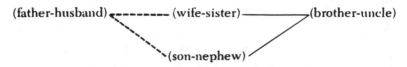

Figure 1. The Irish unit of kinship-patrilineal. Key: dashed line-formal, austere relationship; solid line-mutual, affectionate relationship.

opportunity to own land and the others at least with the desire to maintain rented land within the family, expand its boundaries, and pass it on intact to other generations. The pattern of inheritance was changed and, with it, the structure of the family. This alteration in the distribution of land, which numbered among its consequences the wholesale emigration of young people, was crisis enough. But when the Great Famine of the late 1840s was superimposed upon it, the result was nothing less than catastrophic. It would be precisely in these circumstances, according to Levi-Strauss, that one would expect the avunculate to reemerge.

The avuncular relationship did reappear, albeit in the disguised form of the male group. The male group became firmly entrenched during this period. It represented the religious interest in chastity, the family interest in celibacy, and the economic interest in single inheritance. Religious teachings demanded a chaste existence for the unmarried, and family economics imposed celibacy on all the male offspring save he who was to inherit. Young men were socialized into all-male groups whose older members established avuncular-type relationships with younger members. The male group as institution, then, provided a framework for the avunculate. Social and emotional needs of young men, especially those of friendship, guidance, and recreation, were met in the male group. It provided a context for the intimate mutual relationship between males of different generations—the maternal uncle and nephew relationship in this case. Thus the generations were linked in a relationship of authority and subordination, father-son, and in a relationship of friendship, maternal uncle (bachelor-group member) -nephew (bachelor-group initiate).

A sense of the part the avunculate played within the male group is essential for an understanding of rural Irish life. Previous Irish studies have brought out the conflict among the different male generations without fully drawing out the source of their unity. The all-male group functioned to make palatable the system of single inheritance, few and late marriages, and chastity to young males not naturally inclined toward delayed gratification. Older males socialized younger males into the "bachelor group" traditions, attitudes, and norms that served to elevate the unmarried state at the expense of the married. The avunculate worked to unite the different male generations in support of the new economic and familial relationships. The all-male group, then, proved the cornerstone of rural Irish social order.

5

Irish Drinking as Cultural Remission

"Would you like a drink, boy?" "If you please, sir," said the boy.
The old man opened another bottle grudgingly, and handed it to
the boy. "What age are you?" he asked. "Seventeen," said the boy.

As the old man said nothing further, the boy took the bottle,
said: "Here's my best respects, sir, to Mr. Henchy," drank the con-
tents, put the bottle back on the table and wiped his mouth with
his sleeve. Then he took up the corkscrew and went out of the door
sideways, muttering some form of salutation.

"That's the way it begins," said the old man.
"The thin edge of the wedge," said Mr. Henchy.

James Joyce,
Dubliners

No matther . . . what any one may say . . . Irelan' sober . . . is
Irelan' . . . free.

Sean O'Casey,
Juno and the Paycock

To the non-Irish world perhaps no behavior is more associated
with the Irish than drinking. It is therefore with great trepida-
tion that one undertakes an analysis of Irish drinking. I will formu-
late a historically specific ideal type of Irish male drinking for the
period from the 1870s through the 1930s, although its beginning can
be dated to the 1840s and the rise of a new Irish family system.[1] The
Irish male group grew in importance in direct proportion to the
emergence of the new single inheritance farm economy and the pattern of a low marriage rate and late age at marriage. Without press-
ing the analogy too hard, one could regard the male group as the
avunculate in the Irish family.

Much of the information on which my theory is based has been
gathered and presented by Patrick McNabb and associates in *The
Limerick Rural Survey*. County Limerick in the Province of Munster

is a well-to-do agricultural area. While it might not be the most typical Irish county, it is certainly not markedly atypical. Whatever
unique traits Limerick male groups possess are relatively unimportant compared to the great similarities they share with male groups
all over Ireland. Supporting evidence drawn from literary sources,
travelers' accounts, and social histories appears congruent with
many of McNabb's observations about male groups. Of great interest is McNabb's report (1958–64) that the older men in the community remember a time in the past when the boundaries of the male
groups were much more definitively drawn and their leaders more
clearly recognized. These community informants contrasted male
groups in the present with those in the past. "A capacity to drink or
to fight is no longer a norm," they argue, although it once was, and
the leaders of the male groups now are closer to one's own age group
than they once were.[2] McNabb wisely points out that such an organization of males could exist "only in a closed community."[3] On the
other hand, certain customs of the rural Irish male group (1870s–
1930s) have survived. With these qualifications in mind, I shall con-
struct an ideal type of the rural Irish male drinking group partly
from older men's memories of the past and partly from observations
about the present-day male group by those in the community and by
researchers.

The Bachelor Group

McNabb referred to the male group as the "bachelor group" even
though married men were among its members. Although he used
the term descriptively, it will be used here explicatively—as a
Weberian ideal type. The bachelor group is an ideal type of a historical particular in that it is peculiar to Irish society during a specific
time period, 1870 to 1940.

Relatively few marriages, a late age at marriage among those
who did marry, a religiously imposed chastity on the unmarried, an
extensive segregation of the sexes, negative (authoritarian and hos-
tile) relationships between father and son and between husband

and wife combined to make all-male groups even more important
in the maintenance of communal social order than they had been
before the Great Famine. To compensate the large number of
unmarried males, the status of marriage was devalued and that of
the single state revalued. McNabb described this rather unusual
condition:

> The higher percentage single, even in the older age groups, means
> that there is no stigma attached to the single state. This is sup-
> ported to a great extent by the example of a celibate clergy. It is
> possible that the very high status which the clergyman has, by
> virtue of his office, also attaches to certain conditions in his life. It
> is not suggested that the presence of the clergyman acts as any-
> thing more than an example in this respect, or that lay people aim
> at celibacy in the same sense as does the clergyman. Where the
> single status is an acceptable one, and where the higher propor-
> tion of the adult population are single, it is inevitable that the
> society will be organized primarily for their benefit.[4]

McNabb, however, qualified this conclusion later my saying that the
benefits and privileges accrued to being a single male and a member
of the bachelor group. Prestige was low and activities few for the
unmarried female.

In a family system in which infrequent and late marriage is customary, the unmarried are granted longer periods of fewer responsibilities than they would otherwise possess. Fewer responsibilities
mean greater opportunity for leisure-time activities. However, in a
patrilineal and patriarchal system of kinship, single males will be
given preference over single females for the satisfaction of recreational needs. Moreover, in a society where chastity and segregation
of the sexes among the unmarried are considered necessary to maintain the family system according to religious teachings, unmarried
males will bond together more extensively and intensely than they
would in a society where unfettered interaction between males and
females is the rule.

Not merely the need for sexual adjustment but also general
emotional and recreational needs were provided for within the
bachelor group. For men it provided a context for all nonwork and

nonfamily activities. Furthermore, one's larger status within the community was partially determined by membership and continued participation in the bachelor group. Leaders of the all-male groups were also community leaders. Perhaps the most critical fact helping to expose community underlife is that married men could participate fully in the activities of the bachelor group.

That married men of all ages could carry full membership in the group demonstrates that the division between male and female was greater than that between young and old, unmarried and married. Continued bachelor-group membership functioned as a reward to those who married. In a society where the status of marriage was devalued, where propaganda against marriage was quite pervasive, and marriage was not a positive goal for most males, inducements to marry had to be provided. The obvious inducements were the acquisition of full economic status (inheritance of the land) and sexual privileges. A less manifest reward was continued membership in the male group after marriage, which might be viewed as partial compensation for the negative husband-wife relationship. Thus many "bachelors" were married men, and the segregation of the sexes remained intact even after marriage; moreover, married men's male-group participation proved essential for maintaining community order within the demands of kinship and religion.

The bachelor group is an Irish institution, but within its overall structure exist diverse "bachelor groups"—social groups that can be differentiated according to location, class, marital status, and age. Although such groups are similar in their maleness, they differ with respect to the other social characteristics of their members.

Age is perhaps the most important social characteristic next to sex. Conrad Arensberg emphasized the conflicts between the various generations of males.[5] Antagonisms between the young and the old, between the "boys" and the "men," were a critical component in his study. In the previous chapter I described the father-son relationship in Ireland for the 100 years after the 1830s as being negative. However, sex as a source of social differentiation provided to be of overriding importance in Irish society and thus diminished the total impact of the age status. The salience of the sex differential made age differentials less important than they would otherwise have been.

Thus sex as an attraction proved stronger than age as a repellant. Moreover, the avunculate in the form of bachelor-group socialization of prospective members by older members established the positive relationship between the two generations of males that previous analyses of Irish family life have largely overlooked. Thus the same individual, who in his role as father had a negative relationship with his own sons, might, in the role of bachelor-group member, establish a positive and enduring relationship with someone else's son.

The hapless situation of the "boy," the unmarried man in his forties or fifties still "looking" for a wife, reflects much of the Irish ambivalence about their social order. The "boy," often the butt of jokes, was made out to be a comical figure. Yet his real significance was that he was the victim of a harsh system of single inheritance and few and late marriages. Here is a pathetic/comical character who finally inherits his father's land but at an age when interest in the opposite sex has already begun to wane. So when he advertises for a wife in the local newspaper, it can only provoke laughter and at times scorn; in the "boy" the Irish understood the great sacrifices they had forced their own to make in the interest of a more prosperous farm economy.

In the closed communities that existed before the 1940s, the bachelor group helped to keep open conflict between younger and older men to a minimum. All men, both those who were destined to marry and those who were not, fell under the auspices of this institution. Therefore only married men could act as a bridge between the unmarried and married by acting like and socializing with bachelors. As McNabb observed: "In this group, differences are not made according to age. At one time it had recognized leaders. These leaders were usually married men who had been exceptional in some way in the past. . . ."[6]

However, there were male cliques based on class, marital status, and age. Each of these social differentiations helped to determine one's close associations under the institutional umbrella of the bachelor group. Because the barriers between cliques were not rigid, older members associated quite intimately with younger unmarried members.[7] The cliques simply represented a preference for one's own. Married men had more in common with other married men than with unmarried men, and such was the case for the other sources of social differentiation. In some communities, it would appear, the boundaries between cliques were more sharply drawn than in others. But the fact of one's maleness was more important than any of the differences one had with the other male members of the community. Thus bachelor group membership provided for a constantly shifting set of friendships and associations.

With the disappearance of the closed communities, however, the bachelor group as institution began to disintegrate. Both *The Limerick Rural Survey* and Hugh Brody's *Inishkillane,* a study of the west of Ireland, point to this.[8] In the traditional bachelor group, married men often served as leaders in a rather forceful way and were "chosen" for their feats of drinking, fighting, and storytelling. Today the male group is more amorphous, its leaders more transient, and its members more nearly one's own age and social standing. Indeed, Brody's study indicates that because of the large percentage of unmarried householders in the west of Ireland, bachelors have moved to the very center of community life. Moreover, bars are now frequented mostly by householders, married and unmarried, while those who are unwilling or unable to remain on the land steer clear of the bars. Rather than being a center of social control and male cohesiveness, the pub has become a symbol of differentiation between those destined to remain on the land and those who leave.[9]

In the traditional community, the pub did serve as a center of social control for the enforcement of community standards:

> The pubs are great places for gossip, and for this reason are often centers of trouble. The men drink heavily and their tongues loosen. There is an unfortunate habit of taking a rise out of some person. A group of men made overconfident by drink may chafe one of the company on his shortcomings. During moments of temper, gossip may be repeated. . . . The groups in bars have developed an interesting method of community criticism and ostracism. The offending party is allowed to sit on his own. The men are polite but restrained. On such occasion there is always an air of tension in the public house. Later in the night, a group of men will begin to talk in stage whispers (loud enough to be heard by the offender), in

general terms and in derogatory manner about people who commit offenses similar to the one which he has committed. The offender may choose to ignore the indirect criticism. If so, he loses face. It is more common for the offender to challenge the group to "say what's in their minds." Here we have the very essence of expression in this community; the fear of giving direct offense even to one who by his actions has merited exclusion, and the inability to step outside accustomed behaviour without the support of the group.[10]

Not drinking with an individual was a means of punishing his violation of community norms. Essentially this form of ostracism was a temporary measure. It was also a direct means of social control in contrast with the indirect criticism also used by public-house devotees. The means of social control that took place within the pub, then, were representative of the control tactics of a highly integrated community.

Institutionalized Drinking

Bachelor social groups for the period 1870–1940 have been described briefly, but their institutional context needs to be explained. That way we can begin to see hard drinking among Irish males in its larger cultural context. If an institution, put very simply, is a "regulatory agency, channeling human actions," then the Irish male group certainly qualifies.[11]

Drinking as a Rite of Passage

Institutions such as marriage and the family involve individuals in assuming new positions. The taking of a new status or the transition from one status to another is often marked by ritualistic observances. The more important status transitions like marriage, puberty, and adulthood involve rites of passage.

Rites of passage are "ceremonies whose essential purpose is to enable the individual to pass from one defined position to another which is equally well defined."[12] Arnold van Gennep delimited rites of passage as a category and suggested subcategories:

> I have tried to assemble here all the ceremonial patterns which accompany a passage from one situation to another or from one cosmic or social world to another. Because of the importance of these transitions, I think it legitimate to single out rites of passage as a special category, which under further analysis may be subdivided into rites of separation, transition rites, and rites of incorporation. These three subcategories are not developed to the same extent by all peoples or in every ceremonial pattern. Rites of separation are prominent in funeral ceremonies, rites of incorporation at marriages. Transition rites may play an important part, for instance, in pregnancy, betrothal, and initiation; or they may be reduced to a minimum in adoption, in the delivery of a second child, in remarriage, or in the passage from the second to the third age group. Thus, although a complete scheme of rites of passage theoretically includes preliminal rites (rites of separation), liminal rites (rites of transition), and postliminal rites (rites of incorporation), in specific instances these three types are not always equally important or equally elaborated.[13]

Rites of separation are ceremonies that express the divesting of one's former state or position; transition rites are ceremonies by which one readies himself to enter the new state; rites of incorporation represent ceremonies by which one is brought into or established in the new state or position.

During the period from the 1870s through the 1930s the passage from adolescence to manhood was symbolized by entrance into the bachelor group. McNabb described briefly the transition to manhood in rural Ireland: "According to local opinion, a young man was initiated (into the bachelor group) when he took his first drink in the local public house. This was a sign that he had grown up and was acceptable to the male community."[14] The transition to manhood occurs concomitantly with entrance into the bachelor group. In van Gennep's scheme, an initiation rite is a rite of passage.

Prior to or concurrent with entrance into the bachelor group, the male is required to break off any serious romantic relationship. McNabb described the pattern of rural Irish courtship preceding bachelor-group membership:

> By the time the girls have reached sixteen and the boys eighteen, they have begun to pair off, and from this to their twenty-first year is the only period of their lives when their relationship is relatively normal. The pressure against pairing off is so strong in the community that such love affairs are carried on surreptitiously. Every effort is made by couples to hide their relationships from neighbours and parents. They meet outside the home and, if possible, will carry on their courtship away from the neighbourhood. Both young men and women said that they would not ask friends of the opposite sex to their homes. These courtships, although very intense, are short lived. They rarely last beyond the end of adolescence.[15]

Rites of separation may be either prescriptive or proscriptive. The prohibition against romantic involvement is, indeed, a negative rite, but one whose full meaning can be grasped only by considering its relation to other, positive rites.[16]

A rite of transition symbolizes an intermediate stage between the relinquishment of an old status and the assumption of a new one; moreover, it is sometimes spatially designated and accompanied by territorial movement.[17] The new station or position may be designated by a country, territory, village, church, house, or any of their parts. The journey that takes one to the point which sets off the new area from the neutral zone or old territory is part of the rite of transition. This point is referred to as a "threshold," and it sometimes assumes the form of a door, a beam, a stone, a branch, a gate— something that must be crossed or passed over or under. The threshold in the Irish rite of passage from male adolescence to adulthood, bachelor-group initiation, is the entrance to the public house. The journey to this point with a bachelor-group sponsor, who invites the initiate to the public house and accompanies him there, is a rite of transition.

The crossing of the threshold (entering the public house) and the first drinking session with other bachelor-group members are rites of incorporation. Van Gennep mentioned drinking together as a rite of passage, specifically "a rite of incorporation of physical union."[18]

Rites of passage from adolescence to manhood and initiation into the bachelor group follow this sequence:

Rite of Separation	The prohibition against romantic relationships
Rite of Transition	The journey to the public house with a bachelor-group member
Rite of Incorporation	Entrance into the public house and first drink with fellow bachelor-group members.

It is not the alcohol itself or the act of drinking itself that brings the power of manhood. Proof of this is the fact that prior to bachelor-group initiation, young men drink alcoholic beverages, but not in the local public house or with bachelor-group members.[19] Likewise crossing the threshold of the public house alone does not suggest manhood because young boys, strangers, and temperance devotees at various times enter the public house. Nor does merely being in the company of bachelor-group members demonstrate manhood because bachelor-group leaders establish avuncular relationships with young men prior to their initiation. Rather, it is the combination of the drinking of alcoholic beverages, entrance into the public house, and the company of bachelor-group members that establishes the initiate's manhood, his acceptability to the male community, and his membership in the bachelor group. The initiate's first drink in the public house in the company of bachelor-group members is a ceremonial demonstration of his manhood.

Earlier it was noted that Levi-Strauss's hypothesis about the avunculate reasserting itself in times of societal crises could be applied to Ireland in the mid-nineteenth century. Certain family changes precipitated the reemergence of the avunculate, whose form this time was the bachelor group. In this connection, McNabb described certain bachelor-group activities:

> The bachelor group is an interesting phenomenon which arises out of the great number of single males and the lack of common interests between men and women. In this group, differences are not made according to age. At one time it had recognized leaders. These leaders were usually married men who had been exceptional in some way in the past, either in sport or politics or whose imagination was lively enough to capture the interest of the younger people. They handed on much of the folklore of the community and often expanded and added to it. They were the ones who initiated the young people into the attitudes of the group.[20]

From McNabb's description it is evident that one of the roles played by bachelor-group leaders—entertaining the young men and passing on traditions to them—was similar to what maternal uncles might be expected to do for their nephews. That the bachelor-group leaders were primarily responsible for this socialization of the young is true; however, all bachelor-groups members—married or unmarried, leader or follower—shared in the avuncular relationships. Moreover, the maintenance of avuncular relationships between bachelor-group members and young males in the community was a precondition for the continued existence of the bachelor group. New members must be recruited, socialized, and initiated into the attitudes and norms of the bachelor group. The relationship between certain bachelor-group members and the initiate was one of intimacy and friendly mutual dependence because the bachelor group "provides a refuge against loneliness."[21]

If, as Levi-Strauss maintains, the avunculate is a consequence of an incest taboo, the bachelor group as an institution was the direct result of prohibitions against sexuality and marriage. The bachelor group originated when with certain changes in the structure of the Irish family strict religious teachings about sexual relationships were being promulgated in the mid-nineteenth century. The bachelor group developed and spread concomitantly with and in the same places where the pattern of few and late marriages was becoming established.

The father-son relationship in Ireland was a harsh one, distinguished perhaps by the father's intense concern about his authority. The bachelor group, in its avuncular function, balanced the relationship between males of the two generations. Fathers who maintained a negative relationship with their own sons had the opportunity to establish a positive relationship with someone else's son.

Young men in the community were socialized into the attitudes and norms of the bachelor group. McNabb described several of these attitudes, as related by bachelor-group leaders:

> The picture these leaders painted of their own youth became a standard for their listeners. It was one of the gay, irresponsible rakes whose youth was golden age, lacking care, where he always shone either in sport or violence. They told many tales of adventure, particularly if they had been "on the run." These men were brilliant story-tellers, capable of holding the audience even with repeated stories. They embroidered on a basis of hard fact, so that they were proof against the cynical, but whatever stories they told, whether true or false, had the same emphasis, the same psychological effect: the intense awareness that youth, if short, must be filled with as many experiences as possible. The leader's example showed that responsibility was inevitable fate imposed by a harsh world and that the proof of manhood was instinctive action. Responsibility in such an environment could not be seen as a challenge, and this attitude persists even to the present time.[22]

If celibacy was described and defined more attractively than marriage, the bachelor group had to include both married and unmarried to validate its claim. After marriage, men—in the very act of joining together so frequently—exposed the vicissitudes of married life and commended the unmarried state. As McNabb had pointed out, much of the folklore of the male group centers about the themes of freedom from responsibility, "instinctive action," and adventure. Married bachelor-group leaders passed on this set of sentiments and ideas to younger unmarried males. To actualize these ideas and sentiments about marriage, it was necessary that married men socialize the young males and participate in the activities of the male group. By their active presence in the male group, married men helped to diminish the natural attractiveness of marriage.

If so many activities and so much emotional gratification occurred outside of marriage, what then was so attractive about marriage? Obviously, the right to inherit property was the primary inducement for one to marry; sexual gratification was an important but secondary consideration. But the emphasis of married bachelor-group leaders in the socialization of the young was not on the joys of working and managing a farm or on the exhilarating effect of sexual orgasm; rather, the emphasis was on the potential for freedom and adventure in the state of "nonresponsibility"— celibacy. The single state, then, was made as attractive as possible in story and in song. The propaganda that bachelor-group leaders expounded, albeit unintentionally, was quite effective because the rest of the community, especially landowners, had a vested interest in the existence of a large number of single men and women.

The Bachelor-Group Ethic of Hard Drinking

Related to the ethic of hard drinking was the norm of "treating," a generalized phenomenon in the British Isles during the eighteenth and nineteenth centuries. Treating reached a state of perfection in the bachelor group. Basically, it imposed the obligation on each member to buy a drink for all the other individuals in whose immediate company he entered the public house and with whom he was drinking; moreover, it obliged the others not to refuse a drink once offered.[23] Thus, if six individuals entered a pub together, each was expected to buy a round of drinks for all six as well as to accept and consume each of six drinks provided for him. Once the cycle had been completed, a new one might be begun with the same obligations intact.

Treating was a norm of equality in that, as a ritual of masculine renewal, it made all bachelor-group members—whatever their age and even class differences—equal as men. As a norm of equality and solidarity, treating was a reaffirmation of status differences between men and women. It was a means of enforcing the religiously inspired segregation of men and women that even marriage did not break down. To make the celibate state attractive, it was necessary that married men continue their bachelor-group activities. The norm of treating, then, provided for the constant renewal of manliness in the form of a rite of incorporation: the drinking together by bachelor-group members.

The public house was off limits to women and thus a male sanctuary. Eventually, lounges were provided in some drinking establishments so that men and women might drink together. But the lounge was separate from the main drinking area, which was still reserved for men only. Some have viewed the increase in the number of lounges and other mixed drinking areas as a consequence of modernization. More precisely, however, it is the result of the gradual dissolution of the traditional male group over the past 30 years or so.

Actually the norm of treating within the bachelor group had become an ethic of hard drinking. Hard drinking was a criterion for high status within the group. McNabb observed: "The leader's status depended upon his capacity for drink, and it was to him that a young person looked for leadership and tried to emulate."[24] The capacity for drink included features of both consumption and demeanor; that is, prestige accrued to the ability to consume alcoholic beverages frequently, for extended periods of time, and with little outward display of intoxication.[25] One's ability to drink hard demonstrated great powers of manliness, just as athletic prowess or expertise in storytelling did. The more an individual had proved his manliness, the greater his status within the group. Moreover, the ethic of hard drinking imposed minimal standards of hard drinking on all bachelor-group members. McNabb observed: "The men drink heavily. . . . The public houses are drab and uncomfortable. There is no provision for anything but hard drinking, and a respectable woman would not set a foot inside one of these places. . . ."[26]

Hard drinking, however, was not merely a proof of manhood. It was part of a rite of incorporation by which men expressed their solidarity as well as their manliness and hence their separation and

distinctiveness from women. Hard drinking was perhaps more intimately connected with the collective and individual identity of the
male than with his sexual frustration that separation from females
implied. For the group, hard drinking as a rite of incorporation signaled solidarity, a renewal of manliness, and distinctiveness from
women. For the individual, it indicated maturity or manhood through
which one took his place as an adult male in the bachelor group and
in the larger community.

Hard drinking, which occasionally becomes exacerbated in the
forms of drunkenness and alcoholism, might be viewed as an
attempt to reaffirm one's identity in times of collective and individual crisis. The collective crisis in the first instance was one of status. Traditional status arrangements in the community had been
upended by a series of dramatic changes in Irish society. Single
inheritance meant that many males were left without land, the customary means of support. The economic status of those unfortunate
enough not to acquire land was in jeopardy. Intertwined with inheritance was, of course, marriage. Relatively few married, so many
were denied this social status. Work and marriage as statuses for
the individual have long been crucial sources of identity. That so
many were systematically denied the historical responsibilities
expected of all was nothing less than a collective crisis of identity.
What was a man if not a landowner, a farmer, a husband, and a
father?

New avenues for establishing and enhancing status and molding
identity had to be provided. If the conventional roles of landowner,
husband, and father were closed off to many new roles—such as that
of hard drinker—were eventually more positively rewarded. This
interpretation makes sense of the bachelor-group code of freedom
from responsibility, instinctive action, adventure, and the devalua-
tion of marriage. It was partly a case of sour grapes, of not valuing
and wanting what one cannot have to begin with, and partly a consequence of the contrast between the old means of gaining prestige
and the new. Young males had to be made to believe that little was
lost by their inability to own land or marry. The virtues of hard
drinking, excellence in sports, storytelling, and witty conversation
were extolled. Therefore a man could rise to prominence even

without land, wife, and children. His hard drinking commanded prestige from fellow males and helped anchor his identity as a man. If he suffered frustration, it was probably more status frustration—his inability to own land, marry, and rear a family—than strictly sexual frustration.

We can also speculate that this collective crisis of identity (status frustration) was more intense in the mid-nineteenth century, when the new inheritance and kinship patterns were first being implemented, than it was later, when alternative modes of acquiring status had been institutionalized and became highly valued. The old statuses seemed less attractive with the passing of time,[27] while the new ones beckoned seductively—as expressed in bachelor-group folklore and song. Hard drinking had become a source of bachelor-group status and, in this sense, represented a collective search for identity. Bachelor-group membership and manhood were one and the same.

Irish Culture and the Meaning of Hard Drinking

Culture, according to Philip Rieff, controls the members of society through a system of moral demands. In Ireland, as we have seen, the personifications of the moral demand system were the priest in the community and the mother in the home, both of whom enforced, at times with a vengeance, a strict sexual code. But in addition to moral demands, every culture provides institutionalized releases from such demands:

> To speak of a moral culture would be redundant. Every culture has two main functions: (1) to organize the moral demands men make upon themselves into a system of symbols that make men intelligible and trustworthy to each other, thus rendering also the world intelligible and trustworthy; (2) to organize the expressive remission by which men release themselves, in some degree, from

the strain of conforming to the controlling symbolic, internalized variant readings of culture that constitute individual character. The process by which a culture changes at its profoundest level may be traced in the shifting balance of controls and releases which constitute a system of moral demands.[28]

Hard drinking in Ireland was cultural remission, that is, a release from the difficulty of adhering to the dominant symbols of culture by which personality is socially constructed. It was a release from sexual puritanism. Erik Erikson cautioned that "puritanism was once a system of values designed to check men and women of eruptive vitality, of strong appetites as well as of strong individuality."[29] But with the onslaught of political and economic forces, such as improved agricultural techniques, migration, urbanization, and class stratification, puritanism expanded its domain to the "total sphere of bodily living."[30]

Puritanism as an overarching aspect of Irish culture was a response to the demands of a single inheritance farm economy, especially in the face of a pattern of widespread and early marriage. Subdivision of the land had sustained the previous system. Now indiscriminate sexual involvement ran the risk of illegitimacy and forced marriage, thus threatening the foundation of the new social order. It was imperative that young men and women be kept from marrying until the proper economic arrangements could be made by their families. One is tempted to suggest that nineteenth-century sexual puritanism in general was largely the result of the desire for improved standards of living titillated by industrialization on the one hand and improved farming techniques on the other hand. Marriage, then, must be postponed until economic security was attained, and the most direct way of keeping people single was by stressing the evil and danger of sex.

Male drinking was a moral demand in Irish culture, a cultural remission. Likewise, it was compensation for the paucity of customary opportunities to attain adulthood: marriage, family, and landownership. But its remissive quality can best be understood by analyzing the conflict between drinkers and nondrinkers and the role of the Catholic church as mediator in this dispute.

Bachelor-Group Devotees and Temperance Advocates

In those societies that feature the organization of nondrinking, drinking behavior cannot be fully understood apart from an analysis of temperance movements and societies. Such is the case in Ireland. Father Mathew's prodigious temperance movement of the 1830s culminated in the fusion of temperance and repeal in the interest of Irish nationalism. In the aftermath of O'Connell's defeat, the appeal of temperance declined dramatically.

Remnant groups from the Mathew movement survived, but by and large the temperance cause remained dormant until the Pioneer Total Abstinence Association of the Sacred Heart (Pioneers) emerged in Dublin in 1901.[31] The founder, Fr. James Cullen, S. J., had been associated with temperance work in the late nineteenth century. Reflecting on the failure of Mathew's movement to endure, Father Cullen decided to build a well-structured and disciplined organization. He was willing to forgo the immediate success a wildly emotional movement could generate in order to insure long-term results.[32] In his initial temperance labors, Father Cullen restricted membership to women because he felt he could be assured of their faithfulness. Father Cullen admitted men later, but even then he was less interested in quantity than in the quality of his membership. Pioneers had to prove themselves during a period of probation. Father Cullen hoped to establish an organization of dedicated followers whose ranks would swell slowly and through selective proselytizing efforts. It was to become a self-consciously elitist organization and has survived to this day.

Of specific interest to our analysis is the nature of the relationship that developed between the bachelor-group devotee and the temperance advocate. The bachelor-group member's distrust of the total abstainer has been noted by several writers. De la Fontaine remarked:

> I have heard from responsible Irish people that the danger to society lies not in the drunkard or the young man who frequents the public house with his companions of his own age and class, but

with the teetotaler. The latter is a lone young man, in a sense outcast by his age group, and the argument is that he will be a menace to the sexual standards, which in the country districts are also
standards of farm prestige and economic unity. Drinking is thus a
socially approved recreation.[33]

Citing de la Fontaine, Bales emphasized the sexual meaning of this
distrust: that the total abstainer posed a threat to the chastity of the
unmarried female.[34] The man who did not imbibe had rejected an
acceptable substitute for heterosexual intercourse; thus the teetotaler was suspect as a potential chastity breaker. Teetotalers, on the
other had, suspected drinkers of the same sexual deviance.

In a discussion of the recent success of the several formal associations for leisure in rural Ireland, McNabb reported the feelings of
a non-drinker about his exclusion from bachelor-group associations:

> One of the reasons for the increasing popularity of Macra na
> Feirme is that it enables some young people to short-circuit the
> bachelor group. Another young man said, "I don't drink, and for
> this reason, I found it difficult to make friends with lads of my own
> age. They don't think much of you if you don't drink, and anyway,
> the lads here lead an immoral life. I tell you I was lonely. But
> when Macra was set up I joined it, and so did a lot who had no
> time for drinking and immorality. Some of the wild boys joined it,
> too. Now I have plenty of friends, both boys and girls, and we have
> a great social life without drinking."[35]

From the nondrinker's standpoint, the bachelor-group member
is the threat to sexual standards. This is implied by the reference to
the "immoral life" led by the drinkers in the preceding quotation. If
the drinker sometimes suspects the teetotaler of being a sexual
deviant, the teetotaler in turn suspects the drinker of the same. The
drinker's suspicion of the teetotaler as a sexual deviant is both a
justification for the exclusion of the nondrinker and rationalization
for his own heavy drinking. Thus the drinker may be guilty on occasion of the sin of drunkenness, but the nondrinker commits the
most serious sin—the one against chastity. The teetotaler on the
other hand, partly in self-defense and partly because of a belief in

the generalizing immoral effects of hard drinking, infers that the drinker is the sexual deviant.

How are we to interpret this comedy of errors? Bales apparently was not aware of the teetotaler's suspicion of the drinker as a sexual deviant. His argument was cast in neo-Freudian terms: The teetotaler was suspect because he had rejected drinking, which was functionally equivalent to sexual intercourse. I maintain that although drinking may function at times as a substitute for sex, and although the non-drinker may be suspected on occasion of sexual indiscretions, this is but one function of drink and one attitude toward the nondrinker—both of which must be interpreted in their more general contexts. Along these lines, McNabb noted the general distrust of nondrinkers by drinkers: "At night, they visit the local public house (very few of the older farmers are non-drinkers. In fact, there is a tendency to distrust the abstainer)."[36] This distrust, however, is general and not specifically centered about the teetotaler's potential sexual deviance.[37] The male nondrinker, in rejecting the auspices of the bachelor group, has jeopardized community traditions by remaining outside its control in that the bachelor group is a primary basis of social order. From this perspective the teetotaler is a general, and not a specific, deviant.

I have deduced this from personal observations and past reports of the real behavior of drinkers toward nondrinkers, not just from their verbal behavior. Moreover, that drinkers and nondrinkers regarded each other as sexually deviant casts strong doubt about accepting their verbal statements at face value. They were essentially ideological maneuverings, attempts to discredit their rivals. With chastity extolled as the primary Irish virtue, it is not surprising that each side hurled the invective of "sexual deviant" at the other.

The ideological nature of the distrust of the teetotaler can be inferred from the following facts: Catholic and Protestant denominations alike supported teetotalism and the teetotaler. It is common knowledge that for Catholics, membership in the Pioneer Total Abstinence Society (demonstrated by the wearing of a pin) saved the nondrinker from excessive ridicule. It made his nondrinking somewhat respectable. In addition, the sanctions against nondrinkers were usually mild (e.g., avoidance). Stronger measures, such as ridicule and ostracism, were less frequently used. The dominant means of dealing with the nondrinker included a subtle process of exclusion in which the nondrinker was cut off from bachelor-group activities and friendships. The nondrinker missed out not only on drinking but on other activities as well. His opportunity for securing friendship was severely restricted. Thus the reported fear of the teetotaler's potential sexual deviance was a justification for his exclusion and a rationalization for hard drinking on the part of his excluders. If the community actually believed the nondrinker was a sexual deviant, more stringent means of control would have been used.

Two other facts support my position about the general nature of the teetotaler's deviance. Total abstainers were thought to be less manly than drinkers. Were the "less manly" the sexual threat? The final irony lies in the fact that, historically, there has not been much illegitimacy—by drinkers or teetotalers.

Bales used the contention that the teetotaler was suspect as a sexual deviant as proof for a hypothesis about the psychological meaning of Irish male drinking, claiming: "The function of drinking as a sexual substitute is indicated quite clearly by the attitude toward the teetotaler."[38] Bales, however, has confused ideology with motivation. Taking the drinker's suspicion of the teetotaler at face value, he made an inference about the motivation of the drinking of the "boys." Even if most people thought that drinking functioned as a substitute for sex, this fact would not prove that this was drinking's chief psychological function. Actually the conviction that drinking was a substitute for sex and prevents sexual indiscretion was the ideological justification for permitting hard drinking. The questions ultimately became: What evils would occur if hard drinking were not allowed? The answer: sexual deviance.

If we add to this idea the Irish (and Irish-American) adage that "drink is a good man's failing," we have then the clearest evidence for considering Irish drinking as cultural remission. In this saying the community was acknowledging the fact that the man who may on occasion drink too much is at the same time the solid man of the community, the bachelor-group member by whose sacrifice Irish social order was constructed. He has conformed to the most important standards of his community, especially sexual asceticism, and his drinking cannot take away from his general goodness. These two cultural attitudes complement each other: On the one hand, the man who does not drink is a sexual threat and thus a threat to the social order; on the other hand, the man who does drink is in conformity with community standards. Therefore a man's drinking lapses are much preferred to the potential destruction his nondrinking poses. Consequently, one cannot infer individual motivation from collective ideology, at least in a straightforward manner. More often ideology conceals motivation. There are two more objections to regarding drinking as a psychological substitute for sex. Carrying Bale's argument to its logical conclusion, must we not also argue that because the teetotaler suspects the drinker of sexual infraction, nondrinking also functions as a substitute for sex? Ultimately we would end up maintaining that both drinking and nondrinking are functional equivalents to sexual intercourse. Moreover, that men after marriage continue to drink hard as members of the bachelor group appears to weaken the sexual frustration argument even further unless one further assumes that Irish marriage provides little relief from the tension of the sexual instinct. But of course this does not coincide with two related facts: (1) the sometimes Catholic teaching that spouses are required under pain of sin to submit to the sexual overtures of their mate and (2) the high fertility rate in Ireland. By itself the second fact might indicate just the reverse of my argument, but taken in tandem with the first it provides strong evidence against a sexual frustration argument conceived of in largely physical terms.

The problem of sexual frustration is not being dismissed, only qualified. I am assuming that the sexual urge, while partly a biological drive, is significantly influenced by culture; that is, the psychological intensity of the drive can be altered according to the cultural meaning with which it is endowed. Ironically where a culturally permissive attitude toward sex exists, it can create more, not less, frustration. Continually bombarded with sexual images, titillated at every turn, hounded by the performance standards of more effective sexual techniques, it is a small wonder that many today are frustrated. Needless to say Ireland's culture has kept such sexual stimuli to a minimum. Furthermore, when sex becomes a cult if not a religion for some and when it is revered as a spiritual value, it is quite easy to overestimate its importance. I am not denying that drinking may be for some, on some occasions, a substitute for sex. What I am saying is that one is not justified in overstressing this specific function of drink to the exclusion of others. The constellation of facts about Irish drinking points to a related but quite different interpretation.

One might just as well argue a status frustration or deprivation position, that is, hard drinking as a substitute for the statuses of landowner, husband, and father—which assured a man of adult standing in the rural community. Yet once again the continued drinking of married men poses a problem. Hence hard drinking, culturally remitted as an integral part of male identity, moves us beyond the rather superficial argument of sexual frustration narrowly conceived or even status frustration.

The Church as Mediator between Definitions of Drinking and Nondrinking

Insofar as bachelor-group devotees and temperance advocates define one another as deviant, and given the preponderance of drinkers, temperance membership can be seen in part as the realization of the need of social outcasts for group support. The Irish Catholic church takes a somewhat ambivalent position on drinking: It blesses the religiously based total abstinence work of such groups as the Pioneer Total Abstinence Association of the Sacred Heart; at the same time it recognizes the virtue of *moderate* drinking. Moderate drinking is of course a broad enough category to include bachelor-group drinking. Since the bachelor group is an informal institution, the Catholic church does not support or denounce it officially. But many clergymen participate in all-male drinking while being covertly unsympathetic to the "fanatical" temperance arguments.

The theme of moderate drinking is the rubric under which the institutional conflict between the bachelor group and temperance is mediated by the church. All involved parties support moderate drinking in principle. Thus one reads in Pioneer temperance literature:

> Pioneers do not deny that drink in moderation is all right; they know that many excellent people who drink, not only do no wrong, but practise the virtue of temperance. Pioneers therefore, are not extremists who condemn drink in itself and do not wish to interfere with the legitimate enjoyment of others. They see nothing wrong in the moderate use of alcohol but the evil in its abuse.[39]

The formal position of the Catholic church is exactly that of the Pioneers: moderation in drinking is virtuous. The bachelor group is in favor of drinking, with special prestige accruing to the drinker who can "hold his liquor." Where then is the conflict? It centers precisely on the several life-styles and proselytizing efforts of the bachelor groups and temperance groups that compete for the loyalties of the young.

In Ireland part of the ceremony surrounding the sacrament of confirmation for the young is a pledge to abstain from alcoholic beverages until the age of 21. (This pledge is not regarded by the church as binding under pain of mortal sin.) In addition, during secondary school or vocational school, young people are usually urged by their teachers to become Pioneer probationers, who must meet the following conditions:

1. Willingness to take the pledge for life;
2. To have been of previous temperate habits;
3. Have already reached your fourteenth birthday.[40]

A few years later the young male is under considerable pressure to drink in order to gain admittance to the bachelor group. Most adolescent males forsake their confirmation pledge to become bachelor-group members. Irish social structure, in a sense, conspires against the forces of temperance.

Temperance advocates qualify the concept of moderate drinking, but not to the same extent as did Father Mathew, who almost claimed it was impossible. Pioneer literature notes:

> Moderate drinking is praised but carefully silenced is the fact that many moderate drinkers become inebriates. Various are the figures given of the moderate drinkers who become alcoholics; one estimate is one in every twenty. Whatever is the correct figure the percentage is very high and puts us on our guard against the propagators of moderate drinking for all, even though it may help in business.[41]

The dangers of moderate drinking are heavily emphasized. To the temperance advocate, the bachelor-group member is an excessive drinker. Also disturbing to the temperance advocate is the community tolerance for an individual's occasional lapses into inebriety.[42] This demonstrates the favored position of the bachelor group in community life.

The Catholic church advocates either moderate drinking or abstention from drink for religious reasons. Thus both structures of drink in Ireland—the bachelor group and temperance—can lay claim to church support. The theme of moderate drinking provides the basis for minimal agreement on both sides, some degree of order. But the agreement is only apparent. What really matters is that an ethic of moderate drinking is free-floating; it is not embedded in a structure of orientation. There is no organization or reference group that is built on an ethic of moderate drinking. The Catholic church is a religious institution and can claim among its members almost the entire Republic of Ireland. But it is not a viable reference group in terms of drinking. With few exceptions, bachelor-group devotees and temperance advocates are both Catholic.

But the bachelor group and temperance (to a much lesser extent) do provide social groupings of orientation. The bachelor group can be characterized by an ethic of hard drinking; temperance, by an ethic of nondrinking. The drinker who drinks moderately must do so on his own because there is no organization or reference group that can provide support for this type of drinking. Men are forced to choose between the bachelor group and temperance early in their lives. The man who rejects both is an individual indeed.

The result of the institutional conflict between the bachelor group and temperance is that the individual male is pressured, in terms of group participation, to choose between hard drinking and no drinking. The bachelor group pushes the more moderate drinker toward total abstinence, while temperance propels the less moderate drinker in the direction of bachelor-group hard drinking.

With the exception of the few years when Father Mathew's movement was at its zenith, the Irish clergy by and large has supported bachelor-group drinking more than total abstinence. It would have been unusual if a clergy composed largely of peasant origin had felt otherwise. The bachelor group had full community support. Wit the advent of a new family pattern in the nineteenth century, it was imperative that the potentially explosive situation of the large number who must remain unmarried for a long period by checked by the clergy, who held preeminent position in community life. Chastity was promulgated as the paramount virtue; drunkenness was a less serious offense. It appears that some of the clergy regarded a night's drinking with the boys as the best safeguard against sexual indiscretion. All in all the bachelor group and its ethic of hard drinking were rarely challenged. Occasional upsurges of temperance enthusiasm proved but a transient threat to bachelor-group drinking.

The Psychocultural Meaning of Intoxication

The term "intoxication" does not imply drunkenness, legal or otherwise; rather, intoxication is seen as falling within a continuum with drunkenness, or the inebriated state, at one pole and a mild "high" at the other pole. Thus hard drinking almost invariably implies intoxication, but not necessarily drunkenness.

As if in the possession of an original insight, many have proclaimed that drinking provides an escape from reality. Simplistic perhaps, but true as far as it goes. Horkheimer and Adorno commented on such an escape from reality:

> Men had to do fearful things to themselves before the self, the identical, purposive, and virile nature of man, was formed, and something of that recurs in every childhood. The strain of holding the I together adheres to the I in all stages; and the temptation to lose it has always been there with the blind determination to maintain it. The narcotic intoxication which permits the atonement of deathlike sleep for the euphoria in which the self is suspended, is one of the oldest social arrangements which mediate between self-preservation and self-destruction—an attempt of the self to survive itself. The dread of losing the self and of abrogating together with the self the barrier between one-self and the other life, the fear of death and destruction, is intimately associated with a promise of happiness which threatened civilization in every moment. Its road was that of obedience and labor, over which fulfillment shines forth perpetually—but only as illusive appearance, as devitalized beauty.[43]

In a historical sense, self-preservation for Ireland meant conforming to the tyrannical rule of England without political autonomy, without land, without the free practice of religion, without self-respect. Self-destruction, on the other hand, was rebellion, the perpetual readiness to fight England even when it appeared to be suicidal. Ireland vacillated between a hopeless self-preservation and a hopeful self-destruction. Communal hard drinking was a way to mediate these conflicting demands, but institutionalized, it too became a means of self-destruction—albeit a slow and gradual process. It is in this sense that Father Mathew and later Sean O'Casey declared that "an Ireland free is an Ireland sober."

In a similar vein, the purported Irish tendency to fluctuate back and forth between a mystical romanticism and a grim realism can be understood. The romantic side of Irish culture—with its emphasis on imagination and introspection, love of the past, and finely honed wit—was always intermixed with a tough realism about Ireland's actual situation.[44] Romanticism itself is a form of intoxication and has its ridiculous expressions, sometimes in the interest of self-preservation. Self-effacement, humor turned inward, playing the fool, evasive answers, even lying gave rise to a stereotyped comical Irishman, a romanticized figure, but one which at times loomed large in conformity to English rule. G. B. Shaw saw this romanticized Irishman as a trick the Irish played on the English that helped mitigate the extremes of the oppressors' cruelty. Here romanticism and realism form a dialectic. So, if intoxication is a mediation between self-preservation and self-destruction, Ireland's history strongly counterpointed these opposing tendencies and provided a lush setting for the institutionalization of hard drinking.

But hard drinking also became important when a relaxation of English oppression occurred. Hard drinking was remitted culturally to release men permanently doomed to less than full adult status from the stringencies of Irish social structure and a puritan culture. The bachelor-group drinker was the good solid man because, through his sacrifice, the progress of an Irish-owned farm economy was forged. Rural men without land did not often marry and therefore were required to be segregated from their female counterparts. Ultimately the unmarried male, by his participation in the bachelor group, was tacitly acknowledging the legitimacy of the new system of single inheritance, few and late marriages, and the religiously imposed sexual taboo. Married men who participated in the bachelor group were a bridge between conventional society and the unmarried male's marginal standing. But by taking the lead in bachelor-group activities, the married man ratified a cultural definition of masculinity in terms other than those of the usual adult responsibilities of land ownership, marriage, and family. Freedom from responsibility, as in the adventure of story, sports, and hard drinking, was extolled. Hard drinking, even as freedom from responsibility, made one responsible to the moral community of the bachelor group and ultimately the large community. Those males who were not bachelor-group members stood outside the purview of the community and this posed a threat to the newly founded social order. Hard drinking for men was morally demanded as a cultural release from sexual puritanism, as a solution to the problem of male marginality, and in support of a single-inheritance farm economy.

With the emergence of the bachelor group as institution, it is evident that a continuity exists from the Irish drinking customs of the eighteenth and early nineteenth centuries through those of the early decades of the twentieth century. Hard drinking was an integral part of the cultural definition of masculinity, at least among the working classes in the eighteenth and nineteenth centuries in the British Isles. From the middle of the nineteenth century onward, temperance as part of a larger middle class movement made an inroad on the definition of masculinity in most western European countries. However, by this time in Ireland temperance and its complement, repeal, were dead. In the other countries masculinity among the lower middle class and "respectable" working class came more and more to reflect the assumption of industrial responsibility: hard work, diligence, thrift, sobriety, prudence, and success.

6

The Cult of Irish-American Drinking

Sobriety diminishes, discriminates, and says no; drunkenness
expands, unites, and says yes. It is in fact the great exciter of the
Yes function in man. It brings its votary from the chill periphery
of things to the radiant core. It makes him for the moment one
with truth. Not through mere perversity do men run after it. To
the poor and the unlettered it stands in the place of symphony
concerts and literature; and it is part of the deeper mystery and
tragedy of life that whiffs and gleams of something that we immediately recognize as excellent should be vouchsafed to so many of
us only in the fleeting earlier phases of what in its totality is one
degrading a poisoning. The drunken consciousness is one bit of the
mystic consciousness, and our total opinion of it must find its
place in our opinion of that larger whole.

William James,
The Varieties of Religious Experience

The Irish were the first in that great wave of immigrants to flood
American's shores, to work its industry, and to inhabit its
urban slums in the mid-nineteenth century. Examination of the
probable impact of immigration and the sociohistorical organization
of Irish-American settlements will allow us better understand Irish-
American drinking.

Irish Emigration

The Great Famine dramatized the ruinous consequences of the
indiscriminate subdivision of land, early and widespread marriage,
and the maintenance of a large population in an impoverished country.[1] The famine was the immediate occasion for much emigration.
The consolidation of farm holdings and the new marriage pattern

(few and late marriages) should not be viewed as "causes" of emigration; but both the former and the latter were products of the desire to escape extreme poverty, the desire for a better life, and, with the death of the repeal movement, a hopelessness that a better life could be found in Ireland.[2]

The geographic areas in which the new marriage pattern first became established were also the major sources of emigration. As early as 1820 and especially after 1830 the marriage rate began to decline:

> The new, lower pattern of nuptiality established itself first in the relatively prosperous areas of the East and Central Plains, where postponing marriage and thereby limiting family size offered the greatest prospects of achieving land ownership and improved economic conditions. Only after the second great agricultural depression of the century, in the 1870's, was this lead followed by the poorer areas of the Western Seaboard, and high levels of permanent celibacy, together with late average age at marriage, became a national characteristic.[3]

During the Great Famine, state and landlord aid in emigration was minimal; consequently, individuals from the poorer areas were least able to sustain the cost of emigration. The west of Ireland was the single most impoverished area in Ireland. Emigrants came mostly from eastern and central areas.[4] Moreover, this trend of emigration from the more "prosperous" areas continued throughout the early 1880s until, finally, widespread emigration from the west of Ireland came to dominate the overall migration picture.[5] That emigration from the west predominated after 1880 can be explained by the interaction of the following factors: (1) more readily obtained financing of emigration; (2) considerable population increase in the west concurrent with a decrease in the east and central areas from 1850 to 1880; (3) occasional crop failures in the west, which still was dependent on the potato to support a large population; (4) the gradual institutionalization of the pattern of few and late marriages in the west; and (5) the almost irresistible pressure to emigrate because of the increasing desire to acquire living standards comparable to those in the east and central areas.

Both "emigration and celibacy were alternative solutions to the problem of maintaining a certain desired way of life," observed Kennedy.[6] But either solution could only occur where the problem was recognized. Thus relative economic prosperity had a direct bearing on emigration in the beginning: The more prosperous areas, which first accepted the new marriage and family system, were also the most capable of supporting emigrants, many of who went to America.

The fact that during the latter half of the nineteenth century and into the twentieth century the Irish possessed the lowest rate of marriage in western Europe perhaps suggests that the Irish pattern of emigration was more one of unmarried individuals than of family units. But this is not entirely true. S. H. Cousens observed that "the impressions gained from the immigration statistics that family movement was more common in times of crisis . . . is confirmed by the local press."[7]

However, in less than a crisis situation, most of the emigrants were young adults, unmarried and without children.[8] What constituted a crisis? The Great Famine of 1846–51 and the sporadic crop failures of the 1860s certainly qualify as crises. In noncrisis situations, Irish emigration represented the normal draining off of young males and females not destined to inherit land or marry. As noted previously, extensive emigration was a solution to the new family pattern of single inheritance and a low marriage rate. It took a crisis to uproot a peasant family from the soil.

To find the extent to which emigration consisted of family units or unmarried individuals, Cousens determined the percentage that children under 15 formed among all emigrants. Illustrating the point about the tendency of family units to emigrate only during periods of crisis (1863 and 1864), Cousens presented data for two Irish counties, Mayo and Kerry (see Table 6). There was a greater proportion of child emigrants to adult emigrants during years of crises than in other years. But even during a crisis emigrants were predominantly young unmarrieds.

In a study of ethnic groups in Boston, Bushee gives a breakdown for 1900–1901 of newly arrived immigrants by age composition (Table 7). During a noncrisis year, the Irish emigrant contingency to Boston numbered comparatively few family units as measured by the

TABLE 6   Emigrants—Percentage of Children Aged Under 15

County	1863	1864	1868	1869
Mayo	20.2	21.9	12.1	10.6
Kerry	17.6	17.7	11.5	6.8

percentage that those under age 14 comprised out of all emigrants for each ethnic group. Given the data in Tables 6 and 7, it would perhaps be safe to conclude that even during a crisis the Irish would rank lowest among ethnic groups in respect to the percentage of family units among the total number of its emigrants. With the relative infrequency of marriage in Ireland and the tendency of family units to emigrate only during crises, Irish immigration consisted primarily of young unmarried adults who had no future in the Old World and faced the bleak reality of discrimination in the New World.

Of singular import is the fact that before the pattern of few and late marriages was institutionalized for Irish society as a whole (the 1880s), emigrants came from precisely those areas in which this marriage pattern was first being established. And, as I have argued, the all-male group became structurally and culturally most significant in relation to that marriage pattern. As a permanent institution, it

TABLE 7   Percentages of the Various Nationalities Belonging to the Three Age Periods

	Between 14 and 45 Years	Under 14 Years	Over 45 Years
Irish	92.13%	4.14%	3.73%
Scandinavians	86.92	7.66	5.42
Northern Italians	86.20	8.64	5.16
Southern Italians	77.74	14.16	8.09
Germans	73.84	18.82	7.34
Scotch	73.68	15.82	10.50
English	72.87	15.44	11.69
Hebrews	70.74	23.40	5.86
Portuguese	65.96	25.37	8.67

became an epiphenomenon of a pattern of few and late marriages coactive with high expectations of chastity for the unmarried.

Irish-American Settlements

Initially the majority of Irish immigrants gravitated to large eastern cities: Boston, New York, and Philadelphia, among others. They usually inhabited boardinghouses and tenements in Irish areas and worked at whatever unskilled jobs were available. The Irish areas were in the most dilapidated sections of the city. In Boston[9] and in New York[10] these sections were most often within or adjacent to the commercial center of the city.

Most infamous, however, were Irish "shanties," whether located in "shantytown" or interspersed among the boardinghouses and tenements. In New York City, especially in southern Manhattan, squatters—partly because of a housing shortage and partly to avoid inflated rent—"occupied barren areas of rocks and hills" and built flimsy one-room dwellings known as shanties. Shantytown, comprised of thousands of Irish squatters, moved outward as the built-up section of the city expanded. Shantytown inhabitants often kept domesticated animals, such as cows, goats, and pigs, and thus maintained the semblance of a rural environment at the edge of the city. Poor sanitation, little warmth in the winter, and the lack of privacy became crushing physical and psychological burdens in shantytown.

Shanties also grew up amid the endless tenements and boardinghouses in the inner city. Tenement apartments were formed out of former middle-class residences, but even this subdivision could not accommodate the throngs of immigrants. Thus every available nook and cranny was used to house an immigrant. In Boston, as Handlin recalled, "within the focal points of Irish concentration . . . the price of real estate was too high to permit tenement construction. Instead, enterprising landowners utilized unremunerative yards, gardens and courts to yield the maximum number of hovels that might pass as homes."[11] These areas became such mazes of makeshift dwellings that one observer claimed they were "full of sheds and shanties."[12]

The shanties were not restricted to the cities, however. They sprang up alongside public works, notably railroad and canal construction sites. Potter, quoting Thoreau, provided a vivid description of "an uncommonly fine" Irish public works shanty:

> "It was of small dimensions, with a peaked cottage roof, and not much else to be seen, the dirt being raised five feet all around, as if it were a compost heap." The window was deep and high. "Doorstill there was none, but a perennial passage for the hens under the door-board." Inside it "was dark, and had a dirt floor for the most part, dank, clammy, and aguish, only here a board and there a board which would not bear removal." The "board floor extended under the bed" and the cellar was "a sort of dust hole two feet deep." "There was a stove, a bed, and a place to sit, an infant in the house where it was born, a silk parasol, a gilt-framed looking-glass, and a patent new coffee-mill nailed to an oak sapling, all told."[13]

Laborers were compelled to buy food and clothes from "company stores" operated by public works contractors, who were reputed to have charged "up to 50 percent over a fair price."[14] The great bulk of the Irish laborers on public works were either "rootless unmarried men" or husbands living away from their families during the work season.[15]

Back in the city, those not living in shanties subsisted in boardinghouses and tenements. Boardinghouse occupants were mainly bachelors, but occasionally families rented a room as a stopgap measure until a permanent residence could be secured. Tenements, more run down than boardinghouses, were often converted mansions and warehouses in various stages of decay. The conversion process involved numerous middlemen:

> In many cases, boardinghouse keepers, wishing to profit by the new demand, took over properties which, after a few alternations, emerged as multiple dwellings. In other cases, a sublease system developed, whereby a contractor, usually Irish himself and frequently a neighborhood tradesman, leased an old building at an annual rental, subdivided it into immigrant flats, and subrented it at weekly rates. Sometimes the structure passed through the

hands of several agents, completely severing control from owner-ship. Solely interested in immediate income, having the welfare of neither the building nor the tenants at heart, sublandlords encouraged a host of evils. . . .[16]

Each room of the tenement, from basement to attic, was packed with one or more families. By mid-century, the 586 rented basements in Boston housed from 5 to 15 persons each.[17] Some of the overcrowd-ing was due to the immigrants' willingness to give temporary shel-ter to newly arrived relatives and friends; but mostly it was simply the result of financial exigency.

Whether in shanty, tenement, or boardinghouse, the problems were much the same: overcrowding, lack of ventilation, poor sanita-tion, cold and dank climate, vermin, and general filth resulting in a high incidence of disease and early death. Indeed, the Irish immi-grant in Boston could expect to live, on the average, only 14 years after arrival.[18]

The Irish-American Family

The Irish family in America was almost a facsimile of its counter-part in Ireland.[19] At the root of family relationships lay the counter-pointing of the male and female sex roles and the awesome emphasis on chastity. The Irish-American woman seems to have maintained her Irish counterpart's chaste image, although not with-out its having become somewhat tarnished. "Irish women are par-ticularly free from offenses against chastity" wrote Bushee, but "Irish women of the second generation are not, however, to the same extent free from these offenses."[20] Other notable observers, such as Maguire and Woods, made the same assertion—but without the qualification about the second generation.[21]

On the other hand, some have pointed to the high proportion of Irish among those suspected of prostitution and to the high incidence of illegitimacy among the Irish. Ernst cited statistics from New York City's venereal hospital:

Of 2,000 prostitutes examined in 1858 at the Penitentiary Hospital on Blackwell's Island . . . 762 were natives of the United States and 1,238, or five-eights of the total were immigrants. The largest proportion was born in British territory: 706 in Ireland, 104 in England, 63 in British North America, 52 in Scotland, and one in Wales. . . . More than 45 per cent of these foreign-born prostitutes had lived in the United States less than five years, and of these 21 per cent were residents of less than one year. Of the 2,000 women, native and immigrant, three-eights were between the ages of fifteen and twenty, and fully three-quarters were younger than twenty-six.[22]

Furthermore, Handlin commented that "by 1860 illegitimate births were probably more frequent among them [the Irish] than among any other nationality."[23]

Raw frequency statistics, however, do not begin to tell the story. Immediately suspect are data that do not allow for the proportion formed by each ethnic group in respect to the overall population of the city. Furthermore, statistically minded sociologists would want the variables of age and social class held constant. As Ernst himself noted, most crime in the mid-nineteenth century was committed by those between 20 and 40 years of age of lower-class standing.[24] These categories of age and class were filled largely by immigrants, especially the Irish. This abstract and formalistic approach to the problem by itself is inadequate, however, because the real issue is the meaning of being a young female Irish immigrant in the early nineteenth century.

Many young Irish girls emigrated with few material possessions and, because some were duped into buying bogus tickets and certificates, were overcharged room and board upon arrival, and even had their possessions stolen, they became indebted to those desiring to exploit them—a prostitution conspiracy. In 1864 Thurlow Weed, a long-time advocate for emigrants, claimed that "innocent and unprotected girls came consigned to houses of prostitution."[25] He was referring to an earlier period of emigration dominated by the Irish. A visitor to American during that period observed that "panderers to the lust of the great cities are constantly on the watch to drag into their dens of infamy the young, the innocent, and the unsuspecting."[26] Worth repeating is the story of

> . . . a young and handsome Irish girl who was lately trapped into
> hiring, in a Western city, with a person of infamous character. She
> was fortunately observed by a poor old Irish woman, who knowing
> the peril in which the young creature stood, boldly rushed to her
> rescue, and at personal risk to herself, literally tore the prey from
> the grasp of the enemy . . . and though the girl lost all her clothes,
> save those in which she then stood, she congratulated herself that
> she had never crossed the threshold of the house of ill-fame.[27]

Illegitimacy was the result of prostitution, the reluctance to
marry, or a forced condition of slum life. No one has better dramatized the plight of the young female Irish-American than Stephen
Crane, in his brilliant short novel *Maggie: A Girl of the Streets*.[28]
Overwhelmed by a brutal slum environment, her alcoholic mother,
and her cruel brother, Maggie seeks escape by going with a con-
temptible young man whom she nonetheless idealizes. While still
chaste, she acquires the reputation of a tramp. Initially she resists
his sexual advances and, when finally she succumbs, Maggie desper-
ately urges her exploiter to admit his love for her. Discovered by a
neighbor who spreads the news of her degradation, Maggie is cursed
and thrown out by her mother and brother to lead a life of sin.

Part of Crane's genius is his felicity in depicting the societal
reaction to Maggie's deviant behavior. As Eric Solomon comments,
"Maggie is a victim, bearing the brunt of others' lusts and hypo-
crisies."[29] Her brother, a past master of seduction, and her degraded
mother hypocritically uphold the strong Irish tradition of chastity.
As Solomon further comments, "Since her family and her lover have
failed to recognize her identity, Maggie must assume the only role
available, the traditional role of fallen women in which they have
cast her."[30] Maggie was never allowed an identity apart from what
her family thrust upon her; so, as she had been previously, she
remained but a "cipher."[31] Thus Crane, in one scene, has Maggie
perceiving with horror her future state in a "brief encounter with two
painted women."[32]

The apparent contradiction between the reputation of Irish girls
for chastity and their seemingly high propensity for prostitution and
illegitimacy can be reconciled. The overwhelming majority of Irish-
American girls were chaste to the point that some came to denigrate

sex even within marriage. But total rejection was the lot of those who, by circumstance or choice, deviated from this ideal. If one could not sustain the role of the chaste Irish woman, one was automatically regarded as a harlot. Nothing in between was admitted. As long as chastity remained the very foundation of the Irish woman's positive identity, its complement, the negative identity of fallen woman, posed a threat to each woman. Whether Irish-Americans practiced this virtue as religiously as the Irish in Ireland, chastity was still extolled above all other virtues.[33]

Irish-Americans' reluctance to marry was notorious. The Irish were the standard against which ethnic celibacy was judged. In regard to the Italians' disdain for the single state, Glazer and Moynihan pointed out that "bachelors and spinsters are few, much fewer than among the Irish."[34] De la Fontaine discovered that in New York city "the correlation between the proportion of unmarried men to total men and the proportion of Irish foreign white stock to the total foreign-born white stock in these areas showed a high positive correlation (plus .715)."[35] Bagenal likewise said, "For the year 1873, in New York, only ten per thousand of the Irish indulged in matrimony against forty-two per thousand of the Germans," and he concluded that the Irish were "less given to marriage than any others."[36]

Reticence about marriage was still intact by the turn of the century. From the vantage point of a South Boston settlement house, Woods and Kennedy observed that many Irish families numbered several bachelors "between the ages of twenty and forty-five" living at home.[37] Even into the twentieth century, observers were in agreement on this point. In the 1920s a series of articles in *America* focused on the reluctance of Irish-Americans to marry.[38] Walsh, for instance, gathered data on this subject for a decade; all the data pointed to an inordinate number of bachelors and spinsters in Irish families.

There also appears to have been little divergence from the Irish pattern of late age at marriage. In a study of Irish mobility in Buffalo, Mattis discovered that from 1877 to 1882 the average age at marriage for men was 35 and for women 31 when both partners were Irish and 32 for men and 27 for women when only one partner was Irish. Neither other ethnic groups nor native Americans (whites who were born in America) approximated the Irish age at marriage.[39]

There is a certain amount of evidence about the nature and quality of Irish family relationships, albeit much of it is contained in casual observation and fiction. Even so, it all seems in agreement. In Ireland, as discussed previously, a negative husband-wife relationship and a negative father-son relationship were counterbalanced by a positive brother-sister relationship and a positive maternal uncle-nephew relationship. But the mother-son relationship and the husband-wife relationship are most central to my argument.

Greeley has written on a tendency of Irish-American mothers to dominate the household and to manipulate their husbands and children by appealing to their guilt and sympathy.[40] Both the estrangement of husband and wife and the mother's singular part in child rearing have been vividly captured in the writing of Irish-American novelists and playwrights.[41] Crane's realistic portrayal of Irish-American life in the nineteenth century is unsurpassed. *Maggie* and *George's Mother* are detailed depictions of Irish-American slum families, taking to their logical conclusion certain tendencies in both the Irish family and the American slum.[42] In *Maggie,* the drunken father and alcoholic mother are the masters of his or her own province: the household, child rearing, and religion in the mother's case and work and leisure in the father's instance. The husband-wife relationship is even more a void, the absence of a relationship, than it is the acrimonious relationship overtly dramatized. The husband frequently flees the household for the companionship of his tavern colleagues during or after a fight with his wife. The fights range from disagreements about the children to those about the husband's absence and his drinking. The wife, family and religion centered, sees her husband as an intrafamily predator, egotistically inclined and posing a great threat to her interests. The husband on the other hand is more defensive, resenting his wife's intrusion into his domain.

But concurrently there was a tendency borne out of necessity for Irish-American husbands and wives to depend on each other more and to do more together. *In The Uprooted,* Oscar Handlin persuasively argues that immigrants torn away from their peasant community and extended family had only their immediate family to rely on. One might argue that at times the slum destroyed this fragile source of support. Hence *Maggie* and *George's Mother* represent not so much

"typical" Irish-American families but the end products of the concatenation of the Irish family and extreme slum conditions. Such
conditions could weaken and negate even marital relationships much
stronger than those of the Irish. Actually there was more husband-
wife interaction in America than there had been in Ireland. For this
reason and for political and economic reasons to be discussed later,
family drinking in the Irish-American home was not uncommon, as
it had been in Ireland.

George's Mother focuses on the mother-son relationship. George
is torn between his mother's attempt to make him a religious and
dutiful son and his desire to become one of the boys, to be accepted
by older drinking companions. Finally he resists both efforts to mold
him into something he does not really desire to become. His mother
hoped to realize her thwarted ambitions in her son. If her husband
was a failure, at least her son could be her constant companion, a
decent and upstanding credit to religion and community.

If, as is apparently the case, the Irish-American family resembled
the Irish family, there was one factor in America that could serve
only to exacerbate any prior estrangement of husband from his wife
and sons. This was the forced absence of fathers from the home.
Those who worked on the canals, railroads, and highways were often
forced—because of low wages and exploitive living arrangements—to
leave their families behind in the city with relatives and friends until
they returned in the off-season. Therefore the mother had to assume
an even larger role in the family. This factor might have prevented
many men from even contemplating marriage.

The Political Organization of the Irish-American Neighborhood

This section is based on descriptions of Irish-American politics during
the end of the nineteenth century and characterizes the beginning of
the twentieth century as well.

Although every ethnic group had its share of street gangs, they
apparently were most prevalent among the Irish. "It is the Irish boys

that form street gangs," wrote Bushee.[43] What actually set the Irish apart from other immigrant groups was the older men's continued participation in street gangs, even if married, plus the propensity of the Irish for organized political activity, especially at the ward level. Of course, the two were related. The strength of Irish-American political activity centered about the extensive and intensive organization of men willing to take direction. The street gangs operated under the umbrella of the ward political association. The Irish political association was composed of street gangs, social clubs, and machine clubs, all to varying degrees under the tutelage of the ward boss and his associates.

Most male Irish-Americans became members of street gangs early in life. When their members reached 18 years of age, some gangs became formalized as social clubs having official meetings, elected officers, and dues. Such clubs provided a basis of organization for the larger ward political organization: "The description thus far of the gang, the social club, and the dance hall, shows that the politician does not need to deal with individuals. Ready at hand are these various social centres for him to make use of."[44]

Over the various gangs and social clubs stood the "machine club." All those in the ward having good political appointments were members; the ward boss was its leader. The ward boss had "lieutenants" and "heelers" under him. The lieutenants were political aids entrusted with the implementation of high-level decisions; the heelers performed the legwork and put pressure on people to vote for their candidate. The street gangs and social clubs also had leaders, many of whom were involved in ward politics as members of the machine club.

Woods made a distinction between the "respectable" social gangs and the "disreputable" ones. The respectable gangs often banded together as social clubs, while the disreputable gangs preferred "to use what little money they have in carousing."[45] The disreputable outnumbered the respectable. The respectable gang members appeared more attracted to politics as a career and "legitimate" activities and opportunities; the disreputable gang members, many of whom were employed sporadically or unemployed, were content to reap the spoils of politics. Respectable as well as disreputable street gangs and social clubs fell under the political and economic influence of the ward boss, who established reciprocal relationships with his people by providing services, jobs, food, and drink in exchange for votes. Woods described this relationship:

> In these wards there is a large number of men in the employ of the City, chiefly as laborers. I have already referred to the loafers and semi-criminal class. Many of them live in lodging houses. It is a tradition among these men to stand in with the boss. If they get into trouble with the police, he frequently comes to their assistance. Through his help, the case is sometimes quashed or the sentence is abridged.[46]

But it was not just the unemployed who became obligated to the machine:

> On the whole, partly for the love of position and power, and partly from a good heart, the boss enjoys doing good turns for men. . . . He has been known to pay the funeral expense of poor people who have no insurance. At Christmas time and Thanksgiving he gives turkey to needy families. Dance tickets, baseball passes, tickets to the theatre, railway passes, and so forth,—which cost him nothing, being simply incidental results of his tools in the common council or the legislature voting "right"—are distributed with wise discrimination. He is always ready to treat. . . . This all sounds very generous; but the chief admirers of the boss cannot deny that when the supremacy of the ward is at all endangered, he makes capital of all his good deeds. In other words, every man to whom he has granted a favor is made to feel that the boss expects a vote.[47]

However well-intentioned the boss might be, the dictates of the system in which he was enmeshed demanded that he regard people as votes, that he gauge the potential utility of those with whom he came in contact. As Woods observed:

> The boss can never be a disinterested member of society. He is forced to make men act and vote with him,—the weaker their wills, the fewer their convictions, the better for him. He gives another drink to the drunkard: he has a vote. The only morality he seeks in men is loyalty to him.[48]

The ward was only a microcosm of the larger American society in that economic and political considerations were dominant. The extended family had been the basis of community in the rural peasant village. Helping one another at harvest time and in emergencies had been regulated by a set of reciprocal norms embedded in the kinship system. In the leaving and resettlement, kinship had been torn asunder—and with it the community.[49] The problem of social integration was further confounded by the utilitarian character of the New World. With reciprocal kin relationships shriveled to their nuclear core, the ward political association performed many of the same helping activities that had been performed previously in the name of family and community. But now there was an asking price: a vote. The ward political association provided for the survival needs of many in the district: Those receiving goods and services incurred political debts that could be erased at the next election. But the relationship, no matter how outwardly avuncular between the boss and his wards, was principally a political one from his point of view and an economic one from their point of view.

"Political association" is an apt term. The Irish rural community possessed a vast network of primary or personal relationships and a modicum of secondary associations. In America, however, the ward political association was comprised of secondary relationships. This does not mean that members of political clubs and neighbors did not know each other and were not friendly. It means that personal relationships were by-products of and subsidiary to secondary, utilitarian relationships. Increasingly immigrants were forced to use each other to compete in American society. The Irish-American neighborhood dominated by the political association supplanted to a great extent the Irish community that depended on kinship and religion.

Irish immigrants were attempting to adapt to the larger American society. By and large the Irish, like some other immigrant groups, accepted the goal of economic success if for no other reason than that not to do so would mean continued poverty and powerlessness. In a society that pitted ethnic group against ethnic group in striving for the scare goods of respectability, money, and power, a non-competing group would have remained outcast and downtrodden.

The Irish had to compete if only to survive. Ultimately political and economic relationships displaced those of kinship and religion as the mainstay of community order. The Irish peasant community had been dominated by religious interests, the extensive role of the priest, and kinship interests as in single inheritance, whereas the immigrant community was shaped by political and economic considerations partially freed from the restraints of kinship and religion.

A brief comparison of Italian and Jewish immigrants with the Irish should prove instructive. Italian and Jewish moral communities in the old country present an important contrast with that of the Irish. For one, both groups have long been singled out for their unusually low rates of alcoholism. Also, the moral community in Ireland was centered in the social roles of priest and mother; in Italian and Jewish circles, the moral community was embedded in the extended family. For different historical reasons, moral control and solidarity were much more concentrated within the family for Jews and Italians.

"Amoral familism" is the name Edward Banfield applied to rural southern Italian morality.[50] The principal idea here is that moral obligations apply only to one's family, leaving one free to be immoral toward strangers. This suggests a takeover of moral interpretation by the family at the expense of the Catholic church, which explicitly states Christian morality must be applied to all men. The dictates of organized religion are altered to suit family interests; the church's influence was mitigated in Italian culture.

For the Jews, on the other hand, there was no major conflict between family and organized religion. The history of the Jewish people is a history of almost continuous migration, transplantation, and oppression. In such a history the family was often the only structure the individual could depend on. Communities were a luxury that only the secure could enjoy. Moreover, the family had always been at the very seat of the religion, the point at which race and religion were most cogently intertwined. The family, then, was "sacred" to the Jews and the very seat of religious ceremony. Everyday religious ritual took place within the home.

The solidarity of the Italian and Jewish families was more intense than it was for many other nationalities. Glazer and Moynihan noted the similarity in the solidarity of the two families: "The Italian family resembles in some ways the Jewish one, in its strength, its heightened and uninhibited emotional quality, and even in some of its inner alliances."[51] Italian male grouping tended to terminate at marriage, so the family eventually captured the full attention of the adult male.

Thus, for Italians and Jews, the family was the center of both moral control and solidarity. For the Irish, on the other hand, organized religion in the person of the priest and the mother was the major source of moral control, and solidarity for adult males resided to a great extent within the male group. The implications of this contrast are of great import to the social meaning of immigration. Jewish and Italian reliance on the family tended to mitigate somewhat the inherently uprooted effects of immigration, especially when entire families emigrated together. The greater the reliance on the family, the less traumatic was the dissolution of the larger community Nationalities that had struck more of a balance between the inner controls of the family and the outer controls of the community experienced more profound shock from the migration experience. The weakness of the Irish family, together with the alienating effects of emigration, meant that the Irish more than many immigrant groups relied on politics as a way of organizing their settlements and neighborhoods.

Politics as Relgion: The Social Role of the Irish Boss

Religion and politics have always been intimately connected it would appear. During the Middle Ages Christendom represented a deliberate attempt on the part of Christians to make society conform to Christian beliefs. All institutions were to reflect Christ's Lordship over history. In this instance politics was subordinate to religion.

However, politics and religion are not in this relationship today. Ellul has described the dominance of politics:

. . . instead of the consoling presence—that experience so much desired by religious people—man now experiences faith and religious conversion thanks to his participation in politics. What was lost by the church has been found by the parties, at least those worthy of the name. Faith in attainable ends, in the improvement of the social order, in the establishment of a just and peaceful system—by political means—is a most profound, and undoubtedly new, characteristic in our society. Among the many basic definitions of man, two are joined together at this point: *homo politicus* is by his very nature *homo religiosus.* And this faith takes shape in active virtues that can only arouse the jealousy of Christians. Look how full of devotion they are, how full of the spirit of sacrifice, these passionate men who are obsessed with politics. But people never ask whether all this is worthwhile. Because these witnesses are so devoted, they invest the object of their service with their passion. In this fashion a nation becomes a cult by virtue of the millions of dead who were sacrificed for it. It must all be true, as so many agreed (did they?) to die for it. The same goes for the state, or national independence, or the victory of a political ideology.[52]

The twentieth century has witnessed the development of apparently contradictory secular religious attitudes: the quest for consumer goods and services in the private sphere and veneration of the nation-state in the public sphere. Thus "civil religion in America"[53] might be concerned either with a consumption-oriented life-style or with the deeply emotional and irrational adoration of America as a political and economic giant. But these are not really contradictory because the goal of political life in the past two centuries has been man's happiness, defined in terms of increased levels of production and consumption. Technology and its products have become a spiritual power partly because man attaches a spiritual value to them. Politics under the auspices of the state became the means of funding and organizing technological advances. Furthermore, even the politically apathetic, who seem to be retreating into the private sphere, are still political true believers. Ellul comments on the phenomenon of depolitization:

Depolitization, as discussed by most political scientists, is really concerned only with actual participation of a democratic nature.

> Yet, for example, to put oneself in the hands of the state not by
> default but because of loyalty is the height of politization . . . sim-
> ilarly, in a democracy, politization in the general concept of social
> life is more important than participation in election meetings.[54]

Those who become cynical about politics and disdain political involvement still look to the state to solve their problems and make them
happier. Today people's deepest sentiments and beliefs center about
politics; it is truly a religion. What we generally call religion, on the
other hand, finds it necessary to draw out continually the political
implications of a particular faith. However, these political implications are almost invariably defined in secular terms. Hence, religion
becomes politicized while politics becomes a religion.

In regard to Irish politics in the late nineteenth and early twentieth centuries, it is not being argued that politics was the singular
religion of the Irish; rather, it had equal footing with Catholicism
and, for some (especially men), it was more truly *the* religion. Irish
nationalism had been long frustrated by English rule. Even though
the main thrust of the opposition was against the English because
they were also mostly Protestant, the battle was between Catholic
Ireland and Protestant England. Catholicism was an integral part of
being Irish; so in a certain sense religion was an ally, perhaps only
an adjunct to politics, in the holy cause of Irish nationalism.

The sources seem to agree that among American ethnic groups,
the "greatest degree of political activity is found among the Irish."[55]
Woods claimed:

> The political interest of the Irish people is shown not only in the
> large proportion of Irish voters, but also in the greater activity of
> these voters. They are not merely the most easily organized of any
> nationality, but they are the most capable organizers. According
> to their own account, this political capacity is the result of the
> struggle for independence.[56]

Moreover, in the celebration of national heritage, "a folklore of fond
remembrance for their native land," the Irish far outstrip other
immigrant groups.[57] When politics begins to function as a religion, it
becomes totally autonomous:

> The Irishman regards politics as a separate department of life. It is an end in itself, and is undertaken for its own sake. To be sure, he hopes by its means to be able to gain a living, but that is the stake of a game which has a fascination all its own.[58]

In rural Ireland the social role of the priest was potentially a strong one, as we have already seen. The priest was looked to for assistance in other than religious matters partly because he was educated and partly because he was believed to have special powers. However, his forte was religion, and his desire to be a good clergyman as defined by the church hierarchy was countered by his previous upbringing in the traditional Irish community. He was not a tyrant except on occasion and only in regard to religious concerns.

The social role of the Irish ward boss in America was an enlargement on the social role of the priest in Ireland. To an extent, the ward boss supplanted the priest as the dominant figure in the Irish-American neighborhood. The boss was an autocrat who made little pretense about being otherwise. Assuredly most of the Irish bosses were deeply concerned about their fellow countrymen, but the fact remains that they ruled in an authoritarian fashion. Too often the Irish political boss has been sentimentalized and the pernicious effects of his authoritarianism played down. The boss's influence on the criminally inclined was notorious because his connections allowed him to get them out of jail. Those who worked for the city voted for the boss and reaped the spoils of the victor, but even those who were honestly unemployed were pawns of the boss:

> The number of men who are almost ready to fawn upon one for a job is simply appalling. . . . Some of these men are looking for political jobs. Consider the hold the boss can gain upon them. The few secure a job; the many get promises. Those who get jobs are the slaves of the boss. . . . According to the ethics of the district, a man who receives a job is under the most sacred obligations to the politician who bestowed it.[59]

With great insight, Woods perceived that the ward boss too was a servant of the political system he engineered:

> I do not see how any man in his position, however good his char-
> acter to begin with, could do otherwise than use men as checkers
> on a board. His ambition to boss the party in his ward necessitates
> his looking upon men continually from the point of view of votes.
> The logic of the boss system demands this. Votes are his busi-
> ness,—they mean money, power.[60]

The boss sometimes had to bully and domineer recalcitrant supporters:

> A group of men got together, put up a fairly strong ward and city
> committee, and selected one of their number to run for warden, as
> a guarantee of an honest caucus. The boss grew suddenly active.
> He quickly visited about half the men on the ticket. Some he
> warned that if they ever wished a City job, he would oppose them;
> others he smiled upon, promising them election to an office later
> on, or a position in a City department if they would only with-
> draw. He came to the room of their leader, having learned that he
> had some intention of running for a certain office later on. Almost
> before greeting this man, the boss demanded that he withdraw his
> name as warden from the opposition ticket. Bringing his fist down
> on the table, and growing purple in the face, he swore with a hor-
> rible oath, that if this man did not withdraw his name, he could
> never be elected to any office in the ward.[61]

The role of ward boss could be traced back to the role of "counselor" in the street gang. The counselor was the brains of the gang
who planned its activities, whether legitimate or illegitimate; sometimes he was also the gang's "judge," settling its disputes. The counselor was "the ward boss in embryo."[62] The ward was organized and
operated like a gang and in reality was composed of many gangs,
disreputable and respectable, young and old.

But what about the Irish-American priest? He was still a force
to be reckoned with, but his more extensive role in Ireland had been
pared in America. He was now in charge of the private sector of
life—religion and family. In Ireland, where Catholicism became a
source of national identity and a rallying point against Protestant
England, the priest was the enforcer of a Christian morality that up
to a point covered the private and public spheres of life. However,

the reduction of religion to a fixed morality is itself a political act. In America religion had shrunk to Sunday worship and child rearing; it had become family centered and was now a private matter, even though it was still a sign of national identity.

The shrinking role of religion corresponds to the ascendancy of a middle-class morality in the nineteenth century. A major tenet of this morality was the strict separation of life into private and public domains. In the world of work and politics, men followed the dictates of utility in striving for success; in the world of leisure and the family, they tacitly adhered to a pseudo-Christian morality.[63] Thus religion was put in its place, the private sphere; but its role even there was rapidly diminishing.

Irish-Americans adapted so completely to the necessities of American industrialism that they eventually earned the grudging admiration of native Americans for their political exploits. They had become more American than the natives. And the Irish boss and his regime simply represented the logical conclusion of that bifurcated morality, at least insofar at it applied to an exploited and downtrodden group attempting to compete with those in power. The Irish could only come to power if they became tougher and stronger than those they hoped to displace. The Irish became the living embodiment of a middle-class morality and American way of life, and they had their own guides; the boss for the give-and-take of the political and economic world and the priest for life within the home and the church.

The Economics and Politics of Drink

The role of drink in the economics and politics of Irish-American settlements has an important bearing on a full understanding of Irish-American drinking. The Irish were notorious in the large cities for their grogshops, taverns, and saloons. By 1851 the overwhelming majority of grogshops in Boston were operated by the Irish.[64] The *New York Tribune* reported that in 1854 as many as three-fourths of that city's saloons were run by Catholics who made up only one-fourth of its population.[65] Irish boardinghouses often featured a grogshop on the first floor. It is said that the landlord profited more from the sale of drink than from room rent. Sometimes the newly arrived Irish immigrant was met at the docks by runners employed by Irish boardinghouses and was led straight out to the groggery for a drink with some of his own.

The tenements also contained numerous grogshops. Handlin mentions that "numerous Irish families sold gin as a sideline, without license."[66] Furthermore, the cellars of old mansions more often than not housed "a grocery and vegetable shop; and not infrequently, a groggery and dancing hall."[67] Maguire, an Irish visitor to America, offered this description about the pervasiveness and dangers of the drink business.

> The "liquor business" is most pernicious, either directly or indirectly, to the Irish. Requiring little capital, at least to commence with, the Irish rush into it; and the temptation to excess which it offers is often more than the virtue of the proprietor of the business can withstand. If the evil were confined to the individual himself, the result would be a matter of comparatively trifling consequence; but the Irishman attracts the Irishman to his saloon or his bar, and so the evil spreads. Almost invariably the lowest class of groggery or liquor-store—that which supplies the most villanous and destructive mixtures to its unfortunate customers—is planted right in the centre of the densely-crowded Irish quarters of a great city. . . . In America, as in Ireland, there are men in the trade who are a credit to their country . . . but, on the other hand, there are others whose connection with it is injurious to themselves and prejudicial to their countrymen. The bad liquor of the native American or the Dutchman is far less perilous to poor Pat than what is sold by the barkeeper whose name has in it a flavour of the shamrock.[68]

For a number of the Irish, the liquor business was a means of mobility, if not social, at least economic and political. Woods observed that "the business has been a very lucrative one in times past, and many well-to-do Irish families throughout the city own their use in life to it."[69] If the drink trade proved the surest means of acquiring capital, it also provided a power base for politics.

Along with the home and church, the saloon was the focal point of community life.[70] Many saloons were owned and operated by Irish politicians; indeed, the saloon owner fully expected to enter the political arena directly or indirectly. Matthew Breen, in his ruminations on New York politics, had this to say about the involvement of the Irish liquor dealer in politics:

> As a rule the liquor dealer in politics makes headway by no false pretenses. He is no better or no worse than he appears. He is free from hypocrisy and cant. He is in politics as a matter of business and he makes no disguises of it. He laughs to scorn those who sanctimoniously publish to the world that they accept political station for the benefit of the people. . . . Such declarations he regards (and justly in most cases) as the merest sham.[71]

One could just as well say that the politician was in the drink business as a matter of politics Because ward bosses and their associates could assure many men of jobs with the city or the machine, men frequented their establishments hoping to secure better positions:

> . . . the working man is seduced into that most tempting, yet most fatal of all moral maelstroms.—the whirlpool of pothouse politics . . . fascinated by the coarse Sirens—Drink and Politics—many an Irishman . . . has first become a tool, then a slave, then a victim: helping to build up the fortunes of some worthless fellow on his own ruin, and sacrificing the legitimate gain of honest industry for the expectation of some paltry office, which, miserable at best, ever eludes his desperate clutch.[72]

Treating others to drink became a favorite technique of bosses to keep in good standing with the boys. Also, political opinion was often formed and fermented at the saloon:

> In each ward . . . there are five or six hundred men who are more or less influenced by the political talk of the saloon. . . . The men who frequent the saloons are, almost without exception, the men who attend the caucus . . . if a barkeeper is given money with which to treat the boys, even the fairly respectable men who are at the bar, after a round of drinks, look with favor upon the saloon keeper's

candidate. The saloon is thus the place where political opinion is formed very quickly and the opinions formed there are soon circulated through the community by the "saloon gossips." No man who wishes to become elected in these wards disregards the saloon. Other things being at all equal, the man who has the greater number of saloon keepers on his side will surely be elected.[73]

It was also essential for the boss to make an occasional personal appearance in the local saloons, where his supporters could hear firsthand what was happening at city hall and could see he was one of them:

> There is something very flattering in having the boss retail to you the political gossip of "downtown." He does this the most effectively at the club, or at a saloon, where a crowd quickly gathers. In this role he is quite at his best when he speaks in scathing terms of some opponent, or perhaps the "fight" at a recent convention. It is racy, pugilistic talk. It is cheap, but it keeps the boss in touch with the crowd. If washed down with a drink, it makes the boss a good fellow, "one of our kind," the idol of the tough element,—and the tough element tell mightily in a caucus.[74]

Usually the boss delegated his drinking responsibilities to his heelers, however. Woods offered this derogatory profile of the heeler:

> As a rule, a "heeler" is a brokendown "bum," afraid of work, fond of his cups, in touch with loafers and the semi-criminal class . . . glad to be lifted into temporary importance by having money to spend on the "boys." . . . Perhaps his ambition stopped short of a clean shirt—it meant just so much drink. . . . He is a hard drinker and noted fighter. . . . He knows how to throw down a half dollar in this or that saloon in the most approved fashion and call for a general toast to the success of some "regular" candidate.[75]

The heelers were recruited from the disreputable gangs and had plenty of experience in strong-arm tactics. These gangs sometimes badgered or even forced strangers in their area to buy them drinks. Edward Steiner, a Jewish immigrant who later became a college professor, recalled that as a young man:

There was one Irish lad in the group who belonged to that species called "low down" Irish. His wit was vitriolic and his delight in my sufferings made him invent new cruelties, every hour. He compelled me to treat him and his comrades to drink, and when he discovered that I had a twenty-dollar gold piece in my pocket easily possessed himself to it.[76]

The heeler and his boss had a reputation as hard drinkers. The heeler's renown was deserved it appears, but not the boss's. Without qualification Glazer and Moynihan state that the "stereotype of the Irish politician as a beer-guzzling back slapper is nonsense"; instead, "sobriety was the mark of successful leaders."[77] How is it that the boss was known as a hard drinker but was not so in reality? Obviously it was expedient that the boss project an image that he was one of the boys: rough, a good fighter, and a hard drinker. Because Irish politicians were of working-class backgrounds, such an image was plausible. But the demands of politics militated against the boss's having the time to drink hard and against any impaired functioning on his part. One way of projecting the image of hard drinker while remaining cold sober was treated humorously by that master of the political sketch, Finley Peter Dunne, through the mouth of his most famous character—"Mr. Dooley," an Irish-American saloonkeeper:

In me day I niver knew a gr-reat statesman that dhrank, or if he did he niver landed anny job betther thin clerk in th' weather office. But as Hogan says Shakespere says, they pretended a vice if they had it not. A polytician was a baten man if th' story wint around that he was seldom see dhrunk in public. His aim was to create an impressyon that he was a gay fellow, a jovyal toss pot, that thought nawthin' iv puttin' a gallon iv paint into him durin' an avenin's intertainment. They had to exercise diplomacy, d'ye mind, to keep their repytations goin'. Whin Higgins was runnin' f'r sheriff he always ordhered gin an' I always give him wather. Ye undherstand, don't ye? Ye know what gin looks like? Well, wather looks like gin. Wan day Gallagher took up his glass be mistake an' Higgins lost th' precinct be forty votes. Sinitor O'Brien held a bolder coorse. He used to dump th' stuff on th' flure whin no wan was lookin' an' go home with a light foot while I swept out his constitooents. Yes, sire, I've seen him pour into th' sawdust quarts an' gallons iv me precious old Remorse Rye, aged be me own hands on th' premises.[78]

The boss could maintain his image as a hard drinker for a number of reasons: his working-class origins and hard drinking when younger; his association with his hard-drinking associates, the heelers; and his pity on the drunkard whose family he looked after. But paramount was the desire on the part of his supporters to believe that their leader personified the quintessence of Irish manhood. The boss was the projected image his supporters had of themselves.

The concatenation of the economics and politics of drink illustrate a sad law: Exploited groups first exploit their own in the attempt to better themselves. Many Irish families became moderately wealthy by selling liquor that was sometimes of poor quality to their neighbors. In addition, the saloonkeeper in politics encouraged men to drink as the asking price for jobs. Finally, the ward boss used drink as a wedge to control his electorate. Daniel Bell once called organized crime in America "a queer ladder of social mobility" for numerous ethnic groups.[79] What is sometimes underemphasized is the fact that the ethnic organized crime began in the ethnic neighborhood before it spread outward. Its first victims were its own.

Adjustment, Identity, and Drink

A brief comparison of Irish-Americans and Italian-Americans is necessary for my argument in this section. Italian immigrants provide as neat a natural control group as can be found for examining some of the stock variables used to explain drunkenness and alcoholism. Italian immigrants, who possessed an extremely low rate of alcoholism among ethic groups, came to America during the late nineteenth and early twentieth centuries, primarily from the southern regions of Italy. The south of Italy had been impoverished for centuries. Its people were principally laborers and farm workers. At least three-quarters of the Italian immigrants were farm workers or semiskilled laborers. Emigrating with few skills and little education, they became the mainstay of the large urban industrial centers, which greatly needed unskilled manpower. With few exceptions they were Catholic. Italians suffered considerable discrimination, as did the Irish. The description of Italian immigrants does not differ critically from that of Irish immigrants: an uneducated, unskilled, lower-class, rural, Catholic people who settled in the large American cities.

All immigrants faced dire circumstances to which they were forced to adjust. However, some sociological studies of deviant behavior have equated adjustment with out-and-out conformity.[80] Therefore, adjustment often connotes a high degree of passivity.[81] Adjustment so defined does not involve continued struggle as with the concepts of transcendence and overcoming. Many have pointed out that by theoretically treating adjustment as conformity, by minimizing conflict, and by making the socialization process total and impregnable, one is ideologically justifying the status quo.

This is why we must look at the concrete realities that the concepts "adjustment" and "group identity" refer to in each particular context. That adjustment and group identity are dialectically related seems a truism. Erikson defined group identity as a group's "basic ways of organizing experience."[82] In the organization of experience, a group is sometimes faced with the demands of a new social order sustained by strict moral controls. Thus in Ireland hard drinking was a form of cultural remission; that is, it was a morally regulated form of release for Irish males who were put upon by dramatic changes in farm economy, kinship, and marriage patterns. Hard drinking as an aspect of male identity was a way of organizing the experience of being a man so that it did not threaten the new and fragile social order: a single-inheritance farm economy regulated by strict sexual taboos.

But in the uprootedness of emigration, the individual was increasingly on his own. Handlin's great work, *The Uprooted,* describes this stripping away of communal support to its bare bones, one's immediate family. He wrote, "Although entire communities were uprooted at the same times, although the whole life of the Old World has been communal, the act of migration was individual."[83] Earlier the individual's ego identity had been integrated with his larger group identity:

Ego identity then, in its subjective aspect, is the awareness of the fact that there is a self-sameness and continuity to the ego's synthesizing methods, *the style of one's individuality,* and that this style coincides with the sameness and continuity of one's *meaning for significant others* in the immediate community.[84]

As Erikson points out, there is a "mutual complementation of group identity and ego identity, of ethos and ego."[85] But this complementation is precisely what was momentarily lost in emigration. Moreover, when a previous source of a well-regulated group identity is expunged from the individual's worldview, it grows in intensity and significance to the individual. It can become an exaggerated way of differentiating oneself from others. Handlin spoke of the general phenomenon among the immigrants:

> The old folk knew then they would not come to belong, not through their own experience nor through their offspring. The only adjustment they had been able to make to life in the United States had been one that involved the separateness of their group, one that increased their awareness of the differences between themselves and the rest of the society. In that adjustment they had always suffered from the consciousness they were strangers. The demands that they assimilate, that they surrender their separateness, condemned them always to be outsiders. In practice, the free structure of American life permitted them with few restraints to go their own way, but under the shadow of a consciousness that they would never belong. They had thus completed their alienation from the culture to which they had come, as from that which they had left.[86]

The nationalistic group consciousness of the Irish confirmed them as assimilated into American life, albeit as separate but not equal Americans. "Nationalistic leaders accepted almost without exception the dominant ideals and assumptions of Americans," wrote Thomas Brown.[87] Irish-Americans made Ireland's history over in the ideal image of America and exaggerated their former group traits by treating their origins in caricatured fashion. Ultimately then, "Immigrant nationalism, which is to say Irish self-consciousness and sense of group identity, was a powerful agency of assimilation, while at the same time giving the appearance of isolating the immigrant from American life."[88] Irish-American culture was more American than Irish. By concomitantly proffering and accepting a "positive" stereotype of themselves (i.e., stage Irish), they compensated for the stark reality of the present and created a bond of acceptance between themselves and native Americans.

But the old culture is never dissolved all at once; rather, it is transformed, idealized, and romanticized to meet the new conditions of the New World. Thus hard drinking, disembodied from its previous context of meaning in Ireland, grew in significance in America as a means of identification among Irish-Americans and as a synthesis of group identity and individual and group adjustment. After all, identity is an adjustment of sorts.

Drinking now made one more Irish; it distinguished one from other ethnic groups. Hence in the act of drinking, in the affirmation of a life-style, one was truly nationalistic. Ultimately drink—even more than it had in Ireland—acquired a spiritual value; it had become sacred. No one better understood this than Stephen Crane, who captured the essence of Irish-American drinking in *George's Mother.* In this short novel, Crane depicts the initiation of a young man into the moral community of drinkers. Crane wrote that his hero's newfound friends "drank reverently."[89] George's subjective reaction was that

> he was all at once an enthusiast, as if he were at a festival of religion. He felt that there was something fine and thrilling in this affair isolated from a stern world, and from which the laughter arose like incense.[90]

And again:

> [George] Kelcey sometimes wondered whether he liked beer. He had been obliged to cultivate a talent for imbibing it. He was born with an abhorrence which he had steadily battled until it had come to pass that he could drink from ten to twenty glasses of beer without the act of swallowing causing him to shiver. He understood that drink was an essential joy, to the coveted position of a man of the world and of the streets. The saloon contained the mystery of

a street for him. When he knew its saloons, he comprehended the street. Drink and its surroundings were the eyes of a superb green dragon to him. He followed a fascinating glitter, and the glitter required no explanation.[91]

Eugene O'Neill also portrayed a sense of drink's sacredness in *A Long Day's Journey into Night.* Critic John Henry Raleigh observed that "the bottle is the most important object in the room" for the entire family in this great drama.[92] To know what religion someone adheres to, one must know what that person holds sacred. Drink was a spiritual value and, as something sacred, was part of a larger religion of Irish nationalism and Irish life-style. It was the exact point at which nationalism and life-style were intertwined. In the past drinking had been the overflow or consequence of communal conviviality; now it had become the mystical means of community, of creating an imaginary one to fill the void where real community once stood. Drinking among men or in the family was the occasion for recalling memories of Ireland. It was compensation for the grim reality of Irish-American life.

Drink in Irish-American culture was related of course to drink in Irish culture. But in America it became more sacred. It became idealized to the extent it became an important source of differentiating the Irish from other ethnic groups in a society that assimilated immigrants by domesticating them as caricatured ethnics. Irish-American culture centered around an exaggerated and idealized self-consciousness, much of which was only what Americans wanted to believe about them anyway. In Ireland drink was largely a sign of male identity; in American it was a symbol of Irish identity.

In that hard drinking was now more an Irish than simply a masculine province, women and children were more readily admitted to the company of hard drinkers. O'Neill, especially in *Long Day's Journey,* provided us with lush examples of Irish-American family drinking as a religious or at least ritualistic endeavor. Stephen Grecco writes of the autobiographical origin of the play:

> Like his character Jimmy, O'Neill began drinking—and getting drunk—at a very early age. In retrospect, it seems he had little choice in the matter: become intoxicated by one means or another

was almost a family ritual. His brother Jamie was a confirmed alcoholic at twenty and predictably died a drunkard's death; his mother became addicted to morphine shortly after (and because of the difficulty of) Eugene's birth, and spent most of the remainder of her life in a semi-narcotized state; and his father, who normally started the day with a pre-breakfast cocktail, became so possessive about his liquor that he decided to lock it up in the cellar out of reach of his perpetually thirsty sons.[93]

Drinking had attained the status of the sacred, whether in a male-group or family context. Drink and Irish were inexorably linked; the more one drank, the more Irish one became. And because nationalism as a religion led people to worship the collective image of themselves, whatever set one apart from other nationalities became sacred.

The upshot of this is that whereas hard drinking had been culturally remitted in Ireland, it was now under the province of direct moral control. Remissions and controls both go to make up the moral demands of a culture, but there is an important difference between them. Hard drinking as cultural remission was a release from the dominant symbolism of religious devotionalism/puritanism and was tolerated by the Catholic church as long as it could be seen as falling short of drunkenness. This, of course, served as a check on the hard drinking and encouraged drinkers at least to simulate sobriety. But in America, Irish drinking as a cult embodied nationalistic self-consciousness and individual life-style. Drinking was truly a religious phenomenon, under direct moral control, and as such implied strict obligations to oneself and others. Hard drinking had all the appearances of a religious obligation—the obligation to be Irish and to promote one's Irishness. The implication was that the more one drank, the more Irish one became. In this sense the habitual drunkard was at least a religious true believer and at most only a religious fanatic. On the social level, hard drinking was encouraged by saloonkeepers and liquor dealers for economic reasons and by politicians in the quest of a power base of voters. Irish-American drinking was under intense and strict social control.

But as religion always creates its extremists, so also did the (political) religion of Irish drinking. Hard drinking as Irish group identity provided the opportunity for excess for the troubled individual. Alcoholic drinking, was an "invisible" adaptation to stress. An addicted drinker blends right in with a community of hard drinkers.

In chapter 5, attention was called to what was regarded as the primary psychological function of intoxication: a mediation between "self-preservation and self-destruction—an attempt of the self to survive itself."[94] Once again, Crane's *George's Mother* offers insight. In describing his protagonist's anticipation of an impending drinking spree, Crane wrote: "He was about to taste the delicious revenge of a partial self-destruction. The universe would regret its position when it saw him drunk."[95] In the same vein, Raleigh characterized the drinking in *Long Day's Journey* as "suicide without death."[96] Hard drinking as group identity acted as a lodestone for the already existing tendencies and needs of the individual to escape reality whether temporarily, as in the case of occasional intoxication, or permanently, as in the case of alcohol addiction.

"Momism" and "Bossism"

Although the main trust of this study is on the sociological level, the psychological implications of my argument need to be explored—if only tentatively. Such is the case with "momism" and "bossism" as defined by Erik Erikson. Momism and bossism are two sociological trends that together "have usurped the place of paternalism: momism in alliance with the autocratic rigor of a new continent, and bossism with the autocracy of the machine and the 'machines.'"[97] ("Machines" refers to political and business machines, which individual autocrats dominated; "machine" refers to the tendency in modern societies to organize everything, including humans, in a machinelike, efficient manner.) Although Erikson wrote about these trends in the context of the larger American society and in relation to American identity, these trends are very pronounced among Irish-Americans.

Momism is a tendency in families for the mother to assume the roles of both mother and father. This places a certain pressure on her, as expressed in the rigidity she displays in the moral upbringing of her children. Erikson argues that the American frontier environment helped create a strict division of labor between mother and father. "Mom" had to become

> . . . the cultural censor, the religious conscience, the aesthetic arbiter, and the teacher. In that early rough economy hewn out of hard nature it was she who contributed the finer graces of living and that spirituality without which the community falls apart. In her children, she saw future men and women who would face contrasts of rigid sedentary and shifting migratory life. They must be prepared for any number of extreme opposites in milieu, and always ready to seek new goals and to fight for them in merciless competition. For, after all, worse than a sinner was a sucker.[98]

And again:

> Mother became "Mom" only when Father became "Pop" under the impact of the identical historical discontinuities. For, if you come down to it, Momism is only misplaced paternalism. American mothers stepped into the role of the grandfathers as the fathers abdicated their dominant place in the family, in the field of education and in cultural life.[99]

Erikson suggests that puritanism was the "decisive force in the creation of American motherhood and its modern caricature 'Mom.'"[100] The transition of a vital puritanism to its stultified facsimile has been noted:

> This much-maligned puritanism, we should remember, was once a system of values designed to check men and women of eruptive vitality, of strong appetites, as well as of strong individuality . . . a living culture has its own balance which makes it durable and bearable to the majority of its members. But changing history endangers the balance. During the short course of American history, rapid developments fused with puritanism in such a way that they contributed to the emotional tension of mother and child. Among these were the continued migration of the native population, unchecked immigration, urbanization, class stratification, and female emancipation. These are some of the influences which put

puritanism on the defensive—and a system is apt to become rigid when it becomes defensive. Puritanism, beyond defining sexual sin for full-blooded and strong-willed people, gradually extended itself to the total sphere of bodily living, compromising all sensuality—including marital relationships and spreading its frigidity over the tasks of pregnancy, childbirth, nursing, and training. The result was that men were born who failed to learn from their mothers to love the goodness of sensuality before they learned to hate its sinful uses. Instead of hating sin, they learned to mistrust life. Many became puritans without faith or zest.[101]

Momism is readily apparent trend among the Irish both in Ireland and in America. A puritanical sexual code is upheld by the mother in the Irish family; in fact sin in general is almost equated with sexual sin in particular. The Irish mother often functions as an autocrat in the home, even though she is concomitantly gentle and loving toward her children. The sociohistorical origins of this trend lay within the agrarian economy that stressed single inheritance. For a number of reasons mentioned previously, the end result was a pattern of few and late marriages. Sexual indiscretion, early marriage, and universal marriage were a direct threat to his system; thus puritanism reinforced by Catholic teaching prevailed.

Up to this point we have not analyzed the relationship of the priest to the Irish mother. The mother appears to be a representative of the church in the family. Erikson sagely observed that with the onset of a defensive, atrophying puritanism, "the church community becomes a frigid and punitive Mom."[102] No wonder then that the Irish priest was sometimes referred to as "she." The priest often acted just like one's mother with respect to the enforcement of a rigorous moral code. That the Irish mother strongly desired that at least one son become a priest is commonly known. The priest was the mother's male ideal.

The "boss" is the male counterpart to "Mom." According to Erikson machine bosses are

> self-made autocrats and, therefore, consider themselves and one another the crown of democracy. As far as is necessary, a "boss" stays within the law, and as far as is possible he enters boldly into

the vacuum left by the emancipated sons in their endeavor to restrict themselves in fairness to others. He looks for areas where the law has been deliberately uncharted (in order to leave room for checks, balances, and amendments) and tries to use it and abuse it for his own purposes. He is the one who—to speak in highway terms—passes and cuts in where others leave a little space for decency's and safety's sake.[103]

Because the machine boss did so much to help those in his own ethnic group, his criminal and quasi-criminal offenses appeared to be a function of his great zeal to help his own. And this is the dilemma. His self-interest was equated with the interests of his ethnic group. But in the overwhelming task of improving his own and his group's station in a highly competitive society, the boss turned his electorate into a machine, thereby rendering them irresponsible. Erikson has described certain of the social and psychological consequences of bosses and political machines:

"Bosses" and "machines," I have learned, are a danger to the American identity, and thus to the mental health of the nation. For they present to the emancipated generations, to the generations with tentative identities, the ideal of an autocracy of irresponsibility. In them is seen the apparently successful model, "he who measures himself solely by what 'works,' by what he can get away with and by what he can appear to be." They make "functioning" itself a value above all other values. In their positions of autocratic power in legislation, in industry, in the press, and in the entertainment would, they knowingly and unknowingly use superior machinery to put something over on the naïve sons of democracy. They thrive on the complication of "machinery"—a machinery kept deliberately complicated in order that it may remain dependent on the hard-bitten professional and expert of the "inside track." That these men run themselves like machinery is a matter for their doctor, psychiatrist, or undertaker. That they view the world and run the people as machinery becomes a danger to man.[104]

As previously cited, Woods, near the turn of the century, concluded that the Irish are the "most easily organized of any nationality" and concurrently the "most capable organizers" when it comes to politics.[105] Moreover, they taught other ethnic groups the intricacies of political organization. The Irish-American mother, with the tacit support of the priest, was at times a moral tyrant in the home, while the Irish boss dominated political and economic life with the saloon as his base of operation. Home, church, and saloon were the mainstays of the Irish community, its paramount local institutions; yet these same institutions were permeated with the autocracy of momism and bossism.

The probable psychological consequences of the complementary sociological trends of momism and bossism have been explored by Erikson:

> Where the resulting self-definition, for personal or for collective reasons, becomes too difficult, a *sense of role confusion* results: the young person counterpoints rather than synthesizes his sexual, ethnic, occupational, and typological alternatives and is often driven definitely and totally for one side or the other.[106]

Thus, in the Irish-American family, the mother held up to her children two ideal sexual roles: the chase Irish woman and the saintly Irish man (the priest). In contradistinction to this, adult males proffered to the adolescent male the hero of the political boss, reputed to be the epitome of a man of the world, a force to be reckoned with, and among other things, a hard drinker. Irish-American literature indicates also that some mothers caviled about their husband's or brother's drunkenness to their sons. So, hard drinking or drunkenness also became a negative identity, something to be avoided at all costs.

In a sense, then, many Irish adolescent males were placed in the position of having to choose between their mother and their male drinking companions. Crane's *George's Mother* is exceedingly insightful on this point. Of course, some mothers did not counterpoint the sexual alternatives of priestliness and worldliness as much as others, thus affording their sons a chance to synthesize the two roles. But those mothers (obviously a small minority) who had psychologically stifled their sons' ability to synthesize or even choose between the contrasting roles inadvertently confirmed their sons as drunkards through their continual harping about drink's pernicious consequences. Erikson has observed, in the clinical setting, that a negative identity can be the surest sense of identity when in fact positive identity choices cancel each other out. The negative identity is offered as "undesirable or dangerous and yet as most real."[107] Erikson alludes to a case of a would-be alcoholic to illustrate this point:

> A mother who was filled with unconscious ambivalence toward a brother who had disintegrated into alcoholism, again and again responded selectively only to those traits in her son which seemed to point to a repetition of her brother's fate, with the result that this "negative" identity sometimes seemed to have more reality for the son than all his natural attempts at being good. He worked hard at becoming a drunkard. . . .[108]

The upshot of this discussion is that some adolescent males could handle the positive identity of hard drinker provided by adult male companions and synthesize it together with their mother's valuation of priestliness; but others were doomed to choose the negative identity of drunkard, which on the surface met the requisites of the male group. It was their mothers' inability to distinguish between drinking and drunkenness and their inability to tolerate their sons' drinking in any form that contributed to their choice of the negative identity. Added to this was the stereotype of the Irish-American as drunkard, which confirmed on the cultural level what was in some instances being foisted on the Irish male on the psychological level.

7

"A Religion of Saloonkeepers": The Stereotype of the Irish-American as Drunkard

For people generally, moralism is surely the greatest force in the destruction of the person. It is a destruction of the person of others through judgment, classification, the refusal to consider individual determinations.

Jacques Ellul,
To Will and to Do

C oncerned about the image of Irish-Americans, several leaders of the Hibernian movement against liquor in the latter half of the nineteenth century sadly commented, "We are known as a religion of saloonkeepers, of men who drink and men who provide the means of drinking."[1] We need to examine, then, the stereotype of the Irish-American as drunkard against its historical and social backdrop—if not to separate fact from fiction, at least to understand when fiction became fact.

The antipathy toward the Irish in the form of discriminatory practices, cultural prejudice, and occasional outbursts of violence is perhaps unmatched in the history of American reaction to European immigrant groups. In one sense Irish and immigrant were synonymous because the Irish in the late 1840s were the first great wave of immigrants to reach American shores.[2] They became the personification of the "outsider," the "stranger," the "foreigner"—types that Americans had had an exaggerated fear of ever since the time of colonization.[3] Several social scientists have maintained that "no other immigrant was proscribed as the Catholic Irish were."[4] Another highly proscribed group, blacks, were said to be preferred to the Irish for many jobs. More often than not, however, these two groups were compared to one another in highly stereotyped terms as being inferior races. As early as the eighteenth century the Irish were being referred to as "white Negroes" in English literature.[5]

If the Irish were the most maligned ethnic group throughout much of the nineteenth century, their reputed drunkenness contributed mightily to their general denigration.[6] Numerous historians of Irish immigration have reported on their reputation for drink. For instance, Clark noted that "drunken" as modifier for Irish became a stereotype, and Potter suggested that "Americans marked down drunkenness as natural to the Irish as their brogue."[7] "For a time," commented Wittke, a "stage Irishman and a drunkard were practically synonymous."[8]

General Discriminatory Practices against the Irish

Perhaps because of unrealistic letters from relatives and friends who had already immigrated urging them to do the same and because they had been promised so much at the port of embarkment by unscrupulous shipowners, Irish emigrants arrived in American ports largely unwary and vulnerable to exploitation.[9] Boardinghouses near the wharves employed runners, sometimes of Irish descent, to entice the immigrant to become a lodger, promising him pleasant surroundings and reasonable rates. Overcharged for the room and for storage of personal belongings, the immigrant often had his property confiscated if he could not pay. With an instinct for overkill, some boardinghouse proprietors misinformed their clients about job opportunities and transportation routes to their destination points. An Irish visitor to America vividly described the plight of the newly arrived immigrant, who was often done in because

> ... the runners, and brokers, and ticket-sellers, and money-sellers, and money-changers, had everything their own way; and terrible were the consequences of their practical immunity. Swarming

about the wharves, which they literally infested, all—the emigrant passenger, his luggage, his money, his very future—was at their mercy. The stranger knew nothing of the value of exchange, nor how many dollars he should receive for his gold; but his new-found friend did, and gave him just as much as he could not venture to withhold from him. Then there were the tickets for the inland journey to be purchased, and the new-found friend with the green necktie and the genuine brogue could procure these for him on terms the most advantageous: indeed, it was fortunate for the emigrant that he fell into the hands of "an honest man at any rate"—"for, Lord bless us! There are so many rogues to be met with now-a-days."[10]

Even when the immigrant finally departed (if he ever left New York or Boston), he might discover that his ticket was worthless or only took him partway to his destination.

The Irish, like other immigrants, discovered that their tenement housing was quite similar to the conditions on board ship. Crowded together in basements with little ventilation and no running water, they faced the daily problem of raw sewage in the streets and alleys outside or in its overflow inside. Subject not only to the dangers of disease and vermin, the Irish also had to face high rents and arbitrary eviction.

Urban slums and tenement living were by-products of an industrializing society in great need of a cheap labor force. Ostensibly brought to America to meet the need, the Irish still found difficulty in obtaining employment, at least of the gainful type. Catholic Irish girls looking for domestic work scanned the help-wanted section of the newspaper only to find they had already been eliminated by the qualifier "Irish people need not apply."[11] One newspaper advertisement read:

WOMAN WANTED.—To do general housework. . . . English, Scotch, Welsh, German, or any country or color except Irish.12

Irish males fared worse in the employment market. Sporadic employment threatened many, and those who worked were refused anything but the unskilled jobs that other Americans disdained. Handlin observed that there was a "reluctance to employ Irishmen in any but the lowest capacities," such as longshoremen, hod carriers, quarriers, canal diggers, and railroad workers.[13] An important factor in his exclusion was the Irishman's reputation for hard drinking and fighting.

If only being hired for the most menial of work was not enough, the Irish were sometimes underpaid or not paid at all. This was especially true for those who labored on public works such as canals and railroads. One ploy on the part of contractors was to advertise for twice as many men as they needed in order to "beat down the wages" of those they finally hired.[14] During the winter, when laborers needed higher wages to survive and with the work force reduced because of the weather, contractors used the surplus labor pool to whittle down wages even further. A practice that created instant Irish paupers was the embezzlement of the laborer's wages and life savings by the major contractor. It was a crude form of embezzlement that merely involved absconding with the money. Furthermore, sub-contractors, many of whom were in financial straits themselves, usually worked the laborers unmercifully and sometimes embezzled their wages. Irish strikes to protest against embezzlement, wage cuts, or delays in wage payments were the cause of the riots and resultant property destruction for which the Irish became notorious.

The exploitation of the Irish laborer increased with the beginning of the great wave of Irish emigrants arriving in the 1840s to the extent that, in one writer's words, the contractors had "systematized the swindling."[15] One railroad even employed private police to keep the Irish in line. The overzealous police often provoked the laborers, it appeared, to drum up business and thus justify their presence.

It was difficult enough for the adult Irish to weather discrimination, but when their children were also the victims, it became unbearable. Irish Catholic schoolchildren were often mocked as "Paddies" by their peers. Public-school teachers sometimes ridiculed their Catholic religion, possibly helping to drive a wedge between the children and their parents.[16]

Discriminatory Practices Involving Drinking

The discrimination of the Irish had to face in securing housing, employment, and education for their children is important as the context within which actual drinking practices and the reputation for drinking were foisted on them. Under certain circumstances Irish laborers were literally forced to become hard drinkers, if not drunkards. Irish laborers, especially those working on canals and railroads, were often paid a portion of their wages in rotgut whiskey. Those working on the Dwight Canal in 1841 were paid 75 cents a day and three "jiggers."[17] The following describes both the policy and its rationale:

> The contractor supplied whiskey as a routine of the work. The jigger, a dram of less than a gill, was downed first at sunrise, when the work started, then at ten o'clock, another at noon, and the last on the job at supper time. Some contractors offered six whiskey breaks a day. The whiskey was not a solace given in good heart; the jiggers supposed that the Irishman's shovel flew into the work after a belt of whiskey and that without it he grew morose and idling.[18]

The dispensing of cheap whiskey on the job was related to the embezzlement of wages. Near payday whiskey was distributed generously to laborers, who were then incited to start a fight among themselves, usually over a fictitious issue. When the police arrived the men, fearing arrest, scattered. The contractor became "free" to claim their wages.[19]

The Irish laborer was also encouraged to drink heartily off the job as a means of maintaining a class of indentured servants. Grogshops owned by contractors encouraged hard drinking by providing the laborer with unlimited credit. Moreover, some of the men who ran up credit at the contractors' grogshop also did the same, it would appear, at a saloon, a boardinghouse grogshop, or at their local Irish grocer:

> Agents met incoming ships to hire emigrants for public works. Irish grocers, who also sold liquor, allowed their countrymen to

run up bills and bargained with contractors to supply laborers from these debtors. Saloons acted as labor recruiting offices.[20]

For all intents and purposes this was conspiracy—a conspiracy of mutual greed between the affluent native and the aspiring Irishman. These overtly exploitative uses of alcohol to control the Irish were related to the more covert means that Irish ward bosses used, such as purchasing votes with drinks and doling out free drinks to the boys.

Next to forced drinking, other discriminatory practices involving drinking seem pale by comparison. However, the custom called "Paddy making" was a further blow to the Irishman's already beleaguered sense of dignity:

> An effigy dressed in rags, its mouth smeared with molasses, sometimes wearing a string of potatoes around its neck or a codfish to mock the Friday fasting and with a whiskey bottle stuck out of one pocket, was set up in a public place on the eve of St. Patrick's Day and in the morning the outraged Irish charged it.[21]

Paddy making was so widespread and provocative (it sometimes incited the Irish to riot) that the mayor of New York prohibited it in 1812. However, it continued unabated through the middle of the nineteenth century.[22]

Police attitudes and actions toward Irish drinking must be seen as "an extension of existing civic corruption in our large cities."[23] A historian of early immigrant life in New York City, Robert Ernst, concluded that "immigrants were easy prey for policemen who, unwilling to risk their jobs by raiding gambling dens, brothels, and criminal hideouts, kept a sharp eye for slight misdemeanors committed by persons of no political influence."[24] The police were "no more prejudiced than other groups" toward the Irish, concluded Roger Lane in his study of the Boston police in the nineteenth century.[25] Hardly a consolation as illustrated by the following newspaper report:

> The *Pilot* acknowledged with shame the truth of the record cited by a nativist paper that seven-eighths of the arrests for drunkenness were foreigners, that is, Irish, but asserted that "if the native

constables and watchmen of this city looked as sharp after natives as they do foreigners," the story would be different. Constables shushed native boisterousness; they arrested the boisterous Irish. They helped home a native drunk; the Irish drunk landed behind the bars.[26]

The police also discriminated against the Irish for resisting arrest and for liquor-license violations. Statistics on crime indicated that the Irish were the most criminally inclined group, largely because of their drunkenness. But the public was scarcely aware of the differential treatment the Irish received from the police. It is no wonder that in the early twentieth century a slang expression for a police patrol wagon was "paddy wagon." The clients of police wagons were often Irish drunks, and by this time many of the drivers were also Irish policemen.[27]

Cultural Prejudice: The Irish-American as Drunkard

If socially exploitive and discriminatory practices toward the Irish with respect to their drinking was one means of collapsing the distance between them and their drinking, so too was cultural prejudice in the form of the stereotype of the Irish-American as drunkard.

Stereotypes are part and parcel of ethnic prejudice, cognitive[28] definitions rooted wholly in affective reactions, which thus render them irrational. Ultimately then:

> A stereotype is a seeming value judgment, acquired by belonging to a group, without any intellectual labor, and reproducing itself automatically with each specific stimulation. The stereotype arises from feelings one has for one's own group, or against the "out-group." Man attaches himself passionately to the values represented by his group and rejects the clichés of the outgroup. . . . "Stereotypes correspond to situations which the individual occupies in society, to his groups and his métier."[29]

These value judgments or fixed opinions take the form of "labels, slogans, ready-made judgments."[30] Gordon Allport observes that, "the stereotype acts both as a justificatory device for categorical acceptance or rejection of a group, and a screening or selective device to maintain simplicity in perception and thinking."[31]

I must take issue with Allport, however, when he claims that "a stereotype is not identical with a category; it is rather a fixed idea that accompanies the category."[32] There exists strong evidence that through much of the nineteenth century Irish and drunkard were next to interchangeable terms, that the one implied the other. Let us look at the evidence as it appeared in language, newspaper stories and cartoons, nonfiction, social science, songs, plays and novels.

Language, especially in the form of slang, colloquialisms, clichés, and commonplaces, contains strong conative and moral dimensions. Obviously language can express prejudice and can be used against certain groups. With respect to the Irish victims of language, H.L. Mencken wrote, "In the United States, in the days of the great Irish immigration, the designation of almost anything unpleasant was hung with the adjective Irish, and it was converted into a noun to signify quick temper."[33] For instance, *Irish evidence* was false evidence; *Irish promotion* was a reduction in pay; an *Irish theater* was a guardroom; and an *Irish wedding* was the emptying of a cesspool.[34]

Newspapers sometimes exaggerated the seriousness of Irish misdemeanors. Ironically, they often demonstrated inadvertently the triviality of the crime by burlesquing the Irish criminal in court in order to write a more humorous story. Take the case of an Irish drunk as recorded in one newspaper:

> Police Court—*Yesterday*—Justice Rogers.
> –The court, during the morning, had several spicy cases before it.
> Pat Rooney, c.d., 2m H.C. [common drunk, two months in the House of Correction]. "Gard bless me! From the likes o' this defend me hereafter!," and away he went.[35]

Newspapers either poked fun at or moralized about "Paddy funerals" and "Irish wakes." For instance, on several occasions in 1854 the Boston *Pilot* and Brownson's *Review* "castigated the Irish for their lack of cleanliness, and particularly for their disgraceful conduct" at wakes and funerals.[36] As late as 1860 a prominent journalist referred to the Irishman as a "jolly, reckless, good-natured, passionate, priest-ridden, whiskey-loving, thriftless Paddy."[37]

Perhaps the most vivid source of the stereotype of the Irish-American as drunkard was the newspaper sketch and cartoon. The Irishman was often caricatured as drunkard, thus providing viewers with a living, concrete referent for their image of the drunkard. Now the image had an Irish brogue, carried a shillelagh, and was named Pat or Mike. Bourget, a French traveler to America, in his enumeration of Irish traits, commented that "it is noteworthy that the caricaturists only show the drunkenness and disorder."[38]

Thomas Nast, Frederick Opper, and Joseph Keppler were among the most famous American caricaturists of Paddy.[39] After 1860 the Irish-American was sketched with exaggerated simian features.[40] In keeping with the racial and evolutionary theories of the day, the Irish were often compared to the blacks and were viewed as a race whose physical, intellectual, and emotional development had been arrested at a primitive stage. The Irishman was even regarded as a link between the gorilla and the black. In cartoons, this simian beast was often seen drinking and brawling. L.P. Curtis's excellent study, *Apes and Angels,* contains numerous examples of the caricature of the Irish by the English and of Irish-Americans by "fellow" Americans. The caricature prior to the 1890s tended to satirize the beastly consequences of the Irishman's drinking. During the 1890s, if not slightly earlier, the caricature turned less savage and more thoroughly humorous (see Figures 2 and 3). Increasingly, the simian caricature was transformed into that of a comical human or even that of the leprechaun.[41] And of course a leprechaun's drinking was only good fun and not to be taken seriously.

Here are the verbal descriptions of caricatures from the 1890s made by a contemporary onlooker:

> . . . policemen, themselves Celtic, preside at this carnival of tramps, Negroes, and Irishmen, drinking hard and hitting like the others, and shouting "Take that!" as they progress in their game of head-breaking. . . . Again, it is an Irishman coming home intoxicated,

Figure 2. "The Day We Celebrate": Saint Patrick's Day, 1867. Thomas Nast portrays the Irish as simians who attack the police and respectable citizens on Saint Patrick's Day. The motivation for this act is readily apparent: Observe the bottle off rum in the coat pocket of the Celt on the far right, also the word *rum* in the lower left-hand corner. (Source: *Harper's Weekly, 6* April 1867, p. 212.)

whose state the sketcher represents by multiplying the head of his wife seven times, as she looks at her husband and, out of her seven mouths, says: "If you saw yourself as I see you, you would be disgusted."—"And if you saw yourself as I see you," replies the drunkard, "you would also be astonished."[42]

Another source of the stereotype was travelers' impressions, histories, and autobiographies. Making a Teutonic-Celtic contrast, so typical of the Victorian period, one writer said, "Of them [the Germans] it may be said that they are the opposite of the Irish, being generally a self-reliant, sober, frugal, thrifty people."[43] An English traveler concluded, "Poor food and hard work have had terrible effects upon the American-born children of Irish parents,

Figure 3. "Suppression." By 1900 the Irishman's features were depicted as more human and less apelike. The vicious side of Irish drinking has been downplayed in favor of its more gentle and humorous side. "Pat" and "Mike" are simply engaged in their favorite recreation. (Source: *Puck*, vol. 48, 24 October 1900, p. 6.)

especially when the parents succumbed to the one gigantic temptation of the country—drink."[44] A German traveler and historian given to easy generalization was not unduly optimistic about the intermarriage of Germans and Irish:

> No matter how unfortunate may be the marriage of Germans in America, shines by comparison with the marriage of a German

and an Irishwoman. Language, in truth, is a barrier easily over-come—but, Irish and German habits. . . . Ten times out of eleven she is drunk when you come home, and if you deprive her of money and warn the grocer to give her no credit, she will simply pawn one piece of furniture, one garment after another to be able to buy whiskey.[45]

Among the social scientists, historian Henry Cabot Lodge was quite representative of the Brahmin position in his portrayal of the Irish:

. . . a very undesirable addition at that period [the colonial period]. Scarcely more than a third of the latter succeeded as farmers; and they were a hard-drinking, idle, quarrelsome, and disorderly class, always at odds with the government. . . .[46]

Economist Francis Walker made reference to the urban immi-grant, but especially the Irish, as a "wretched beer guzzler."[47] However, most of the social scientists, committed to objective schol-arship as they were, were less crude and more circumspect in the expression of their prejudice.

Popular songs, whether written by the American Irish or by others, were an important source of the stereotype. Irish songs proved universally popular from 1860 to 1900. After a thorough review of such songs, Wittke reported that "dozens of Irish songs represent the Irish as good-natured, roistering, and brawling indi-viduals who get drunk, meet their friend, and for love knock him down."[48] Many of the humorous songs had as their theme "the Celt's presumably irresistible love of whiskey," examples being "Sprig of Shillelagh," "Donnybrook Fair," "The History of Paddy Denny's Wife and His Pig," and "Tim Finnegan's Wake."[49] "Finnegan's Wake," as it is known today (the song has gained the status of a folk song), recounts the story of Tim Finnegan, a work-ingman who while drunk falls from a ladder and lands on his head. Thinking he is dead, his wife arranges for a wake. Amid much drinking and fighting, Finnegan's body is accidentally doused with whiskey, whereupon the "corpse" jumps up and reprimands his friends for spilling good whiskey.

The Irish did not fare much better in American writing. Thomas Beer, in his fascinating collection of essays on the Mauve Decade (1890–1900), said: "As to American writing on the Irish, it has always been bad and is bad today. It either flatters them for possessing the ordinary virtues of decent people or it turns them into comic supplements."[50] Not so was Harold Frederic's *The Damnation of Theron Ware* written in 1896. This now acclaimed minor classic was the only work of any consequence which showed Irish Catholicism triumph over American Protestantism. The difference between Irish-Americans and their stereotype was discerned in the novel. Frederic portrayed the Irish-American characters realistically. But the novel's protagonist, a young Methodist minister, prior to meeting Irish-Americans close-up, held the stereotype common to native-born Protestant Americans.

With the notable exception of Stephen Crane, Irish-American writers were unwilling to portray their own in realistic terms. But the Irish literature emerging in the second half of the nineteenth century was not so much the work of immigrants as it was that of native Americans, who "exploited the characteristics of Irish immigration for their literary purposes."[51] "Allusions to the proverbial Irish faults of violence, indolence, and intemperance are strewn through novels, pamphlet literature, works of history, and cartoons or prints," wrote Curtis, summarizing the English and to a large extent the American view of the Irish during the Victorian period.[52]

Along with newspaper and magazine cartoons, the stage play was perhaps the most important conveyor of the stereotype of the Irish-American as drunkard. The second half of the nineteenth century witnessed a prodigious growth in the popularity of the stage Irishman, a type that 'threatened to dwarf all other types, including the Negro and the Yankee."[53] The stage Irishman was one of England's cultural gifts to America. The Irish were satirized as "wild Irish" from the twelfth century onward in English writing.[54] The stage Irishman as part of the cultural tradition of the "wild Irish" is of such long-standing that several writers began their treatment of the type with a reference to Shakespeare, who at times used this type as a minor character in his plays.[55] By the eighteenth century, the stage Irishman was a major character.[56] Bourgeois provided an extensive definition of the type:

The stage Irishman habitually bears the generic name of Pat Paddy or Teague. He has an atrocious Irish brogue, makes perpetual jokes, blunders and bulls in speaking, and never fails to utter, by way of Hibernian seasoning, some wild screech or oath of Gaelic origin at every third word; he has an unsurpassable gift of "blarney" and cadges for tips and free drinks. His hair is of a fiery red; he is rosy-cheeked, massive and whiskey-loving. His face is one of simian bestiality, with an expression of diabolical archness written all over it. He wears a tall felt hat (billicock or wideawake) with a cutty clay pipe stuck in front, an open shirt-collar, a three-caped coat, knee-breeches, worsted stockings and cockaded brogue-shoes. In his right had he brandishes a stout blackthorn or a sprig of shillelagh, and threatens to belabour therewith the daring person who will "tread on the tails of his coat."[57]

Irish characters were seen on the American stage in the late eighteenth century, but it was with the arrival of the famous Irish actor Tyrone Power in the 1830s that Irish characters in Irish plays became well established.[58] One of his first appearances was in *O'Flannigan and the Fairies,* or *A Midsummer's Night Dream, Not Shakespeare's,* a fairy story set to music that had as a major theme the Irish love of whiskey.[59] The two playwrights most responsible for the vogue of the Irish drama were John Brougham and Dion Boucicault. Brougham, who like Boucicault was also an actor, often played the part of the stage Irishman himself.[60] Boucicault, on the other hand, was offended by certain aspects of the stage Irishman; so he discarded many of the negative traits in his plays in favor of highly romanticized accounts of Irish history and life.[61] He once remonstrated that "England lies when she brands Ireland as a nation of whiskey-drinking, fight-loving vagabonds."[62] Notwithstanding the success of Boucicault's plays, American audiences, counting among its numbers many Irish-Americans, still loved to see the boisterous, hard-drinking, stage Irishman.

The playwrights Harrigan and Hart did not restrict their repertoire to Irish characters or plays. But they did provide many successful vaudeville sketches and plays in which several nationalities were contrasted with the "honest, impulsive, irascible, and sometimes intemperate, but always generous, Irishmen."[63] Apparently no plays with major Irish characters achieved the popularity and at times critical success of those written by Edward Harrigan and Tony Hart, such as *Squatter Sovereingnty* and *The Mulligan Guard.*

Yet not everyone was laughing. At a performance of *The Fatal Wedding* in 1904, an Irishman from the audience rushed to the stage to protest as "an insult to Irish womanhood" a scene with a drunken Irish servant girl.[64] In 1875 the great Henry James, with a touch of sarcasm, wrote:

> Our drama seems fated, when it repairs to foreign parts for its types, to seek them first of all in the land of brogue and "bulls." A cynic might say that it is our privilege to see Irish types in the sacred glow of our domestic hearths and it is therefore rather cruel to condemn us to find them so inveterately in that consoling glamour of the footlights.[65]

And that staunch defender of his fellow immigrant, Thomas D'Arcy McGee, delivering a lecture on "The Social Duties of Irishmen in America," reminded his audience:

> The first difficulty which the Irish in America experienced as a whole was that there existed in the United States a false estimate of their character arising partly from the inheritance of a British literature and English ideas, partly from stage representation and partly from the eccentric conduct of some of the emigrants themselves.[66]

The Irish middle class and its representative, the Irish press, apparently resented the stereotype or at least its negative aspects much more than the workingman. And given that Irish-Americans were overwhelmingly working class, they were by and large enthusiastic supports of stage Irish productions. However, by 1890 the stock Irish play was beginning to decline in popularity.

Stephen Crane appeared to be ambivalent toward hard drinking and drunkenness, sometimes poking kindly fun at it, other times dramatizing its pernicious effects.[67] Noteworthy was his dramatic sketch, "At Clancy's Wake," which appeared in the humor magazine *Truth* in 1893.[68] It was seemingly a satire on the Irish wake and a parody of its representation on the stage. In the sketch, a newspaperman—in his attempt to obtain the needed information for an obituary on Clancy the deceased—is pressed into drinking numerous whiskeys by Clancy's widow; she cuts all the newspaperman's questions short in her determined effort to reminisce and be consoled. At the end the newspaperman is drunk and with great effort asks, "who the blazesh is dead here anyhow?"[69]

All in all the stage Irishman was of immense import in solidifying public opinion about the stereotype of the Irish-American as drunkard. As Wittke observed, "For a time, the stage Irishman and a drunkard were practically synonymous."[70]

Anglo-Saxon Ideology

Stereotypes of the Irish and cultural prejudice against them were bound intimately to an Anglo-Saxon ideology, an amalgam of racial and nationalistic myths and ideas, class and religious sentiments. The second half of the nineteenth century witnessed the confluence of numerous ideologies: Anglo-Saxonsim, Teutonism, social Darwinism, and Americanism. These ideologies contained as their driving force a virulent middle-class morality. The immigrant Irish stood indicted on every count: They were the wrong race, the wrong religion, the wrong class in the "right" country. Curtis provided an extensive definition of the propositions contained within the English variety of Anglo-Saxonism:

> 1. There was an identifiable and historically authenticated race or people known as the Anglo-Saxons who shared common ties of blood, language, geographical origin, and culture and who could be traced right back to the Jutes, Angles, and Saxons who had once inhabited the region between the Baltic and the Black Forest. 2. Civil and religious liberties enjoyed no fuller expression anywhere in the world than in predominantly Anglo-Saxon societies, and this tradition of freedom was directly attributable to the peculiar genius of Anglo-Saxon in political affairs. 3. The Anglo-Saxon peoples of the British Isles possessed a combination of virtues and

talents which made them superior in all important respects to any other comparable racial or cultural group in the world. 4. Such specifically Anglo-Saxon attributes as reason, restraint, self-control, love of freedom and hatred of anarchy, respect for law and distrust of enthusiasm were actually transmissible from one generation of Anglo-Saxons to the next in a kind of biologically determined entailed inheritance. 5. The most serious threats to the inherent superiority of the Anglo-Saxon peoples came not only from international rivalries for markets, and competition for industrial production, overseas empire, and command of the seas, but also from physiological and biological forces inside the nation or race. Among those threats were the likelihood, if not the actuality, of racial deterioration through the strains and pressures of a highly urbanized and industrialized society, or of "race suicide" through a deliberate limitation of family size, or of the adulteration and contamination of Anglo-Saxon blood by mixture with "foreign" blood, whether that of the Irish, Jews, Italians, French, and so on.[71]

Anglo-Saxonism in England and in America regarded the Anglo-Saxon as the "archetype of the most desirable branch of the Teutonic race."[72] The overlap between the Anglo-Saxonism in the two countries, especially between 1860 and 1900, proved, in the words of one student of prejudice, "nothing short of striking."[73] First of all, the British press and intelligentsia were highly critical of the great influx of foreigners to the United States. And Americans tended to see the Catholic Irish through the "eyes of English writings."[74] At a time when cultural origins were being romanticized, it is not surprising that New Englanders were asserting the superiority of their Anglo-Saxon heritage. The American version of Anglo-Saxonism that took root in early nineteenth century was fueled by two longer standings traditions: anti-Catholicism and antiradicalism. Situated as the English colonies had been between French and Spanish settlements (both Catholic), anti-Catholicism had been rife in America from the beginning. Political upheavals in Europe in the late eighteenth and early nineteenth centuries were transformed into an exaggerated fear of foreign radicals.[75]

Anti-Catholicism was the more salient prejudice. Convinced that Roman Catholicism meant to enslave the world and pointing out that Roman bureaucracy was in direct conflict with democratic ideals, Protestant America perceived Catholicism as the greatest threat to it's national autonomy.[76] Thus some historians were led to equate nativism with anti-Catholicism, and in the mid-nineteenth century Catholics in America were more often than not also Irish.

The racism expressed in Anglo-Saxon ideology derived from two major sources: literature and political thought on the one hand and science on the other hand.[77] Earlier Anglo-Saxonism had been more a cultural than a racial attitude. Edward Snyder's article "The Wild Irish" traces the cultural prejudice against the Irish in English literature from the twelfth century to the twentieth century. The rise of romanticism in the late eighteenth century was a catalyst in the identification of national destiny with such past cultural achievements as literature, are, and music; later this was extended to military exploits as well. Therefore Anglo-Saxon ideology was communicated in a nationalistic idiom. Early nineteenth-century Anglo-Saxonism thus stressed the glory of English national culture rather than the English race as a distinct biological unit.

In contrast to this was the rise of "scientific" racism fueled by advances in human biological and physical anthropological science. Classification of "primary" groupings of the human race in terms of physiological traits by naturalists began in the eighteenth and continued through the nineteenth century. The approach tended to reduce the cultural to the physical: Anglo-Saxon culture as a reflection of the Anglo-Saxon race. The contrasting justifications of Anglo-Saxonims were finally joined in the nineteenth century. Nationalistic ideologies so influenced scientists that "every national trait seemed wholly dependent on hereditary transmission."[78]

It was actually with the rise of Darwinian evolutionary theory and its bastardization, social Darwinism, that the merger of the two forms of Anglo-Saxonism was accomplished.[79] Social Darwinism turned evolutionary theory into the study of society. Social Darwinists, especially English philosopher and sociologist Herbert Spencer and to a lesser extent American sociologist William Graham Sumner, had more of an impact on American thought than did the Darwinists.[80]

Social Darwinism reifies society into an organism that develops just like any other biological organism. Furthermore, it assumes that ontogeny (the development of the individual) recapitulates phylogeny (the development of the race). One variant of this had the development of the individual mind parallel the evolutionary stages of human history. Ideas were contingent on social structures, which in turn were grounded in biological factors.[81] The principle of natural selection implied that the conflicts within nature assured that those organisms which survived were the strongest, the most fit, the best able to adjust. All existence was a struggle for survival. Social Darwinism, at least its Spencerian version, brought together the ideas of progress and development; human society and its members were seen to be moving toward a perfected state of equilibrium, industrial society.[82] The Spencerian version of social Darwinism became an apologetic for human competition in all spheres of life— for capitalism for private property, and for a neglect of the poor and the deviant, the unsuccessful. From the 1860s through the 1890s, "the bulk of American 'thought'. . . was but a recapitulation of Spencer."[83]

The reasons for this vogue of social Darwinism seem rather obvious today. Sociology, of which social Darwinism was once a major force, represents, in Raymond Aron's words, "the consciousness of industrial society." Perhaps Hofstadter's answer to the question of why the rugged individualistic form of social Darwinism predominated in America is sufficient:

> The answer is that American society saw its own image in the tooth-and-claw version of natural selection, and that its dominant groups were therefore able to dramatize this vision of competition as a thing good in itself. Ruthless business rivalry and unprincipled politics seemed to be justified by the survival philosophy. As long as the dream of personal conquest and individual assertion motivated the middle class, this philosophy seemed tenable, and its critics remained a minority.[84]

Anglo-Saxonism in both its racial and cultural versions explains why the Irish were so often caricatured, satirized, and polemicized against as inferior. The early Irish immigrants were the very dregs of society. Anglo-Saxonism, but especially social Darwinism, justified the exploitation and neglect of the Irish.

The Anglo-Saxon ideology became embedded in two social movements of unparalleled significance: the nativistic movement and the
temperance movement. The nativistic movement, essentially anti-
Catholic and anti-immigrant, was not convinced that the democratic
ideal of assimilation was viable.[85] The temperance movement, likewise anti-Catholic and anti-immigrant, perceived excessive drinking
to be the root cause of most social problems, especially poverty and
crime.[86] Both of these movements exuded Americanism. For the native
American, the Catholic Irish immigrant was his negative identity.

Celticism: The Irish Response

Celticism, the Irish response to Anglo-Saxonism, proved to be a
counterirritant rather than a salve to the disease of English-Irish
relations:

> Celticism was an ethnocentric form of nationalism with a strong
> measure of race consciousness which many Irishmen used to arm
> themselves against Anglo-Saxonist claims of cultural and racial
> superiority. Celticism refers to that body of assumptions, beliefs,
> and myths, which emphasized not only the uniqueness but the
> sophistication of early Irish culture, and in particular the virtue of
> ancient Irish political, legal, and social institutions.[87]

The surge of romanticism, coupled, as it was with the growth of
nationalistic sentiment, had its effect on Irish intellectuals and artists.
The "Young Ireland" movement of the mid-nineteenth century signaled a return to Celtic origins even more so than the "Celtic-English"
revival of the eighteenth century. Paramount in distinguishing the
Anglo-Saxon ethnocentrism from its Irish counterpart was the fact
that England's nationalistic goals were largely fulfilled while Ireland's
were not. Also, "John Bull" (the Irish stereotype of the Englishman)
was not as atrophied and detailed a character as was Paddy; this suggested that nationalistically speaking, Celticism worried less
about the enemy than about its own autonomous destiny whereas
Anglo-Saxonism was more defensive in its preoccupation with Irish

encroachment. But Celticism was also defensive about the Paddy stereotype. If the Irish were often caricatured as apes by the English, the Irish caricatured themselves as angels or as handsome humans.[88]

American Celticism was a different matter. Irish-American Celticism was more concerned with improving the living conditions and educational opportunities of its own than with mounting an ideological struggle. In fact the Irish press and Irish writers in America were blatantly Anglo-Saxon without the anti-Irish prejudice; that is, as a "force for Americanization," the Irish press reflected the middle-class ideal.[89] The Irish desired to be free from English rule; Irish-Americans wished to be accepted into and become part of Anglo-Saxon America. Middle-class, aspiring Irish-Americans admonished their own to emulate the Yankee virtues of "hard work, perseverance, frugality, and integrity."[90] The Boston *Pilot* argued, "let the Irish-Americans take pattern by the Yankees."[91]

Apparently contradictory to this argument is the Irish opposition to various social reforms and the virtues these movements spawned. But this needs to be carefully interpreted. At times the Irish accepted the reform but repudiated the movement when it proved to be anti-Catholic and anti-Irish. Thus some Irish-American temperance societies were formed; but they often opposed the Protestant native wing of termperance. At other times they opposed the reform itself because its means were considered ineffectual or immoral. As Handlin pointed out, Irish-Americans saw many humanitarian reforms to be "strengthening secular as against religious forces" and, as an adjunct of the state, to be debilitating of the family as an institution.[92] At other times, such as with the reform of deviants, the reform measure was perceived as not strong enough to deter the deviant from his immoral behavior.

Irish-American Celticism turned out to be a sickly version of its Irish twin. As late as the 1880s Irish-American fiction was "rather anemic."[93] Thomas Beer castigated Irish-Americans writers for not speaking of Irish life in realistic terms, claiming that they knew it would never be accepted as such.[94] Nonfiction fared even worse. Money-hungry publishers, playing to their Irish-American audience's predilections, "concentrated on 'the lives of deceased bishops' or 'the lives of St. Patrick and St. Brigid.'"[95] One student of immigrant groups concluded that no other ethnic group had constructed such an elaborate systems for the idealization of its homeland. [96] Irish-American nationalists equated their devotion to Ireland with their rabid patriotism to America.[97] As a consequence they "wanted to make Ireland over and to make it over largely in the image of America."[98]

The Stage/Professional Irishman: The Stereotype and Its Acceptance

Just as the general stereotype of the Irish-American underwent important modifications after 1900, so too did the specific stereotype of the Irish-American as drunkard. By 1890 many reformers and restrictionists, of whom sociologists and social workers were prominent, had begun to ameliorate their stereotypes of the "old" immigrants. They did this partly to do battle with the real enemy, the "new" immigrants, partly as a begrudging recognition of the achievements of the "old" immigrants.[99] The old immigrants counted among their numbers Germans, Irish, English, Scandinavians, and French Canadians; the new immigrants included those from southern and eastern Europe. Those desiring to restrict the numbers and kinds of immigrants (restrictionists) contrasted the old with the new immigrant as a model for distinguishing between those who were capable of being Americanized and those who were not.

The later stereotype of the Irishman was not as vicious as its pre-1890 version:

> ... out of the conflict between Yankees and Irishmen an image of intimate, painful proportions had been generated. The lowly peasant from the Emerald Isle was ignorant, shiftless, credulous, impulsive, mechanically inept, and boastful of the Old Country. The inclination toward drinking and related crimes, elsewhere emphasized with humor, induced gloomy depreciations in New England.[100]

By 1890 the Irish had a broad base of political power and had proved to be good workers. They were a group to be dealt with. Social workers and social scientists now stressed the Irishman's adaptability.

"Social workers and sociologists made light of the old problem of Irish drinking" and instead found him "an attractive weakling."[101] The well-known sociologist E.A. Ross wrote:

> . . . the Celtic offender is a feckless fellow, enemy of himself more than of anyone else. It is usually not cupidity nor brutality nor lust that lodges him in prison, but conviviality and weak control of impulses.[102]

In summary, the new stereotype of the Irishman, superficially more positive, was as follows:

> Stressing the attractive features of the older stereotype, observers manipulated still further Teutonist theory and historical fact to produce an appealing image. The good-natured, fun-loving, imaginative Irishman of stage and cartoon predominated.[103]

The image of the drunken Irishman, although often explicit (especially before 1890), was implicit even when the reference was only to the Irishman's *fondness* for drink. That is, the association of the Irish and drink contained the assumption that the Irishman's drinking led to drunkenness. After 1890 the stereotype of the Irish-American as drunkard gradually became more subtle and implied, though at time its still showed a humorous drunkenness.

It was not only professional social scientists who finally accepted the stage Irish version of the Irishman. In Thomas Beer's words, "The dummy figure had become deeply sacred with Americans."[104] However, the native American acceptance of the Irish-American was ambivalent at best. American alternately flattered and ridiculed them. Beer recalled that "the Nordics held them [Irish-Americans] at arm's length and treated them in a half-humorous, half-condescending way, as the middle class American treats the Catholic Irishman."[105] The Irishmen's political and economic success contradicted their social standing. Half-accepted, half-rejected, they were accepted largely on a stereotyped basis.

There appears to be evidence that many of the Irish embraced this stereotype and some even attempted to live it. Both prior to 1890 and thereafter there was a tendency for the Irish to feel inferior to native Americans and to be quite sensitive to their opinion. As the famous Irish-Canadian politician and writer, Thomas D'Arcy McGee, admonished his audience:

> If the Irish remembered the old maxim, "respect yourself and others will respect you," might rise to a happier life and a higher station in society. The Irish had been flung among people "*seemingly*" very superior, he explained, and they therefore assumed the air and action of inferiors. Nothing was more foolish, more ungenerous to themselves, more cruel to their offspring and more dangerous to the existence of real democracy "than this wanton and willing prostitution."[106]

The Irish possessed a "false submissiveness" toward native Americans which only earned them more contempt. [107] The Irish press was accused of unduly flattering their own, resulting in but illusionary improvement of their situation. Moreover, "Catholic Irishmen frequently prefaced and undertaking with the query, 'What will the Protestants think?'" [108] Thomas Beer, in his recollections of the Mauve Decade, claimed that Irish-Americans "felt superior to other ethnic groups" but possessed "an inferiority complex toward native Americans."[109]

Even the proud protestations of love for the old country implied an underlying feeling of inferiority. Wittke, a historian of several immigrants groups, concluded:

> Among all the immigrant groups in the United States, none has built up a folklore of fond remembrance for their native land comparable to that of the Irish, and their nostalgic memories have been bequeathed to their American-born descendants. Nothing like their St. Patrick's Day celebrations exists among other immigrant groups.[110]

The exaggerated, romanticized, and stereotyped adoration of one's origins belies an underlying uncertainty and anxiety about one's present situation. Ironically those very persons who were most upset over the stage Irish caricature were the most vocal supporters of Irish-American nationalism.

So, paradoxically, "In the 1880's, while chasing the comic Irish out of the theatre," they ended up "creating a new comic Irishman—the Professional Irishman."[111] The origin of the term *professional Irishman* is uncertain. It is possible that it "had been invented before the Civil War, apparently in the music halls of New York."[112] Earlier it seems to have been the equivalent of the traditional "stage Irishman"; later it meant the living embodiment of a somewhat more sophisticated stage Irishman. A professional Irishman makes a career out of a highly romanticized and stereotyped Irishness in part to please others, in part to distinguish himself from others. Two prominent Irish-American sociologists reflected on the professional Irishman in the twentieth century. Moynihan sadly argued: "The Irish are commonly thought to be a friendly, witty, generous people, physically courageous and fond of drink. There is a distinct tendency among many to try to live up to this image."[113] "I am most angry of all at the thought that many of us can only be Irish when we have had too much to drink," Greeley fulminated in agreement.[114]

In 1896 George Bernard Shaw made several caustic yet incisive observations about the stage Irishman-professional Irishman confluence:

> Of all the tricks which the Irish nation have played on the slow-witted Saxon, the most outrageous is the palming off on him of the imaginary Irishman of romance. The worst of it is that when a spurious type gets into literature it strikes the imagination of boys and girls. They form themselves by playing up to it; and thus the unsubstantial fancies of the novelists and music-hall song-writers of one generation are apt to become the unpleasant and mischievous realities of the next. But in the United States, the natives, not the evading Celts, had produced the spurious type. . . .[115]

Thus the Irish gave the English the stage Irishman, whereas native Americans inflicted it on the emigrant Irish. But if the native Americans foisted the stereotyped Irishman on the emigrant Irish, most Irish-Americans willingly accepted it.

But many intellectual Irish-Americans never accepted the popular stereotypes. And the "'lace-curtain Irish" also rejected it. Lace-curtain Irish, middle-class Irish desiring acceptance into Anglo-Saxon society, often played down their Irishness, comical or otherwise. But many middle-class Irish-Americans still desired an ethnic identity. Furthermore, by 1900 the majority of Irish-Americans were still numbered among the working class, which had never resented the comic Irishman.[116] Despite some opposition, then, the stereotypical Irishman was becoming a bond between the Irish and the native Americans.

This can best be illustrated by the acceptance by both Irish and native American of the stage Irish as portrayed in newspaper comic strip and satire in the 1890s and continuing into the twentieth century. The comic strip "Happy Hooligan," a romanticized and comical version of early lower-class immigrant life, was quite popular, as was "Maggie and Jiggs."[117] Paramount among these was the satire of the Irish-American Finley Peter Dunne. "Mr. Dooley," his fictional alter ego and protagonist in his newspaper sketches, achieved an unparalleled popularity. The sketches originally appeared in the *Chicago Evening Post* and were shortly thereafter carried in a host of newpapers across the country. Mr. Dooley, a bachelor bartender, engaged in one-sided discussions with the empty-headed "Hennessy." Many of Dunne's sketches speak to the humorous side of drinking. A policeman in the local community was satirized as one "who dhrinks the beat."[118] Here are a few scenes from a sketch entitled "Alcohol as Food":

> . . . Th' idee ought to take, Hennessy, f'r th' other doctor la-ad has discovered that liquor is food. "A man," says he, "can live f'r months on a little booze taken fr'm time to time," he says. . . . "No," said Mr. Dooley. "Whiskey wudden't be so much iv a luxury if 'twas more iv a necessity." . . . D'ye think ye-ersilf it sustains life?" asked Mr. Hennessey. "It has sustained mine f'r many years," said Mr. Dooley.[119]

In one sketch, "Mr. Dooley at the Bar," Dunne has Mr. Dooley admonishing Hennessy about the responsibility of the bachelor to drink with his married friends when their wives are away. In the story the married friend gets drunk and Mr. Dooley say, "I hook him on a frindly polisman an' sind him thrippen'—th' polisman—down th' sthreet."[120]

Dunne used Mr. Dooley to make comments on many national and international topics, albeit satirically through Irish caricatures. But even if Dunne perceived a deep human reality underneath the Irish burlesque, his readers—both Irish and native—fell in love with the humorous caricature. Unintentionally the stereotype of the Irish-American as drunkard, now the "happy drunk," was being proffered and accepted interchangeably by native and Irish-Americans; it had become a bond between them.

Culture and Identity: Positive and Negative

It is almost commonplace to note the complemetarity of the Anglo-Saxon and the Celtic stereotypes. The Celt was the negative identity of the Anglo-Saxon. On the psychological level, the Celt represented all the projected traits that English society and culture had repressed in the name of industrialization and middle-class morality. On the cultural level, the Celt was a scapegoat, the symbol of evil:

> . . . the striking antithesis between the Anglo-Saxonist's self-image and his image of the Irish Celt, in terms of both physical and mental characteristics, suggest that the holders of these two complementary images were trying to discharge their own anxieties about feelings of violence, indolence, emotional incontinence, and even femininity onto another people who seemed to bear these stigma only too well. Paddy, that feckless, childish, whimsical, and violent Irishman, who so amused and exasperated the later Victorians, served as a convenient scapegoat for the frustrations which arose out of a code of civilized and gentlemanly conduct that regulated the public lives of countless Englishmen.[121]

Although Paddy's humorous and more positive attributes were emphasized in America after 1890, the reverse was the case in England. The stereotyped Irishman had for centuries been largely a buffoon, but was regarded with some affection by the English; however, with the rise of Irish nationalism and the emergence of the

"Irish question," English prejudice stressed such negative features as violence, drunkenness, and crime.

Before 1890 the American stereotype, especially in New England, had accentuated the dire consequences of the Irishman's drinking—although the stage Irishman competed for attention at this time. After 1890 the stage Irishman, with his more positive traits, was accepted universally even by social scientists. Now the Irishman's drinking behavior was humorous and had consequences only for himself. Thus the stereotypical Irishman contained positive and negative images. Prior to 1850 the negative images were in preponderance; from 1850 to 1890 the negative and positive images competed for recognition; after 1890, the positive images were dominant.

With respect to drinking, we might call these contrasting sets of images the "habitual drunkard" (skid-row alcoholic) syndrome and the "happy drunk" syndrome. The habitual drunkard is a menace to everyone, including himself. His drinking frequently leads to crime, brawls, and loss of income and peace of mind to his family. Finally, he becomes brutalized by alcohol. The happy drunk, on the other hand, harms no one save himself (which is de-emphasized). He is affable and lovable when drunk, a comic figure speaking nonsense one moment, waxing eloquent the next (often about Ireland). He is great entertainment. At worst, he simply collapses at the end of the evening.

Now I am not arguing that the habitual drunkard syndrome was ever an ideal in Irish-American culture. Even in the social organization of Irish ghetto life, with its ethic of drinking, the habitual drunkard was not a positive model for emulation. The Irish press and clergy spoke unceasingly against drunkenness. But negative identities can be internalized when a group faces discrimination and concurrently desires acceptance from the dominant out-group. Erik Erikson, speaking to this point, maintains: "Therapeutic as well as reformist efforts verify the sad truth that, in any system based on suppression, exclusion, and exploitation, the suppressed, excluded, and exploited unconsciously accept the evil image they are made to represent by those who are dominant."[122] In addition there is Erikson's problematic query, "how negative is negative and how positive, positive";[123] that is, there was a relatively short distance from a positive identity as hard drinker in Irish-American culture to the negative identity as habitual drunkard in the American stereotype. Thus when a stereotype, a negative identity, is but an extension of an already existing positive identity, there is a likelihood it will be accepted.

In contradiction to this negative identity is the positive identity of the happy drunk. By the turn of the century both native and Irish-American could revel in the former source of the latter's degradation. Certainly many in the Irish-American community would continue to speak against the stereotype of the Irish-American as drunkard in whatever form and however positive it might become. Yet it was a seductive image. And the distance from the positive identity as hard drinker to that of the happy drunk as almost negligible, much less than the distance from hard drinker to habitual drunkard.

The stage Irishman was acceptable to native American and Irish-American because it enabled both groups to forget what had been done to the Irish: the prejudice, discrimination, exploitation, misery, and suffering. A farcical Irishman was readily acceptable to native Americans because he was not a threat or menace and was still beneath them. It was likewise amenable to the Irish because it was at the same time a source of their distinctiveness and their qualified acceptance into American society. It was as though native Americans could accept only ethnic groups who had been typed, pigeonholed, and thus pacified; and the ethnic groups who desired so much to be accepted were willing to take whatever was proffered.

Therefore the stage Irishman was a bond between them, a source of identity and acceptance for the Irish and a guarantee for the native America. But it was also the native's negative identity in that the Irishman could provide him vicariously with spectacle and the realization of his secret inclinations. So when some Irish-Americans internalized this amalgam of images and sentiments, living it out as professional Irishmen, they became stereotypers and stereotyped.

Stereotypes and Culture

Propoganda forms public opinion to integrate individuals more totally into a mass, to move them to take action against a common enemy, and to justify such action after the fact. Ultimately public opinion categories are stereotypes.[124] In the nineteenth and twentieth centuries, industrializing America often utilized propaganda in the form of sterotypes to both integrate the majority and agitate against minorities. Before 1890 American nativistic and temperance movements condemned the Irish for, among other things, their drinking. The Irish were held accountable for not living up to the Anglo-Saxon ideal and for violating middle-class norms (e.g., sobriety).

After 1890 native Americans released the Irish from some of these demands. As the Irish proved themselves to be hard workers and politically adroit, they could be partically assimilated into American society. Some of their previous failings became peccadilloes and were more humorously treated. Irish drinking was now culturally remitted by native Americans, who permitted and encouraged the Irish to play at being their own caricature. An immigrant group that more of less accepted its caricature was predictable and safe. To the extent that Irish-American culture blended with American stereotypes of the Irish, popular culture transmitted through the mass media had been accepted by native and immigrant alike. The stereotypical Irishman of cartoon, sketch, story, and song was part of a common culture shared by natives and Irish-Americans. Thus the open-ended hard drinking of Irish-Americans, while controlled as an integral aspect of group identity in Irish-American culture, was simultaneously a release from the dominant ethic in American culture. But either way the drinking was demanded in both cultures.

At one time American stereotypes of immigrant groups served to bind together the natives in defense of Americanism against the foreign invasion and to justify the exploitative treatment of immigrants. At another time the then ameliorated stereotypes served to keep the immigrants in their place while apparently offering them acceptance. But whether the immigrants were negatively or positively stereotyped, they were still condemned to a humiliating and degrading conception of themselves—which some managed to live up to.

8

Hair of the Dog: A Dialectical Theory of Irish-American Alcoholism

T he story of the Irish in America demonstrates only too well the dialectical interplay of cultures and cultural definitions. Irish culture, specifically in its remissive identification of manhood with hard drinking, unwittingly made the Irish extremely vulnerable to their stereotype as drunkard (alcoholic) in American culture. And like so many other ethnic groups who eventually achieve some degree of acceptance by the majority, the Irish came to celebrate the former source of their vilification when proffered by the majority in more acceptable terms.

Recapitulation

The reappearance of the avunculate in Ireland in the form of the bachelor group was due to the demands of single inheritance, a pattern of little and late marriage, higher socioeconomic aspirations, and a ferocious emphasis on the virtue of chastity. Irish puritanism was more the result of the necessity and desire to remain single on the part of young people and to have their sons and daughters single on the part of parents than it was the caprice of religious teaching. Even so, there did exist a strong moral foundation on the subject of sexual purity in Catholic doctrine.

Married men as leaders of the bachelor group socialized young men, many of whom were destined to remain permanently celibate, into the ways and lore of segregated male existence. A boy became a man upon initiation into the bachelor group, that is, when first offered a drink in the company of older men in the local public house. Farm and marriage might be a source of male identity for a few, but hard drinking was a more democratic means of achieving manhood.

175

Irish male identity was intimately bound to an ethic of hard drinking. The bachelor group became a means of controlling unmarried males by diverting their interest from the responsibilities of marriage, family, and farm ownership and redirecting it toward the freedom from responsibility found in sports, storytelling, and hard drinking.

If a man were a hard drinker, a drunkard he was not, at least not often. Drunkenness was not culturally sanctioned in a forthright manner. The church defined intemperance as mortal sin, and bachelor-group status went to the man who could hold his own (drink a great amount without showing its influence). But drunkenness was rather narrowly defined: One had to be in a stupor or at least out of control. Even so, there was sympathy for the drunk as expressed in the saying "drink is a good man's failing." The occasional drunk was a good man, but extreme in his goodness.

The Irish attitudes that the teetotaler posed a threat to sexual standards and that men drank to relieve sexual frustration were the ideological justification of hard drinking. It seemed necessary to permit the occasional failing of drunkenness rather than risk the possibility of sexual indiscretion. By contrast with the felony of sexual offense, drunkenness seemed but a misdemeanor. The hard drinker was a stalwart of Irish social structure and culture; his freedom from responsibility made him responsible in that his sacrifice permitted a stem-family farm economy free rein. Irish manhood culturally defined in respect to hard drinking remitted men from a rigorous puritanism and a still more rigorous social structure.

The alienation and anxiety that all immigrants suffered was experienced unduly by the Irish. They emigrated more often than not as unmarried individuals and tended to remain so. Impoverished before they arrived or shortly thereafter, they were forced to work at the most menial jobs. Shunted into tenements and shanties, they felt the full wrath of native discrimination and prejudice. "Irish need not apply" signs appeared in many places of business. Faced with chronic unemployment or sporadic employment at best, they were rendered structurally nonresponsible.

There stereotype of the Irish-American as drunkard became institutionalized in a plethora of ways: (1) employment practices—contractors and employers often paid the Irish part of their wages in rotgut and forced them to drink heavily in order to extort their wages or make them work harder; (2) job discrimination—the Irish were often denied work because their reputed drunkenness made them seem unreliable; (3) police discrimination—the Irish-American was arrested for drunkenness while the native was often left alone, and the Irishman's disorderly conduct was thought to be always the result of inebriety; (4) mass media—the stereotype was transmitted visually and verbally in the form of cartoons, newspaper sketches, and plays.

Synonymous with immigrant in the mid-nineteenth century, the Irish were regarded by nativists, know-nothings, and temperance reformers as the prototype of evil—lazy, dirty, rowdy, and drunken. The Irish drinker was stereotypically depicted as a habitual drunkard, a negative image conveying that the drunkard became brutalized by alcohol. This was congruent with the temperance ideology of the day, which maintained that drinking was the root cause of all other evils and always ended in personal degradation. Hence the immigrant Irish drinker was the personification of evil.

This negative stereotype of the Irish-American as drunkard was a cultural control in that the Irish were judged by the Anglo-Saxon ideal—industrious, clean, peaceful, and sober—and found wanting. It was a severe definition of their life-style and provided the grounds for their exclusion and exploitation.

"Momism" and "bossism" as autocratic social trends made the Irish vulnerable on the psychological level to the negative group identity of drunkard. In particular, those individuals whose mothers most forcefully counterpointed the negative identity of habitual drunkard and the positive identity of holiness were psychologically susceptible to the negative ego identity of habitual drunkard. In competition with the Irish-American mother was the male group and its positive identity of hard drinking. What was hard drinking to the male group was drunkenness to some Irish mothers. The stereotyped Irishman was not always cast in purely negative terms, however. The stage Irishman as portrayed in newspapers, on the stage, and in novels was a more comical figure. But this more positive stereotype was not to become ascendant until the last two decades of the nineteenth century.

Irish-Americans preserved the Irish family structure to some extent. Marriage was infrequent and late, and the virtue of chastity was still paramount. Irish street gangs were notorious in the larger cities. They served as training grounds for political life and were feeders for the ward political machines. The Irish proved most adept at politics, which in turn became a vehicle for organizing the Irish neighborhood. The Irish ward boss, often a former street-gang leader, looked after the economic and social needs of his constituents.

The drink trade was a way of achieving some financial success and was an entry into politics. The saloonkeeper often worked for a particular politician or at least acted as his agent. Those desiring work frequented the saloon associated with a boss who could dispense favors. The boss was reputed to be a hard drinker, although his heelers were usually delegated this role; the boss probably had been a hard drinker in his early life, but the exigencies of his role precluded it in the present. The heelers were given the means to treat the boys. The hard drinker was still the best man.

As the Irish rose to a position of political power and influence, they came to earn the grudging admiration of native Americans. The Irish had proved their industriousness, which, along with success, was the supreme virtue of middle-class morality. In contradistinction to the new immigrants of the late nineteenth century, the Irish and other older immigrants seemed preferable. Social scientists and journalists stressed the more favorable traits of the Irish. The pernicious effects of hard drinking were de-emphasized, and the happy-drunk image in which the insouciant drunk harms no one but himself (and even this harm was minimized) was perpetuated. The stage Irishman of earlier decades had been by now universally popularized. This more positive image was a cultural remission that released the drunkard from the full weight of reprobation. The Irish were no longer totally judged by the Anglo-Saxon ideal; compared to their success and demonstrated capacity for hard work, any vice seemed minor. Stage Irish had become part of the terms for assimilation into American society.

The conditions of American society dictated that any ethnic group that would move up the class ladder and achieve a modicum of respectability would have to use political power if economic advancement was heavily barred. Politics afforded the Irish this success and became sacred as a result. Whatever set the Irish apart from other ethnic groups was heartily endorsed. In this way drinking became a spiritual value in the new religion of Irish nationalism. But if one were Irish when drinking, it followed that one proved most Irish when he had the most to drink. The drinking was now open-ended. The church still caviled against drunkenness, but this meant little to the devotees of the saloon. To drink excessively symbolized one's Irishness, created a community among co-drinkers that the Irish had lost, and was a bond of acceptance into American society. The Irish hard drinker had become the happy drunk.

It is precisely here that Irish culture, American stereotype, and Irish-American culture most cogently intersect: The happy drunk was only a romanticism (as was much of Irish-American culture itself), a bastard born out of the unholy union of Irish culture and American stereotype, and made real in the person of the stage/professional Irishman.

The Mutual Acceptance of the Stereotype

Of great consequence for the period from the 1880s through the mid-twentieth century was the convergence of Irish-American culture and the American stereotype of the Irish: the hard drinker/happy drunk concatenation. The Irish immigrant, like others, desired to be accepted into American society. He was also quite proud of his cultural heritage. And here lies the rub.

By 1890 Americans were more sure of their own identity and of the industrialization and mobility that had earlier threatened it. Social Darwinism provided an apologetic for the conflict that abounded in society. By this time some immigrants had become moderately successful and had not proved as dangerous as anticipated. Therefore the Irish immigrants, through their political exploits, attested to the generosity of American society and of its ability to assimilate immigrants. They were among the older, "fit" immigrants, in contrast with the newer, "unfit" immigrants from eastern and southern Europe.

The Irishman's drinking was more often romanticized; he was the happy drunk who livened up a party but was quite harmless. Thus the natives were willing to accept older immigrants, not necessarily as equals but still not as enemies either. Now the immigrant could be condescendingly treated as a caricature; he had been released from the demands of the Anglo-Saxon ideal. Not being Anglo-Saxon he was inferior, but he was still superior to the new enemy—the southern and eastern European immigrants. Many of the whimsical and farcical traits gleaned from his country of origin were emphasized. The native had to be able to understand, to know what to expect from the immigrant, in order to keep him in his place. The easiest way to do this was to emphasize the romantic caricature that immigrants themselves had perpetuated and accepted.

The immigrants preferred stage Irish to the vile and brutal ways in which they were often depicted. The natives seized on this, and the immigrants who had always accepted to some degree the caricature warmly embraced it. Remember that the caricature of the Irish preceded the great influx of immigration in the 1840s. But since the immigrant could not preserve and live out his old culture anymore, and was not fully an American (an Anglo-Saxon), he was forced to choose between a romanticized version of his origins or the totally negative ways his detractors had portrayed him. It was not just that the caricature was the best choice; it was really the only choice.

Here then is the convergence. The romanticized caricature was welcomed by both the Irish and the natives by at least 1890. There were of course insightful people on both sides who vehemently opposed such nonsense, but still it persisted. Irish-American intellectuals and others among the Irish middle class who aspired to be middle-class Americans opposed it. For the American who had earlier branded the Irish as enemy, the epitome of evil, the positive caricature was a way of taming the wild Irish, of making them safe and secure for American society. For the Irish, the stage/professional Irishman was a way of belonging while simultaneously showing their distinctiveness. It was compensation in part for a reality in which their political and economic power was incongruent with their social standing.[1] It forced them to emphasize Irish culture because they were not totally accepted as American. But in their intense desire to be American, they said that "what was Irish was also American," and they remade Ireland's history in the image of America. In these things they demonstrated their acceptance of the caricature: If they were actually American, they could not have been so rabidly Irish; on the other hand, if they were Irish, they could never have remade Irish history and culture. The Irish, along with other immigrants, were marginal men who had been brought into the mainstream of American life through their entrapment within a caricature.

Perhaps my thesis can be illustrated by a brief analysis of Saint Patrick's Day. The Irish-American and general American celebration of the holiday leaves the Irish in Ireland cynical or, at best, indifferent. They regard the day as a holy day and see the American counterpart as sublimely ridiculous if not sacrilegious. To what do they object? Extravagant parades, shamrocks and leprechauns on napkins and party hats, everyone wearing something green, maudlin Irish-American songs on the radio, and green beer. In America, Saint Patrick's Day also became a celebration of drinking. Obviously the nexus between the Irish and drink is reaffirmed. But adumbrated by all the glitter and hubris is the fact that Saint Patrick's Day is in part an American drinking festival. Of course one can always point out that in some way Saint Patrick's Day is a national immigrant's day, a convenient way of celebrating one's ethnic origins. But this is not completely accurate. Each ethnic group has its own day (e.g., Polish Falcon Day). What Saint Patrick's Day signifies is the mutual acceptance of the Irish caricature, the stage/professional Irishman, by the Irish and other Americans. This day is symbolic of the bond of acceptance: "Everyone's got a little Irish in them"; "I'll drink to that." But while most Irish-Americans play out their stage/professional Irish drinking role only on Saint Patrick's Day, some mange to live out this caricature permanently as happy drunks.

Hair of the Dog That Bit You

Considerations of culture and group identity provide additional dimensions to the folk saying "hair of the dog that bit you," which refers to having one drink or more the morning after a drinking binge to cure one's hangover. In practice it involves the drinker in a vicious cycle of alcohol use.

On both psychological and cultural levels, it is possible to see how Irish-Americans came to involve themselves in the hair of the dog. Until 1890 the negative group identity of drunkard was foisted on Irish-Americans through a cultural stereotype that was extensively institutionalized in American society. The Irish in turn cured themselves of their stereotype as drunkard by accepting it, at least the positive image of happy drunk. By openly accepting the stereotype, they involved themselves on the cultural level in the process of alcoholism. They became both stereotyper and stereotyped. In the sense of a self-fulfilling prophecy, the more they drank and bragged about it the more the stereotype seemed appropriate.

For those tormented individuals who unconsciously held the negative identity of habitual drunkard and also tried to live it out because their sexual identity choices had been too counterpointed (or for whatever reason), the positive group identity of hard drinker/ happy drunk provided the tacit approval for just such an alcoholic adjustment.

On both cultural and psychological levels, the Irish had had a previous source of identity (hard drinking) utilized to enmesh them in the deviant career of drunkard: the happy drunk who could at any moment descent to the depths inhabited by his complement, the habitual drunkard.

Figure 4 summarizes my argument. Thus prior to 1890 the happy drunk image, which though secondary was extant in American culture, was even then helping to modify the Irish-American identity. And simultaneously Irish-American culture was working to ameliorate the American stereotype. By 1890 the transformation had been more obviously effected.

There are two faces to this dialectical movement: positive and negative group identity. More precisely, there are the relatively negative and the relatively positive dimensions of identity with respect to drinking. A particular identity trait such as drinking can be both negative and positive simultaneously. It is difficult to determine which dimension is predominant at any one moment.

(1) from positive (male) identity of hard drinker in Irish culture and Irish-American culture

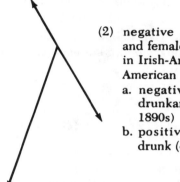

(2) negative (universal, i.e., male and female) identity of drunkard in Irish-American culture and in American stereotype:
   a. negative image of habitual drunkard (dominant prior to 1890s)
   b. positive image of happy drunk (dominant after 1890s)

(3) positive (universal) identity of drunkard in Irish-American culture and in American stereotype: hard drinker/happy drunk convergence

Figure 4. Moments in the dialectic of Irish-American identity from hard drinker to drunkard.

In Ireland the negative identity of drunkard was narrowly defined and quite subordinate to the positive identity of hard drinker. In contrast, before 1890, the negative group identity of drunkard was forced on Irish-Americans through cultural stereotyping and related discriminatory practices. Moreover, it was an extension of an already existing identity of hard drinker. However, certainly by 1890 and even earlier, the negative group identity became simultaneously de-emphasized and more narrowly restricted to that of habitual drunkard. Coeval with this was the gradual transformation of the positive group identity of hard drinker into that of happy drunk. Both the negative identity of habitual drunkard and the positive identity of happy drunk have their identical counterparts in the contrasting negative and positive images encased within the American stereotype of the Irish drunkard. Ultimately, in the convergence of Irish-American culture and American stereotype, the hard drinker became a happy drunk or at least a hard drinker without restrictions.

Thus the dialectic of Irish-American identity reflects the interplay of Irish culture, American stereotype, and Irish-American culture.

Ego Identity and Group Identity

It is important to distinguish between ego identity and group identity. According to Erikson ego identity concerns the "quality of existence" and, in its subjective expression, "the style of one's individuality"; however, "this style coincides with the sameness and continuity of one's *meaning for significant others* in the immediate community." Hence there is a "mutual complementation of group identity and ego identity, of ethos and ego."[2]

Along these lines, I wish to make a distinction between negative and positive group identities and negative and positive ego identities. My study has been centered on the institutional and cultural levels and has dealt with ethos and group identity; only occasionally have I discussed the implications of such for the individual. Hence it is not assumed that the existence of either a negative group identity of habitual drunkard or a positive group identity of happy drunk means that either of these identities dominated each Irishman's ego identity. On the contrary drinking is but one element of Irish group identity and ethos. On the individual level it has been hypothesized, for instance, that the Irish-American mother who counterpointed her son's ego identity choices when one of those choices involved that of drunkard made her son vulnerable to the negative ego identity of habitual drunkard. But there was only a small percentage of individuals for whom the negative ego identity of habitual drunkard or the positive ego identity of happy drunk was a central and dominating enough influence to bring about an alcoholic adjustment.

Generalizations about Cultural Stereotyping and Deviant Group Identity

It is possible to offer limited generalizations about stereotyping and identity from the situation of the Irish-Americans.

1. To the extent that the cultural stereotype is institutionalized, the negative identity will be accepted by the stereotyped group (organized discrimination.)

Discussion. A cultural stereotype can live on in tradition and in interpersonal relations without being fully institutionalized. Not only was the stereotype of the Irish-American as drunkard institutionalized in the mass media via stage play, cartoon, and newspaper sketch, but it also found expression in paying the Irish worker part of his wages in rotgut, in priming him for hard work with drink, in discrimination in work because of his reputation for drinking, and in police arrest patterns. When institutionalized, the stereotype has the force of the entire society—not an isolated individual or group—behind it.

2. To the extent that few alternative sources of positive identity are available, the negative identity will be accepted by the stereotyped group (structured nonresponsiblity).

Discussion. This is a corollary of the first generalization. Occupation has been a major source of identity for many over several centuries. Thus discrimination in obtaining employment and limited leisure-time pursuits (as with Irish-Americans) restricts the range of identity choices.

3. To the extent that a dependent personality type exists, the negative identity will be accepted by the stereotyped group (psychological dependence).

Discussion. Momism and bossism as social trends were evident in Irish-American society. Whether the son has identity choices counterpointed and is dominated by Mom, as in momism, or the individual is kept politically subservient, as in bossism, great dependency needs are engendered. Such dependent types are overly sensitive to the opinion of others and are outmatched when confronted by highly institutionalized stereotypes.

4. To the extent that a negative identity is but an extension or redefinition of an already existing positive identity, it will be accepted by the stereotyped group (dialectic from positive to negative identity).

Discussion. Most stereotypes have some basis in fact, but are premature and highly exaggerated generalizations. The Irish situation exposed a potentially explosive dialectic. While some stereotypes refer to behavior that is not central to group identity, others (e.g., the stereotype of the Irishman as drunkard) refer to behavior of absolute import (hard drinking as male identity) to the group. That the Irish accepted a negative group identity of drunkard does not imply that all or even a majority of individuals would live out this role. On the contrary, relatively few did so.

5. To the extent that the dominate majority comes to accept the stereotyped group, that is, stress the positive (often humorous) image of the stereotype or negative identity, the stereotyped group will perpetuate the negative identity as positive identity (dialectic from negative to positive identity).

Discussion. Stereotypes have both positive and negative images, which reflect the ambivalence of the stereotyping group. This ambivalence is sometimes born out of a secret envy of traits the stereotyped group is thought to possess. Early on, with the Irish as the prototype of evil, the negative image (the habitual drunkard syndrome) was emphasized. But as native Americans reluctantly came to accept the Irish, the positive image (the happy drunk syndrome) became predominant. This more or less positive identity of drunkard was a bond between the Irish minority and the native majority. Proffering this identity of the happy drunk, on the one hand, and accepting it on the other hand, implied reciprocal accommodations. It was as if the Irish said to the majority, "for your acceptance I will be what you say I am" or "since I can only be what you say I am and still have a modicum of respect I accept" (I am purposively rationalizing a largely unconscious process).

Excursus 1: Alcoholism among Irish-American Women

Some of the statistical data used as indicators of alcoholism showed that Irish-American men usually (especially in respect to rate of death from alcoholism and rate of admission for alcoholic psychosis) exceeded Irish-American women in the prevalence of alcoholism. However, Irish women outdistanced women from other ethnic groups more than Irish men outdistanced men from other ethnic groups.[3] How could this be when drinking in Ireland seemed so much a male domain?

First of all, women in Ireland did drink. Although they were excluded from rural pubs, they were allowed and even expected to imbibe on such special communal occasions as weddings. Little drinking occurred in the home. All in all, beginning in the mid-nineteenth century drinking really was part of the male role. One might even speculate that the female Irish drinker (steady or frequent) was in many respects in a similar position to the Mormon who drinks. Since Mormonism strictly prohibits *all* drinking, no guidelines are provided for those who do drink. For Mormons as for all teetotalers, he who drinks is on the road to degradation. Thus there is nothing to prevent the Mormon moderate drinker from becoming an alcoholic; he is nearly one in the eyes of his fellow Mormons.[4] Similarly, the woman in Ireland who drank on other than special occasions was infringing upon the male role and was thus a deviant. Extreme degradation was her lot. Why would she be drinking so unless she were a fallen woman or an alcoholic?

Be that as it may, the role of the Irish woman underwent subtle but profound modification in America. A reluctance to marry and an emphasis on chastity remained intact. For those who did marry, the exigencies of survival meant that many had to work. There had existed a strong taboo against married women working in Ireland. Also, because so many married women were left behind in the city while their husbands went to work on the canals, railroads, and highways, they were required to play both the father and husband roles—to fend for the family, pay the rent, and so forth. In those cases where the mother had previously experienced strong doubts about her sexual identity, it is quite possible that some, given the role into which they had been thrust, found resolution in the male role of hard drinker.

But other factors were even more important. Irish-American wages exceeded Irish wages, while concomitantly the price of liquor was much lower in America. This proved a bonanza to many drinkers. Grogshops invaded Irish tenements, basements, and shanties. Indeed, drink was available in the home and was sold to men and women alike. There are numerous references in both literature and journalistic accounts of Irish women drinking extensively at home and even at times in pubs.[5] Early on, the distinction between home and public house had been blurred amid the glut of grogshops. American life had broken down somewhat the extensive segregation of the sexes that existed in Ireland. But even in Ireland the intensive segregation of the sexes (it did not exist in that form before the Great Famine) was a by-product of the stem family and the necessity to postpone marriage to realize economic ambition. The immigrant without the luxury of community or extended family had to rely more and more on the nuclear family. Male grouping and segregation of the sexes still existed, but segregation had been somewhat mitigated in immigration. Dependence on the nuclear family meant that husband and wife were more dependent on each other, with the result that family-centered drinking was allowable not just on special occasions as in Ireland, but on a day-to-day basis.

But of paramount consequence was the linking of hard drinking with *Irish* identity and not merely male identity. Hard drinking was part and parcel of ethnic status. In the common fate Irish men and women faced as a result of discrimination and prejudice as outsiders, male-female differences were not quite as important as what they shared as Irish. Their collective identity as Irish was a sacred bond between them. Drink as a spiritual value symbolizing national identity extended to women as well as men. The positive group identity of hard drinker/happy drunk was an ethnic seduction even for women. Remember, too, that Irish women were occasionally portrayed as drunkards, especially in plays (e.g., the tippling Irish maid). Nevertheless, because of enduring sentiments, a women's public inebriety was more a disgrace than a man's. Hence the negative identity of habitual drunkard was a greater possibility for women because their public inebriety would not be so generously tolerated. Although an unconscious group identify of hard drinker/happy drunk might be internalized by some women, it could be readily transformed into that of habitual drunkard by the less than full acceptance of women's drinking in Irish-American society. Irish-American women, more so than their counterparts in other ethnic groups, ran the risk of alcoholism.

Excursus 2: Irish versus Irish-American Drinking

Some statistics indicate a relatively low rate of alcoholism for Ireland in contrast to the relatively high rate among Irish-Americans.[6] A conclusion of this kind is possible because America has a higher rate of alcoholism than Ireland and Irish-Americans possess an extremely high rate in comparison with other Americans. But some statistics (namely, the rate of hospital admissions for alcoholic psychoses) indicate a much higher rate of alcoholism in Ireland than do other statistics (e.g., rate of death from liver cirrhosis and rate of arrest for drunkenness). All in all, it seems fair to conclude that alcoholism among Irish-Americans has been more of a problem from the 1870s through the 1950s than it has among the Irish in Ireland during the same period. Assuming this is correct, how can it be accounted for?

Poverty and the price of liquor cannot be underestimated as explanations.[7] Low wages and the high price of liquor in Ireland made hard drinking a less frequent occurrence than in America, where higher wages and a lower price of liquor meant that the opportunity for hard drinking was omnipresent. Nevertheless, men who wish to drink have always found a way, as witnessed by ether drinking in northern Ireland in the nineteenth century and the illicit distillation of poteen in rural Ireland.[8]

More important was the difference in the cultural contexts of hard drinking between Ireland and Irish America. In Ireland hard drinking was a cultural remission, a release from sexual puritanism and the great sacrifice in restraint that a stem family farm economy entailed. Hard drinking was a cultural demand, and status accrued to those who could hold their own and thus keep hard drinking from the label of church-condemned drunkenness. Hard drinking as an integral part of male identity was moral in that it acted to preserve a stem-family farm economy.

In America, on the other hard, hard drinking had been removed from its original context and ceased to be a cultural remission. Now it was a direct control in Irish-American culture. As a sacrament in the religion of Irish-American nationalism, it differentiated the Irish from other ethnic groups. It became a spiritual value symbolizing Irish group identity. It implied that the more one drank the more Irish one became. Drink in Ireland did not fundamentally symbolize one's Irishness or one's Catholicism and thus was not ultimately religious. In America the religion of nationalism superseded that of Catholicism, though they were still united in the minds of the Irish. Therefore the saloon as the point at which ward politics and the lure of the street was most intertwined was more a church than it had been in Ireland. Hard drinking ceased to be modified by the stigma of drunkenness, as it had in Ireland. In Ireland the drunk was ambivalently regarded as the good man with a failing—but he was still a sinner. In America in the give-and-take of ward politics and in saloon and street life, the drunk was no longer a sinner/saint; he had been transformed into a complete saint—the professional Irish inebriate.

In Ireland there was greater insulation from the English stereotype of the Irishman as drunkard because Catholic Ireland had little desire to be assimilated by the English. But in America, the great desire of the Irish to be accepted by native Americans, coupled with the impossibility of remaining authentically Irish, meant that they were doomed to become a caricature—the only terms on which native Americans would accept them.

Afterword: Irish-American Drinking Today

Studies after 1950 (see chapter 1) indicate that Irish-Americans continue to be a relatively heavy-drinking ethnic group, although they are apparently not nearly as outstanding in this respect as they were in the past. Think of it: from the early nineteenth century to the present, this American ethnic group has kept alive its traditional pattern of heavy drinking. Is this a genetically transmitted propensity? Or is it an invariant cultural trait untouched by history or social structure?

As a social scientist who thinks culture to be of the utmost importance in understanding human action, I might be expected to opt for the latter explanation. But even if we assume that culture will provide the clues in understanding Irish-American drinking, are we so sure that this tendency toward heavy drinking has the same meaning today that it did in the nineteenth century? My analysis of the early part of the century emphasized the role that heavy drinking played in relation to ethnic consciousness and ethnic identity. I am not so confident, however, that the resurgence of ethnic consciousness on the part of third and fourth generation "ethnics" has the same significance with regard to Irish drinking. Furthermore, I question if in the decades prior to the ethnic revival of the late 1960s and 1970s (a time of waning ethnic consciousness) heavy drinking had the same traditional meaning of ethnic identity or if it had other meanings. I will argue that the pattern of heavy drinking has taken on different but related meanings since the early twentieth century, and that these different meanings need to be appreciated if one is to understand Irish-American drinking today.

The Secularization/Sacralization of Irish-American Drinking

For several decades prior to the rise of the "new ethnicity" in the late 1960s, there was a lack of interest in ethnicity among social scientists and a prevailing sense that the American "melting pot" had largely assimilated immigrants, at least white immigrants. Nathan Glazer and Daniel Patrick Moynihan's *Beyond the Melting Pot* attempted to show how illusory this complacency about ethnicity was, for they skillfully argued that the immigrants and many of their offspring in the urban centers were still living a ghetto existence.[1] But not to be assimilated is not necessarily not to be acculturated. By this I mean that one can simultaneously be discriminated against in the social structure (unassimilated) and be more or less culturally integrated (acculturated).

Earlier I suggested that Irish-American culture was more American than Irish. This is not to suggest that for the first and second generation Irish-American ghetto dweller, Irish identity was weakening. But for the third and fourth generation Irish-American who was somewhat more assimilated, Irish identity was less decisive, and perhaps for some had even become almost an afterthought.

I maintain that for the third and fourth generation Irish-American and those not confined to a ghetto environment, certain changes in American culture were becoming as much a motivation for heavy drinking as Irish-American identity. For those most removed physically and socially form the time of immigration, cultural changes were perhaps the paramount motivation. This would be difficult to perceive, for the pattern of heavy drinking behaviorally remained the same, but its meaning was being altered. What is to follow is an interpretation of this process, but one based upon well-documented changes in American culture.

As qualities, what is sacred and what is secular vary from culture to culture, and they vary historically. Thus they are dynamic, not static, qualities. Often, secularization refers to that which once was considered sacred but now has become or is being secularized; likewise, sacralization refers to that which as one time was deemed secular but now is in the process of being made sacred. Depending on the period of time, something is more or less sacred, more or less secular.

If drinking were sacralized in relation to Irish-American identity in the nineteenth century, it was becoming secularized in the twentieth century as ethnicity became less important to Irish-Americans.

By itself, however, the above statement is incomplete. For what often happens in the historical process of secularization is the simultaneous process of sacralization: a phenomenon or a relation is secularized in one context concurrent with its being sacralized in a new context. This new context was that of consumption: defining life's meaning in terms of goods and services to be consumed and turning even what is spiritual into something to be consumed. The more Irish-Americans became economically successful, the more they could "afford" to be drawn into this context.

To elaborate on this point, one could look to one of the more profound changes in twentieth century America, a transition from a work ethic to a fun ethic. Martha Wolfenstein documented this transition with respect to child-rearing practices,[2] and David Riesman put the change into its larger cultural setting.[3] This is not to suggest that work ceased to be important to people or that the work ethic disappeared altogether. But increasingly, work came to be less and end in itself, a self-contained ethic, and more a means of self-fulfillment. The movement has been away from production as an end in itself and towards consumption. In Riesman's felicitous phrase, "popular culture is in essence a tutor in consumption."[4]

Indeed, the ethic of fun, so fundamental to the "religion" of consumption, threatens even to eclipse the work ethic. In the 1970s one public opinion poll indicated that a majority of young people in the United States, England, and Germany when given the choice would rather not work than work. Studs Terkle's *Working* indicates that spiritual vacuum most people experience in their work today. Consequently, we turn to leisure, sports, recreation, vacations, etc., to find fulfillment.[5]

As Jacques Ellul has indicated, technology and the consumer goods and services it provides are sacred today.[6] Technology is what guarantees our future, solves our problems, and offers us the good life. Consumer goods and services, as manifestations of technology, provide a "sense of the sacred" in a plethora of ways: for one it is a sports car; for another a stereo; for still another a painting. And for certain Irish-Americans, it was alcohol.

Given a cultural predisposition to view alcohol as symbolic of Irish-American identity, it is very likely that in the age of consumerism some Irish-Americans would choose alcohol to experience the good life. Thus heavy drinking as a symbol of Irish-American identity and heavy drinking as a form of consumerism would be synthesized. This subtle change would be imperceptible, however, because the over behavior pattern of heavy drinking would have remained the same. In sum, I am hypothesizing that the closer we get to the 1960s, the larger the role consumerism as a spiritual value would play in the motivation of Irish-American drinking.

There is a factor in addition to the cultural advocacy of consumerism which might have hastened the sacralization of Irish-American drinking in relation to consumerism: the stereotype of the Irish-American as drunkard. Heavy drinking was a symbol of Irish-American identity albeit not the only one. In chapter 7 I attempted to show how drinking was for a time the chief attribute according to which the Irish were characterized. What this did, of course, was to cause many to equate Irishman with drunkard. The American historian Carl Wittke remarked that for a time in the second half of the nineteenth century "stage Irishman and drunkard were practically synonymous."[7] One effect among Irish-Americans who accepted the stereotype was to make drinking even more important that it had been before. Now it was equivalent to Irish. It would not take much in this situation for the drinking to become even more important than one's Irish-American status, to become an end in itself. Thus, at first one drank heavily because one was Irish, while now one was Irish because one drank heavily. Perhaps this subtle shift in emphasis from Irishness to drinking can be gleaned from the recent confession of a third generation Irish-American to me, "Drinking and the people I drink with are sacred to me." Yet he drank more with non-Irish than with Irish friends, and the drinking was mentioned first. Truly it was the drinking that had become sacred to him.

From the Old to the New Ethnicity

What are the implications of the new ethnicity for Irish-American drinking? Help in answering this question has been provided by

Martin Marty in his *A Nation of Behavers*. In it he has a chapter on ethnic religion, in which, to avoid using pejorative terms, he distinguishes between ethnicity A and ethnicity B. Ethnicity A refers to the cultural situation of a community of immigrants or of an ethnic neighborhood still largely dominated by immigrants, in which identification with and consciousness of one's ethnic heritage is "inescapable, automatic, and reflexive." That is, because of discrimination and prejudice, a group is isolated, forced in upon itself, and in compensation, sacralizes its group identity. Ethnicity B, on the other hand, is "escapable, intentional, and reflective." It involves a conscious decision by third and fourth generation ethnics to reassert their common origin and heritage.[8] Certainly ethnicity A aptly describes the plight of Irish immigrants in the nineteenth century. And, as well, ethnicity B fits the situation of those of the third and fourth generation who are intensely self-conscious of their ethnic identity.

The final word is not in on the percentage of Irish-Americans who have become new ethnics. But let us assume for the moment that at least a sizable minority of later generation Irish-Americans has become intensely ethnic. Should this cause a resurgence of heavy drinking as symbolic of Irish-American identity? It is necessary before answering this question to explore the larger meaning of ethnicity B (the new ethnicity).

The new ethnicity appears to be a form of religion that was anticipated almost forty years ago by the great historian of religion Ernst Troeltsch[9] and articulated by Will Herberg, among others. As Herberg remarks:

> It is "peace of mind" that most Americans expect of religion. "Peace of mind" is today easily the most popular gospel that goes under the name of religion; in one way or another it invades and permeates all other forms of contemporary religiosity. It works in well with the drift toward other-direction characteristic of large sections of American society, since both see in adjustment the supreme good in life. What is desired, and what is promised, is the conquest of insecurity and anxiety, and the overcoming of inner conflict, the shedding of guilt and fear, the translation of the self

to the painless paradise of "normality" and "adjustment!" Religion, in short, is a spiritual anodyne designed to allay the pains and vexations of existence.[10]

For third and fourth generation Irish-Americans outside the confines of a closed ethnic community, the new ethnicity can readily become a religiosity of self-assurance. All of a sudden one's heritage, one's roots, one's ethnic identity, takes on inordinate importance in an effort to shore up one's sagging self-esteem. Especially suspect are the recent converts who are devout Irish-Americans, but know almost nothing about Irish history and their own heritage.[11] They have become consumers of their ethnic heritage. Thomas Luckmann noted this merger of consumerism and private religion:

> The individual, originally socialized into one of the "versions" (church denominations) may continue to be "loyal" to it to a certain extent, in later life. Yet, with the pervasiveness of the consumer orientation and the sense of autonomy, the individual is more likely to confront the culture and sacred cosmos as a "buyer." Once religion is defined as a "private affair" the individual may choose from the assortment of the "ultimate meanings" as he sees fit—guided only by the preferences that are determined by his social biography.[12]

Consumerism and private religions, then, like the new ethnicity, are mutually reinforcing. To select one's own religion is a form of consumerism, and consumerism is a form of private religion. To consume one's ethnic identity and ethnic heritage is but a "denomination" within the larger religion of consumption.

Insofar as the stereotype of the Irish-American as drunkard has not dissipated, the new ethnicity presents an obvious danger to Irish-Americans: once again heavy drinking is identified with being Irish and is sacred. The snare is that the new ethnicity for Irish-Americans might further intensify the tendency toward heavy drinking that consumerism itself has sustained in this century.

Conclusion

In summary, I suggest that heavy drinking among Irish-Americans has had three meanings:

(1) originally heavy drinking was symbolic of Irish-American identity in the nineteenth century;

(2) heavy drinking next was secularized/sacralized as a form of consumerism for Irish-Americans, and finally

(3) heavy drinking becomes a means of consuming one's ethnic identity and heritage.

Therefore, while the pattern of heavy drinking has remained constant, its meaning has significantly changed. To understand this process, it is necessary to understand the transformation of Irish ethnicity as part of an overall national change from a country of immigrants, with their variegated communities and neighborhoods, to a mass society of consumers whose outward expressions of what they consume constitute a large part of their ethnic distinctiveness.

NOTES

Chapter 1: Introduction

1. Andrew M. Greeley, *That Most Distressful Nation* (Chicago: Quadrangle Books, 1972), p. 143.

2. The two most comprehensive and most often cited studies are Robert F. Bales, "The 'Fixation Factor' in Alcohol Addiction: An Hypothesis Derived from a Comparative Study of Irish and Jewish Social Norms" (unpublished Ph.D. dissertation, Harvard University, 1944); and Donald Davison Glad, "Attitudes and Experience of American-Jewish and American-Irish Male Youth as Related to Differences in Adult Rates of Inebriety," *Quarterly Journal of Studies on Alcohol* 8 (December 1947): 406–72.

3. Robin Room, "Cultural Contingencies of Alcoholism: Variations Between and Within Nineteenth-Century Urban Ethnic Groups in Alcohol-Related Death Rates," *Journal of Health and Social Behavior* 9 (June 1968): 110.

4. Ibid., pp. 110–11.

5. Mark Keller, "The Definition of Alcoholism and the Estimation of Its Prevalence," in *Society, Culture and Drinking Patterns*, ed. David J. Pittman and Charles R. Snyder (New York: Wiley, 1962), p. 316.

6. I am well aware of Thomas Szasz's longtime admonition that addiction is a theory, not a fact; but this seems a rather petty observation in the face of the real suffering of those who do not appear able to break the vicious cycle of perpetual alcohol use.

7. How broadly one defines alcoholism is related to what one hopes to accomplish by the definition. A broad definition, when applied in practice, would create a large clientele for alcohol control programs; a narrow definition, on the other hand, would save everyone from the formal stigma of alcoholic except those who were manifestly suffering in a psychological and/or physiological sense. Given the nature of modern technological societies and the proliferation of therapeutic programs that, though purportedly aimed at treating the

198

individual, actually function as systems of total control and manipulation under the aegis of the state, it might be better to restrict the definition. Still, I do not mean to play down the dilemma.

8. Bales, "Fixation Factor," p. 8.

9. Ibid., pp. 4–6.

10. Robert Ernst, *Immigrant Life in New York City, 1825–1863* (New York: King's Crown, 1949), p. 204.

11. Oscar Handlin, *Boston's Immigrants, 1790–1865* (Cambridge: Harvard University Press, 1941), pp. 124–25.

12. See Robert A. Woods, ed., *The City Wilderness* (Boston: Houghton Mifflin, 1898); Robert A. Woods, ed., *Americans in Process* (Boston: Houghton Mifflin, 1903); Robert A. Woods and Albert J. Kennedy, *The Zone of Emergence*, abridged and edited by Sam B. Warner, Jr. (Cambridge: Harvard University Press, 1962).

13. Woods and Kennedy, *Zone of Emergence*, p. 80.

14. Frederick A. Bushee, "Ethnic Factors in the Population of Boston," *Publications of the American Economic Association*, Third Series, 4 (May 1903).

15. Room, "Cultural Contingencies," pp. 106–7.

16. F. Maurice Parmelee, *Inebriety in Boston* (New York: Eagle Press, 1909), p. 30; see also Bales, "Fixation Factor," p. 21.

17. Adolph Meyer, "Alcohol as a Psychiatric Problem," in *Alcohol and Man*, ed. Haven Emerson (New York: Macmillan, 1933), pp. 296–97.

18. Ibid., p. 297.

19. Ibid.

20. Bales, "Fixation Factor," p. 19.

21. Horatio M. Pollock, "The Prevalence of Mental Disease Due to Alcoholism," in *Alcohol and Man*, p. 365.

22. Ibid., p. 364.

23. Benjamin Malzberg, *Social and Biological Aspects of Mental Disease* (Utica, N.Y.: State Hospitals Press, 1940), p. 203.

24. Glad, "American-Jewish and American Irish Rates of Inebriety," p. 408.

25. Benjamin Malzberg, "A Study of First Admissions with Alcoholic Psychoses in New York State, 1943–1944," *Quarterly Journal of Studies on Alcohol* 8 (September 1947): 294.

26. Ibid., p. 293.

27. Robert Straus and Raymond G. McCarthy, "Non-addictive Pathological Drinking Patterns of Homeless Men," *Quarterly Journal of Studies on Alcohol* 12 (December 1951): 601–11.

28. Jerome H. Skolnick, "A Study of the Relation of Ethnic Background to Arrests for Inebriety," *Quarterly Journal of Studies on Alcohol* 15 (December 1954): 622–30.

29. Personal communication from Charles Snyder. The problem involved attempting to ascertain ethnicity on the basis of last names as they appeared in police records.

30. See, for example, Genevieve Knupfer and Robin Room, "Drinking Patterns and Attitudes of Irish, Jewish, and White Protestant American Men," *Quarterly Journal of Studies on Alcohol* 28 (December 1967), pp. 676–700; Don Cahalan, Ira Cisin, and Helen Crossley, *American Drinking Practices* (New Brunswick: Rutgers Center of Alcohol Studies, 1969), pp. 48–53; Andrew M. Greeley, *Why Can't They Be Like Us?* (New York: Dutton, 1971).

31. Andrew Greeley, William McCready, and Gary Theisen, *Ethnic Drinking Subcultures* (New York: Praeger, 1980), p. 3.

Chapter 2 : Drinking Customs in Great Britain and Ireland

1. M. Dorothy George, *London Life in the 18th Century* (New York: Penguin, 1966), p. 303.

2. John Dunlop, *A Philosophy of Artificial and Compulsory Drinking Usages in Great Britain and Ireland* (London: Houlston and Stoneman, 1839), p. 261.

3. See Dunlop, ibid.; Brian Harrison, "The Power of Drink," *The Listener* 1 (13 February 1969): 204–6; George, *London Life*, pp. 287–307; Norman Longmate, *The Waterdrinkers* (London: Hamish Hamilton, 1968), pp. 13–32; and British Parliamentary Papers, Select Committee on Drunkenness (1834).

4. Robert F. Bales, "The 'Fixation Factor' in Alcohol Addiction: An Hypothesis Derived from a Comparative Study of Irish and

Jewish Social Norms" (unpublished Ph.D. dissertation, Harvard University, 1944), p. 154.

5. Dunlop, *Artificial Drinking Usages*, p. 264.

6. British Parliamentary Papers, p. 399.

7. Bales, "Fixation Factor," pp. 155–62.

8. Harrison, "Power of Drink," p. 204.

9. Bales, "Fixation Factor," p. 163.

10. Friedrich Engels, *The Condition of the Working Class in England* (Stanford, Calif.: Stanford University Press, 1958), pp. 116, 143.

11. Longmate, *Waterdrinkers*, p. 16.

12. Bales, "Fixation Factor," pp. 167–74.

13. Longmate, *Waterdrinkers*, p. 182.

14. Harrison, "Power of Drink," p. 205.

15. Bales, "Fixation Factor," pp. 186–88.

16. Longmate, *Waterdrinkers*, p. 18.

17. Bales, "Fixation Factor," p. 194.

18. Harrison, "Power of Drink," p. 204.

19. Bales, "Fixation Factor," pp. 201–6.

20. Harrison, "Power of Drink," p. 205.

21. Sidney Webb and Beatrice Webb, *The History of Liquor Licensing in England, Principally from 1700 to 1830* (London: Longmans, 1903), pp. 98–100.

22. Bales, "Fixation Factor," p. 224.

23. Harrison, "Power of Drink," p. 204.

24. Ibid.

25. Cyril Greenland, "Habitual Drunkards in Scotland, 1879–1918," *Quarterly Journal of Studies on Alcohol* 21(March 1960): 135–36.

26. Dunlop, *Artificial Drinking Usages*, p. 185.

27. Harrison, "The Power of Drink," p. 205.

28. Longmate, *Waterdrinkers*, p. 15.

29. George, *London Life*, p. 303.

30. Webb and Webb, *Liquor Licensing in England*, p. 99.

31. Longmate, *Waterdrinkers*, pp. 16–17.

32. George, *London Life*, p. 293.

33. Ibid., pp. 300–301.

34. Harrison, "Power of Drink," p. 205.

35. Dunlop, *Artificial Drinking Usages*, pp. 27–28, 55.

36. George, *London Life*, p. 293.

37. Much of the information in this section is from Harrison, "Power of Drink," pp. 204–5; and George, *London Life*, pp. 293, 300–302.

38. Engels, *Working Class*, p. 116.

39. Harrison, "Power of Drink," p. 205.

40. Webb and Webb, *Liquor Licensing in England*, p. 86.

41. Harrison, "Power of Drink," p. 205.

42. J. L. Hammond and Barbara Hammond, *The Age of the Chartists: 1832–1854* (New York: August M. Kelly, 1967), p. 144.

43. Webb and Webb, *Liquor Licensing in England*, p. 49.

44. Hammond and Hammond, *Age of the Chartists*, p. 152.

45. George, *London Life*, pp. 286–87.

46. Dunlop, *Artificial Drinking Usages*, pp. 113–15.

47. Ibid., pp. 6–7.

48. Ibid., pp. 256–57.

49. Longmate, *Waterdrinkers*, p. 19.

50. George, *London Life*, p. 292.

51. British Parliamentary Papers, pp. 4–5.

52. Dunlop, *Artificial Drinking Usages*, p. 120.

53. British Parliamentary Papers, p. 4.

54. Longmate, *Waterdrinkers*, p. 19.

55. See Dunlop, *Artificial Drinking Usages*, pp. 12.14.

Chapter 3 : Temperance and the Redefinition of Drinking

1. Patrick Rogers, *Father Theobald Mathew: Apostle of Temperance* (Dublin: Browne and Nolan, 1943), p. 31.

2. Norman Longmate, *The Waterdrinkers* (London: Hamish Hamilton, 1968), p. 35.

3. Rogers, *Father Theobald Mathew*, p. 37.

4. John Maguire, *Father Mathew: A Biography* (London: Longmans, 1865), pp.31–56.

5. Rogers, *Father Theobald Mathew*, p. 71

6. Quoted in Frank J. Mathew, *Father Mathew: His Life and Times* (London: Cassell, 1890), p. 42.

7. John Hamilton, *Sixty Years' Experience as an Irish Landlord* (London: Digby, Long, 1894), p. 199.

8. Mathew, *Father Mathew*, p. 37.

9. James Birmingham, *A Memoir of the Very Rev. Theobald Mathew* (Dublin: Milliken & Son, 1840), p. 28.

10. William Thackeray, *The Irish Sketch-Book*, 2 vols. (London: Chapman & Hall, 1843), 1:115.

11. Rogers, *Father Theobald Mathew*, p. 53.

12. Maguire, *Father Mathew*, p. 86.

13. Mathew, *Father Mathew*, p. 71.

14. Ibid., p. 38.

15. Birmingham, *Memoir of Theobald Mathew*, p. 57.

16. Maguire, *Father Mathew*, p. 100.

17. Mathew, *Father Mathew*, pp. 38–39.

18. Henry B. Stanton, *Sketches of Reforms and Reformers of Great Britain and Ireland* (New York: Wiley, 1849), p. 343.

19. Lambert McKenna, *Life and Work of Rev. James Aloysius Cullen, S.J.* (London: Longmans, 1924), pp. 302–3.

20. Maguire, *Father Mathew*, pp. 75–79.

21. Longmate, *Waterdrinkers*, p. 114.

22. James Haughton, "Ireland and Father Mathew," in Proceedings of the International Temperance and Prohibition Convention, 1862, ed. Rev. J. C. Street, Dr. F. R. Lees, and Rev. D. Burns (London: Job Caudwell, 1862), p. 69. Some estimates have been high as 7,000,000 teetotalers; see Mathew, Father Mathew, p. 9.

23. Dawson Burns, *A Consecutive Narrative of the Rise, Development, and Extension of the Temperance Reform*, 2 vols. (London: National Temperance Publication Depot, 1881), 1:241. (This work has frequently been cited as *Temperance History*.)

24. Longmate, *Waterdrinkers*, p. 114.

25. Ibid.

26. Burns, *Temperance History*, p. 241.

27. Maguire, *Father Mathew*, pp. 130–31.

28. Ibid., p. 134.

29. Ibid., p. 94.

30. Quoted in ibid., p. 95.

31. Ibid., p. 133.

32. Katherine Tynan, *Father Mathew* (London: MacDonald & Evans, 1908), pp. 139–40.

33. Father Senan, ed., *Capuchin Annual 1930* (Dublin: Father Mathew Record Office, 1929), p. 166.

34. Maguire, *Father Mathew*, p. 174.

35. Ibid.

36. Longmate, *Waterdrinkers*, p. 114.

37. Maguire, *Father Mathew*, p. 149, estimated the overlap in membership at nine-tenths, whereas Longmate, *Waterdrinkers*, p. 114, placed it at three-fourths.

38. Maguire, *Father Mathew*, p. 149.

39. Quoted in ibid., p. 152.

40. Ibid., p. 151.

41. Tynan, *Father Mathew*, pp. 139–40.

42. Burns, *Temperance History*, p. 241.

43. McKenna, *Life and Work of Rev. Cullen*, p. 302.

44. Brian Harrison, "The Power of Drink," *The Listener* 1 (13 February 1969): 206.

45. Brian Harrison, *Drink and the Victorians* (Pittsburgh: University of Pittsburgh Press, 1971), pp. 24–27, 395.

46. Ibid., p. 25

47. Ibid., p. 27.

Chapter 4 : The Irish Family and the Remergence of the Avunculate

1. K. H. Connell, *Irish Peasant Society* (Oxford: Clarendon, 1968), pp. 114–15.

2. Michael Drake, "Marriage and Population Growth in Ireland, 1750–1845," *Economic History Review* 16 (1963–64: 303.

3. Connell, *Irish Peasant Society*, p. 116.

4. Ibid., pp. 115–16.

5. Robert E. Kennedy, *The Irish* (Berkeley: University of California Press, 1973), p. 207.

6. Ibid., p. 171.

7. K. H. Connell, "Marriage in Ireland After the Famine: The Diffusion of the Match," *Journal of the Statistical and Social Inquiry Society of Ireland* 19 (1955–56): 82.

8. Conrad Arensberg, *The Irish Countryman* (Garden City, N.Y.: Natural History Press, 1968), pp. 77–80.

9. Connell, *Irish Peasant Society*, pp. 116–17; Kennedy, *The Irish*, pp. 151–52.

10. Kennedy, *The Irish*, p. 155.

11. Connell, *Irish Peasant Society*, pp. 116–17.

12. Kennedy, *The Irish*, p. 14.

13. John T. Noonan, "Intellectual and Demographic History," *Daedalus* 97 (Spring 1968): 477.

14. E. Estyn Evans, *The Personality of Ireland* (New York: Cambridge University Press, 1973), p. 66.

15. Sean O'Faolain, *The Irish: A Character Study* (New York: Deven-Adair, 1949), p. 19.

16. W. B. Yeats, ed., *Irish Folk Stories and Fairy Tales* (New York: Grosset and Dunlap, n.d.), p. xii.

17. Evans, *The Personality of Ireland*, p. 67.

18. Emmet Larkin, "The Devotional Revolution in Ireland, 1850–75," *American Historical Review* 77 (June 1972): 649.

19. Brian Ingles, *The Story of Ireland*, 2nd ed. (London: Faber and Faber, 1965), p. 195.

20. Larkin, "The Devotional Revolution," pp. 627–45.

21. Joseph Lee, *The Modernization of Irish Society 1848–1918* (Dublin: Gill and Macmillan, 1973), p. 43.

22. Larkin, "The Devotional Revolution," pp. 644–45.

23. Ibid., pp. 649–50.

24. Seán O'Súilleabháin, *Irish Folk Custom and Belief* (Dublin: Cultural Relations Committee of Ireland, n.d.), pp. 76–80.

25. Noonan, "Intellectual and Demographic History," p. 477.

26. Ibid.

27. Connell, *Irish Peasant Society*, p. 172.

28. Ibid., pp. 128–29.

29. Ibid., p. 138.

30. J. H. Whyte, "The Influence of the Catholic Clergy on Elections in Nineteenth-Century Ireland," *English Historical Review* 75 (April 1960): 239–44.

31. Connell, *Irish Peasant Society*, p. 144–45.

32. Ibid., pp. 82–83, quoting S. Sundbarg, *Apercus stalistiques internationaux* (1908), mentions that in the 1890s Ireland possessed the lowest rate of illegitimacy of the European countries surveyed.

33. Ibid., pp. 119–20.

34. Conrad Arensberg and Solon Kimball, *Family and Community in Ireland*, 2nd ed. (Cambridge: Harvard University Press, 1968), pp. 199–2000.

35. Kennedy, *The Irish*, p. 172.

36. On this issue see Jacques Ellul, *A Critique of the New Commonplaces*, trans. Helen Weaver (New York: Knopf, 1968).

37. Jacques Ellul, *To Will and to Do*, trans. C. Edward Hopkin (Philadelphia: Pilgrim Press, 1969), p. 115.

38. Patrick McNabb, "Social Structure," Part 4, in *The Limerick Rural Survey, 1958–1964*, ed. Jeremiah Newman (Tipperary, Ireland: Muintir Na Tire Rural Publications, 1964), pp. 222–23.

39. Connell, "Marriage in Ireland," pp. 82–83.

40. Ibid., p. 83.

41. Claude Levi-Strauss, *Structural Anthropology*, trans. Claire Jacobson and Brooke Grundfest Schoepf (Garden City, N.Y.: Anchor Books, 1967), pp. 31–32.

42. Ibid., p. 49.

43. Ibid., pp. 44–45.

44. Arensberg and Kimball, *Family and Community*, p. 55.

45. Ibid., p. 56.

46. Arland Ussher, "The Boundary Between the Sexes," in *The Vanishing Irish*, ed. John O'Brien (London: W. H. Allen, 1954), pp. 154–55.

47. McNabb, "Social Structure," pp. 229–30.

48. Ibid., p. 232.

49. Arensberg and Kimball, *Family and Community*, p. 65.

50. Ibid., p. 66.
51. Levi-Strauss, *Structural Anthropology*, pp. 46–47.
52. Ibid., p. 47.

Chapter 5: Irish Drinking as Cultural Remission

1. See Raymond Aron, *Main Currents in Sociological Thought*, 2 vols., trans. Richard Howard and Helen Weaver (New York: Anchor Books, 1970), 2:244–46, for a discussion of Weber's concept of the ideal type of a historical particular.
2. Patrick McNabb, "Social Structure," Part 4, in *The Limerick Rural Survey, 1958–1964,* ed. Jeremiah Newman (Tipperary, Ireland: Muintir Na Tire Rural Publications, 1964), p. 236.
3. Ibid.
4. Ibid., p. 224.
5. Conrad Arensberg, *The Irish Countryman* (Garden City, N.Y.: Natural History Press, 1968), chap. 4 passim.
6. McNabb, "Social Structure," p. 235.
7. Personal communication from Patrick McNabb.
8. Hugh Brody, *Inishkillane* (London: Allen Lane The Penguin Press, 1973).
9. Ibid., chap. 6 passim.
10. McNabb, "Social Structure," p. 233.
11. Peter L. Berger, *Invitation to Sociology* (Garden City, N.Y.: Anchor Books, 1963), p. 87.
12. Arnold van Gennep, *The Rites of Passage*, trans. Monika B. Vizedom and Gabrielle L. Coffee (Chicago: University of Chicago Press, 1960), p. 3.
13. Ibid., pp. 10–11.
14. McNabb, "Social Structure," p. 236.
15. McNabb, "Social Structure," pp. 218–19.
16. Van Gennep, *Rites of Passage*, pp. 8–9.
17. Ibid., p. 18.
18. Ibid., p. 29.

19. Personal communication from Patrick McNabb.

20. McNabb, "Social Structure," pp. 235–36.

21. Ibid., p. 224.

22. Ibid., 236.

23. Robert F. Bales, "The 'Fixation Factor' in Alcohol Addiction: An Hypothesis Derived from a Comparative Study of Irish and Jewish Social Norms" (unpublished Ph.D. dissertation, Harvard University, 1944), pp. 190–91.

24. McNabb, "Social Structure," p. 236.

25. Personal communication from Patrick McNabb.

26. McNabb, "Social Structure," p. 233.

27. In an early 1970s study Hugh Brody concluded that is difficult to interest a young man in remaining on the land, even as a house-holder. Rural economic insecurity and the attractions of urban life loom too large. Farmers do not marry to the same extent they once did. Hence the bachelor group has lost its raison d'être and is dissolving along with the closed community. See Brody, *Inishkillane*, pp. 119–22.

28. Philip Rieff, *The Triumph of the Therapeutic* (New York: Harper Torchbooks, 1968), pp. 232–33.

29. Erik H. Erikson, *Childhood and Society*, 2nd ed. (New York: Norton, 1963), p. 292.

30. Ibid., p. 293.

31. J. J. Dunne, *The First Pioneer* (Longford, Ireland: Leader Works, 1964), p. 30.

32. Lambert McKenna, *Life and Work of Rev. James Aloysius Cullen, S. J.* (London: Longmans, 1924), p. 306.

33. Elise de la Fontaine, "Cultural and Psychological Implications in Case Work Treatment with Irish Clients," in *Cultural Problems in Social Case Work* (New York: Family Welfare Association of America, 1940), p. 32.

34. Ibid.; Bales, "Fixation Factor," pp. 181–83.

35. McNabb, "Social Structure," p. 237.

36. Ibid., p. 233.

37. Personal Communication from Patrick McNabb.

38. Bales, "Fixation Factor," p. 183.

39. L. O'Neill, S. J., *The Sacred Heart Pioneer Total Abstinence Association* (1963), p. 10.

40. Ibid., p. 25.
41. Ibid., p. 18.
42. Bales, "Fixation Factor," pp. 183–84.
43. Max Horkheimer and Theodor W. Adorno, *Dialectic of Enlightenment*, trans. John Cumming (New York: Herder & Herder, 1972), p. 33.
44. Elsie Leach, "Impressions of the Character of the Irish, of the Irish-Americans, and of the Jewish-Americans" (Berkeley, Calif.: Drinking Practices Study, Paper No. 7, 1964), pp. 1–19 passim.

Chapter 6: The Culture of Irish-American Drinking

1. K. H. Connell, *Irish Peasant Society* (Oxford: Clarendon, 1968), p. 115.
2. Robert E. Kennedy, *The Irish* (Berkeley: University of California Press, 1973), p. 207.
3. Brendan Walsh, "Some Irish Population Problems Reconsidered" (Dublin: Economic and Social Research Institute, Paper No. 42, November 1968), p. 10.
4. S. H. Cousens, "The Regional Pattern of Emigration During the Great Irish Famine, 1846–51," *Institute of British Geographers, Transactions and Papers* (1960): 119–34.
5. S. H. Cousens, "Emigration and Demographic change in Ireland, 1851–1861," *Economic History Review* 14 (1961): 275–88; S. H. Cousens, "the Regional Variations in Population Changes in Ireland, 1861–1881," *Economic History Review* 17 (1964): 300–321.
6. Kennedy, *The Irish*, p. 207.
7. Cousens, "Regional Variations," p. 312; Cousens, "Emigration and Demographic Change," p. 275.
8. Cousens, "Regional Variations," pp. 311–13.
9. Oscar Handlin, *Boston's Immigrants*, 2nd ed. (Cambridge: Harvard University Press, Belknap Press, 1959), p. 91.
10. Robert Ernst, *Immigrant Life in New York City, 1825–1863* (New York: King's Crown, 1949), p. 40.

11. Handlin, *Boston's Immigrants*, pp. 104–5.

12. Quoted in ibid., p. 106.

13. Quoted in George Potter, *To the Golden Door* (Boston: Little, Brown, 1960), pp. 320–21.

14. Ibid., p. 338.

15. Ernst, *Immigrant Life*, p. 63.

16. Handlin, *Boston's Immigrants*, p. 101–2.

17. Ibid., p. 109.

18. Ibid., p. 115.

19. Andrew M. Greeley, *That Most Distressful Nation* (Chicago: Quandrangle Books, 1972), chap. 5 passim.

20. Frederick Bushee, "Ethnic Factors in the Population of Boston," *Publications of the American Economic Association* 4 (May 1903): 114.

21. John F. Maguire, *The Irish in America* (New York: Arno Press, 1969), p. 333; Robert A. Woods, ed., *The City Wilderness* (Boston: Houghton Mifflin, 1898), p. 172.

22. Ernst, *Immigrant Life*, pp. 58–59.

23. Handlin, *Boston's Immigrants*, p. 122.

24. Ernst, *Immigrant Life*, p. 58.

25. Quoted in Maguire, *Irish in America*, p. 340.

26. Ibid.

27. Ibid., p. 341.

28. *The Works of Stephen Crane*, vol. 1, Bowery Tales (Charlottesville: University Press of Virginia, 1969).

29. Eric Solomon, *Stephen Crane* (Cambridge: Harvard University Press, 1966), p. 35.

30. Ibid., pp. 41–42.

31. Ibid., p. 40.

32. Ibid.

33. Elise de la Fontaine, "Cultural and Psychological Implications in Case Work Treatment with Irish Clients," in *Cultural Problems in Social Case Work* (New York: Family Welfare Association of American, 1940), pp. 25–33.

34. Nathan Glazer and Daniel Patrick Moynihan, *Beyond the Melting Pot* (Cambridge: M.I.T. Press, 1963), p. 197.

35. De la Fontaine, "Case Work Treatment," pp. 30–31.

36. Philip H. Bagenal, *The American Irish and Their Influence on Irish Politics* (London: Kegan Paul, Trench, 1882), p. 534.

37. Robert A. Woods and Albert J. Kennedy, *The Zone of Emergence* (Cambridge: Harvard University Press, 1962), p. 145.

38. See James J. Walsh, "Are Irish Catholics Dying Out in This Country?," *America*, 5 August 1922, pp. 365–66; James Walsh, "Catholic Bachelors and Old Maids," *America*, 12 August 1922, pp. 389–90; James Walsh, "The Disappearing Irish in America," *America*, 1 May 1926, pp. 56–57; M. V. Kelly, "The Suicide of the Irish Race," *America*, 17 November 1928, pp. 128–29, 24 November 1928, pp. 155–56, and 1 December 1928, pp. 179–80; and James Walsh, "Shy Irish Bachelors," *America*, 29 March 1930, pp. 592–93.

39. Mary Mattis, "Irish Mobility in Buffalo, New York, 1855–1875," paper presented at the Midwest Sociological Meetings, 10 April 1975, p. 11.

40. Greeley, Most Distressful Nation, p. 110.

41. See especially the work of Stephen Crane, but also that of Eugene O'Neill and James T. Farrell.

42. *Works of Stephen Crane*.

43. Bushee, "Ethnic Factors," p. 151.

44. Woods, *City Wilderness*, p. 122.

45. Ibid., p. 118.

46. Ibid., pp. 135–36.

47. Ibid., p. 126.

48. Ibid., p. 127.

49. Oscar Handlin, *The Uprooted* (New York: Grosset & Dunlap, 1951), chap. 10 passim.

50. Edward C. Banfield, *The Moral Basis of a Backward Society* (New York: Free Press, 1958).

51. Glazer and Moynihan, Melting Pot, p. 197.

52. Jacques Ellul, *The Political Illusion*, trans. Konard Kellen (New York: Vintage Books, 1972), p. 21.

53. See Robert N. Nellah, "Civil Religion in America," in *Religion American Style*, ed. Patrick H. McNamara (New York: Harper & Row, 1974), pp. 73–90; see also Thomas Luckmann, *The Invisible Religion* (New York: Macmillan, 1967).

54. Ellul, *Political Illusion*, p. 23.

55. Woods, *City Wilderness*, p. 134.

56. Robert A. Woods, ed., *Americans in Process* (Boston: Houghton Mifflin, 1903), p. 63.

57. Carl Wittke, *The Irish in America* (Baton Rouge: Louisiana State University Press, 1956), p. 161.

58. Woods, *Americans in Process*, p. 63.

59. Woods, *City Wilderness*, p. 136.

60. Ibid., p. 127.

61. Ibid., pp. 127–28.

62. Ibid., p. 116.

63. Jacques Ellul, "Technological Morality," in *To Will and to Do*, trans. C. Edward Hopkin (Philadelphia: Pilgrim Press, 1969), pp. 185–98.

64. Handlin, *Boston's Immigrants*, p. 121; Potter, *Golden Door*, p. 518.

65. Potter, *Golden Door*, p. 518.

66. Handlin, *Boston's Immigrants*, p. 121.

67. Ibid., p. 110.

68. Maguire, *Irish in America*, pp. 286–87.

69. Woods, *Americans in Process*, p. 107.

70. William V. Shannon, *The American Irish* (New York: Macmillan, 1963), p. 34.

71. Quoted in Potter, *Golden Door*, p. 519.

72. Maguire, *Irish in America*, p. 287.

73. Woods, *City Wilderness*, p. 138.

74. Ibid., pp. 128–29.

75. Ibid., pp. 129–31.

76. Edward A. Steiner, *From Alien to Citizen* (New York: Revell, 1914), p. 207.

77. Glazer and Moynihan, *Melting Pot*, pp. 226, 228.

78. Finley Peter Dunne, *Mr. Dooley at His Best*, ed. Elmer Ellis (New York: Scribner's, 1942), pp. 114–15.

79. Daniel Bell, "Crime as an American Way of Life," in *The End of Ideology* (New York: Free Press, 1965), pp. 127–50.

80. Functionalism, structural functionalism, systems theory, and symbolic interactionism assume this explicitly or implicitly.

81. Among others, see Erving Goffman, *Asylums* (Garden City, N.Y.: Anchor Books, 1961), pp. 318–20; and Alvin W. Gouldner, "The Sociologist as Partisan: Sociology and the Welfare State," *American Sociologist* 3 (May 1968): 105–7.

82. Erik H. Erikson, *Identity: Youth and Crisis* (New York: Norton, 1968), pp. 47–48.

83. Handlin, *Uprooted*, p. 38.

84. Erikson, *Identity*, p. 50.

85. Ibid.

86. Handlin, *Uprooted*, p. 285.

87. Thomas N. Brown, "Social Discrimination Against the Irish in the United States," mimeographed pamphlet in the Library of Jewish Information (American Jewish Committee, November 1958), p. 18.

88. Ibid.

89. *Bowery Tales*, p. 146.

90. Ibid.

91. Ibid., p. 159.

92. Quoted in Elsie Leach, "Impressions of the Character of the Irish, of the Irish-Americans, and of Jewish-Americans" (Berkeley, Calif.: Drinking Practices Study, Paper No. 7, 1964), p. 23.

93. Stephen R. Grecco, "High Hopes: Eugene O'Neill and Alcohol," *Yale French Studies*, no. 50, Intoxication and Literature (1974), p. 42.

94. Max Horkheimer and Theodor W. Adorno, *Dialectic of Enlightenment*, trans. John Cumming (New York: Herder & Herder, 1972), p. 33.

95. *Bowery Tales*, p. 141.

96. Quoted in Leach, "Impressions," p. 23.

97. Erik H. Erikson, *Childhood and Society*, 2nd ed. (New York: Norton, 1963), pp. 323–24.

98. Ibid., pp. 291–92.

99. Ibid., p. 295.

100. Ibid., p. 292.

101. Ibid., pp. 292–93.

102. Ibid., p. 319.

103. Ibid., p. 322.

104. Ibid.

105. Woods, *Americans in Process*, p. 63

106. Erikson, *Identity*, p. 87.

107. Ibid., p. 174.

108. Ibid., p. 175.

Chapter 7: "A Religion of Saloonkeepers": The Stereotype of the Irish-American as Drunkard

1. Quoted in Sister Joan Bland, *Hibernian Crusade* (Washington, D.C.: Catholic University Press, 1951), p. 127.

2. David Rothman, *The Discovery of the Asylum* (Boston: Little, Brown, 1971), p. 254.

3. George Potter, *To the Golden Door* (Boston: Little, Brown, 1960), p. 170; Rothman, *Asylum*, chap. 1 passim.

4. Robert Ernst, *Immigrant Life in New York City*, 1825–1863 (New York: King's Crown, 1949), p. 66; and David Matza, "The Disreputable Poor," in *The Collective Definition of Deviance*, ed. F. James Davis and Richard Stivers (New York: Free Press, 1975), p. 219.

5. Edward Snyder, "The Wild Irish: A Study of Some English Satires Against the Irish, Scots, and Welsh," *Modern Philology* 17 (April 1920): 160.

6. Carl Wittke, *The Irish in America* (Baton Rouge: Louisiana State University Press, 1956), p. 48.

7. Dennis Clark, *The Irish in Philadelphia* (Philadelphia: Temple University Press, 1973), p. 103; and Potter, *Golden Door*, p. 517.

8. Wittke, *Irish in America*, p. 262.

9. Potter, *Golden Door*, pp. 128–31; W. F. Adams, *Ireland and Irish Emigration to the New World from 1815 to the Famine* (New Haven: Yale University Press, 1932).

10. John Francis Maguire, *The Irish in America* (New York: Arno Press, 1969), pp. 193–94.

11. Ernst, *Immigrant Life*, p. 67.

12. *Daily Sun*, 11 May 1853, quoted in the *Irish American*, 28 May 1853, cited in ibid.

13. Oscar Handlin, *Boston's Immigrants*, 2nd ed. (Cambridge: Harvard University Press, Belknap Press, 1959), p. 62.

14. Potter, *Golden Door*, p., 318. See Potter for a general discussion of Irish labor conditions.

15. Ibid., p. 337.

16. Ibid., p. 411; Wittke, *Irish in America*, p. 42.

17. Vera Shlakman, *Economic History of a Factory Town* (New York: Octagon Books, 1969), p. 49.

18. Potter, *Golden Door*, p. 320.

19. Ibid., p. 338.

20. Ibid., p. 318.

21. Ibid., p. 168.

22. Ibid.; and Wittke, *Irish in America*, p. 47.

23. Lawrence Ellwood, "The Immigrant in American Fiction, 1890–1920" (unpublished Ph.D. dissertation, Western Reserve University, 1943), p. 101.

24. Ernst, *Immigrant Life*, p. 57.

25. Roger Lane, *Policing the City: Boston, 1822–1885* (Cambridge: Harvard University Press, 1967), p. 76.

26. Potter, *Golden Door*, p. 526.

27. Eric Patridge, *A Dictionary of the Underworld* (London: Routledge & Kegan Paul, 1968), p. 492.

28. Howard J. Ehrlich, *The Social Psychology of Prejudice* (New York: Wiley, 1973), p. 20.

29. Jacques Ellul, *Propaganda*, trans. Konard Kellen and Jean Lerner (New York: Knopf, 1969), p. 163.

30. Ibid.

31. Gordon Allport, *The Nature of Prejudice*, (Garden City, N.Y.: Anchor, 1958), p. 188.

32. Ibid., p. 187.

33. H. L. Mencken, *The American Language*, Supplement I (New York: Knopf, 1945), p. 604.

34. Eric Patridge, *The Routledge Dictionary of Historical Slang* (London: Routledge & Kegan Paul, 1973), pp. 478–79.

35. Potter, *Golden Door*, pp. 528–29.

36. Wittke, *Irish in America*, p. 41.

37. An extract from a journalist's letter of 16 March 1859, appearing in Edith Abbot, ed. *Historical Aspects of the Immigration Problem* (Chicago: University of Chicago Press, 1926), p. 516.

38. See Bourget's remarks in Oscar Handlin, ed., *This Was America* (Cambridge: Harvard University Press, 1949), p. 382.

39. L. P. Curtis, *Apes and Angels* (Washington, D.C.: Smithsonian Institution Press, 1971), chap. 5 passim.

40. Ibid., p. 101.

41. See Andrew M. Greeley, *That Most Distressful Nation* (Chicago: Quadrangle Books, 1972), p. 199.

42. Handlin, *This Was America*, p. 382.

43. Abbott, *Immigration Problem*, pp. 831–32.

44. Ibid., pp. 535–36.

45. Handlin, *This Was America*, p. 256.

46. Quoted in Andrew Saveth, *American Historians and European Immigrants* (New York: Columbia University Press, 1948), pp. 56–57

47. Quoted in Barbara Solomon, *Ancestors and Immigrants* (Cambridge: Harvard University Press, 1956), p. 71.

48. Wittke, *Irish in America*, p. 245.

49. Ibid.

50. Thomas Beer, *The Mauve Decade* (New York: Knopf, 1926), p. 165.

51. Wittke, *Irish in America*, p. 247.

52. L. P. Curtis, *Anglo-Saxons and Celts* (Bridgeport, Conn.: Conference on British Studies, 1968), p. 13.

53. Carl Wittke, "The Immigrant Theme on the American Stage," *Mississippi Valley Historical Review* 39 (September 1952): 214.

54. Snyder, "Wild Irish," p. 149.

55. See ibid., pp. 162–63, and Maurice Bourgeois, *John Millington Synge and the Irish Theatre* (New York: Benjamin Bloom, 1965), p. 108.

56. Curtis, *Anglo-Saxons and Celts*, p. 52; Beer, Mauve Decade, p. 149; G. C. Duggan, *The Stage Irishman* (New York: Benjamin Bloom, 1969), p. 290.

57. Bourgeois, *Synge*, pp. 109–10.

58. Wittke, "Immigrant Theme," p. 214.

59. Wittke, *Irish in America*, p. 254.

60. Ibid., p. 255.

61. Margaret G. Mayorga, *A Short History of the American Drama* (New York: Dodd, Mead, 1932), p. 161.

62. Wittke, *Irish in America*, p. 255.

63. Ibid., p. 258.

64. Ibid., p. 263.

65. *Nation*, 11 March 1875.

66. *New York Times*, 27 April 1853.

67. Eric Solomon, *Stephen Crane* (Cambridge: Harvard University Press, 1966), p. 53.

68. R. W. Stallman and E. R. Hagemann, eds., *The New York City Sketches of Stephen Crane* (New York: New York University Press, 1966), p. 22.

69. Ibid., p. 25.

70. Wittke, *Irish in America*, p. 262.

71. Curtis, *Anglo-Saxons and Celts*, pp. 11–12.

72. Solomon, *Ancestors and Immigrants*, p. 60.

73. Curtis, *Anglo-Saxons and Celts*, p. 90.

74. Potter, *Golden Door*, p. 167.

75. John Higham, *Strangers in the Land* (New York: Atheneum, 1963), pp. 5–10.

76. See James Froude, "Romanism and the Irish Race in the United States," *North American Review* 129 (1879): 519–36, and 130 (1880): 31–50.

77. See Higham, *Strangers*, pp. 5 and 132–34, on this subject.

78. Ibid., p. 134.

79. Richard Hofstadter, *Social Darwinism in American Thought* (Boston: Beacon, 1955), pp. 172–73; and Saveth, American Historians, p. 10.

80. Hofstader, *Social Darwinism*, p. 31.

81. Lewis Coser, *Masters of Sociological Thought* (New York: Harcourt Brace, 1971), p. 90; Hofstadter, *Social Darwinism*, pp. 37–38.

82. Hofstadter, *Social Darwinism*, p. 37.

83. Perry Miller, *American Thought: Civil War to World War I* (New York: Holt, Rinehart & Winston, 1957), p. xiii.

84. Hofstadter, *Social Darwinism*, p. 201.

85. See Higham, *Strangers*.

86. See Joseph Gusfield, *Symbolic Crusade* (Urbana: University of Illinois Press, 1963).

87. Curtis, *Anglo-Saxons and Celts*, p. 109.

88. Curtis, *Apes and Angels*, chap. 6 passim.

89. Wittke, *Irish in America*, p. 202.

90. Potter, *Golden Door*, p. 282.

91. Quoted in ibid.

92. Handlin, *Boston's Immigrants*, p. 134.

93. Wittke, *Irish in America*, p. 247.

94. Beer, *Mauve Decade*, p. 159.

95. Wittke, *Irish in America*, p. 247.

96. Ibid., p. 161.

97. William V. Shannon, *The American Irish* (New York: Macmillan, 1963), p. 132.

98. Ibid., p. 133.

99. See Solomon, *Ancestors and Immigrants*, pp. 152–55, on this topic.

100. Ibid., p. 153.

101. Ibid., p. 155.

102. Quoted in ibid.

103. Ibid., p. 154.

104. Beer, *Mauve Decade*, p. 152.

105. Ibid., p. 158.

106. Potter, *Golden Door*, p. 433.

107. Ibid., p. 434.

108. Ibid., p. 433.

109. Beer, *Mauve Decade*, p. 162.

110. Wittke, *Irish in America*, p. 161.

111. Thomas N. Brown, *Irish-American Nationalism, 1870–1890* (Philadelphia: Lippincott, 1966), p. 180.

112. Beer, *Mauve Decade*, p. 151.

113. Nathan Glazer and Daniel Patrick Moynihan, *Beyond the Melting Pot* (Cambridge: M.I.T. Press, 1964), p. 250; Moynihan wrote the section on the Irish.

114. Andrew M. Greeley, *That Most Distressful Nation* (Chicago: Quandrangle Books, 1972), p. 143.

115. Quoted in Beer, *Mauve Decade*, p. 153.

116. See Shannon, *American Irish*, pp. 131, 142–43; and Ernst, *Immigrant* Life, p. 148.

117. Shannon, *American Irish*, pp. 144–45.

118. Quoted in ibid., p. 145.

119. Finley Peter Dunne, *Mr. Dooley on Ivrything and Ivrybody*, ed. Robert Hutchinson (New York: Dover, 1963), pp. 133–34.

120. Finley Peter Dunne, *The World of Mr. Dooley*, ed. Louis Filler (New York: Collier Books, 1962), p. 194.

121. Curtis, *Anglo-Saxons and Celts*, pp. 64–65.

122. Erik H. Erikson, *Identity: Youth and Crisis* (New York: Norton, 1968), p. 59; on this point see also Allport, *Nature of Prejudice*, pp. 147–48.

123. Erikson, *Identity*, p. 304.

124. Daniel J. Boorstin, *Democracy and Its Discontents* (New York: Random House, 1974), pp. 37–40.

125. Ellul, *Propaganda*, p. 111.

126. Boorstin, *Democracy*, pp. 12–15.

127. Ibid., p. 20.

128. Ellul, *Propaganda*, p. 206.

Chapter 8: The Hair of the Dog: A Dialectical Theory of Iris-American Alcoholism

1. Thomas N. Brown, *Irish-American Nationalism, 1870–1890* (Philadelphia: Lippincott, 1966), p. 180.

2. Erik H. Erikson, *Identity: Youth and Crisis* (New York: Norton, 1968), p. 50.

3. I wish to thank Robin Room for bringing the problem of alcoholism among Irish-American women to my attention.

4. Robert Straus and Selden D. Bacon, *Drinking in College* (New Haven: Yale University Press, 1953), pp. 144–45; the hypothesis can be attributed to Isidor Thorner, "Ascetic Protestantism and Alcoholism," *Psychiatry* 16 (1953): 171.

5. See especially *Maggie: A Girl of the Streets*, in *The Works of Stephen Crane*, vol. 1, Bowery Tales, ed. Fredson Bowers (Charlottesville: University Press of Virginia, 1969).

6. On the side of those who maintain that Ireland posesses a high rate of alcoholism, see Dermot Walsh, "Alcoholism in Dublin," *Journal of the Irish Medical Association* 61 (May 1968): 153–56; Dermot Walsh, "Alcoholism in the Republic of Ireland," *British Journal of Psychiatry* 115 (September 1969): 1023–25; and Noreen Kearney, M. P. Lawler, and Dermot Walsh, "Alcoholic Drinking in a Dublin Corporation Housing Estate," *Journal of the Irish Medical Association* 62 (April 1969): 140–42. On the other side are those who maintain that Ireland has a relatively low rate by international comparison. See R. Lynn and S. Hampson, "Alcoholism and Alcohol Consumption in Ireland," *Journal of the Irish Medical Association* 63 (February 1970): 39–42; and R. Lynn, *Personality and National Character* (Oxford: Pergamon Press, 1971).

7. I wish to thank Edmund Dougan for reminding me not to overlook the differential impact of poverty among the Irish in Ireland and the Irish in America.

8. K. H. Connell, "Illicit Distillation" and "Ether-Drinking in Ulster," in *Irish Peasant Society* (Oxford: Clarendon, 1968), pp. 1–50 and 87–111.

Afterword: Irish-American Drinking Today

1. Nathan Glazer and Daniel Patrick Moynihan, *Beyond the Melting Pot* (Cambridge: MIT Press, 1963).

2. Martha Wolfenstein, "The Emergence of Fun Morality," *Journal of Social Issues* 7 (1951): 15–25.

3. David Riesman, *The Lonely Crowd* (New Haven: Yale University Press, 1961).

4. Ibid., p. 189.

5. Studs Terkel, *Working* (New York: Avon, 1975).

6. Jacques Ellul, *The New Demons*, Trans. C. Edward Hopkin (New York: Seabury, 1975), ch. 3.

7. Carl Wittke, *The Irish in America* (Baton Rouge: Louisiana State University Press, 1956), p. 262.

8. Martin Marty, *A Nation of Behavers* (Chicago: University of Chicago Press, 1976), pp. 164–69.

9. Ernst Troeltsch, *The Social Teaching of the Christian Churches*, Vol. 1, Trans. Olive Wyon (New York: Macmillan, 1931).

10. Will Herberg, *Protestant, Catholic, Jew* (Garden City: Anchor Books, 1960), p. 267.

11. Andrew Greeley, *That Most Distressful Nation* (New York: Quadrangle, 1972).

12. Thomas Luckmann, *The Invisible Religion* (New York: Macmillan, 1967).

TABLE SOURCES

1. John Dunlop, *A Philosophy of Artificial and Compulsory Drinking Usages in Great Britain and Ireland* (London: Houlston & Stoneman, 1839), pp. 13–14.
2. John Maguire, *Father Mathew: A Biography* (London: Longmans, 1865), p. 131.
3. K. H. Connell, "Marriage in Ireland After the Famine: The Diffusion of the Match," *Journal of the Statistical and Social Inquiry Society of Ireland* 19 (1955–56): 83.
4. *Reports,* Commission on Emigration and Other Population Problems, 1948–1954 (Dublin: Stationery Office, 1954), p. 63.
5. *Reports,* Commission on Emigration and Other Population Problems, 1948–1954 (Dublin: Stationery Office, 1954), 72.
6. S. H. Cousens, "The Regional Variations in Population Changes in Ireland, 1861–1881," *Economic History Review* 17 (1964): 311.
7. Frederick Bushee, "Ethnic Factors in the Population of Boston," *Publications of the American Economic Association* 4 (May 1903): 17.

ACKNOWLEDGMENTS

This study began at the Social Sciences Research Center, University College Galway, Ireland, where I was a research fellow working on my doctoral dissertation from Southern Illinois University. I am grateful to Herman Lantz, Peter Munch, Edmund Dougan, and especially Charles Snyder for their comments and encouragement at that stage of my research. Later Robin Room made a detailed critique of my dissertation for which I am much indebted.

Subsequent research was completed at Illinois State University in the mid 1970s with the assistance of Andrew Churchirillo and John Moore.

For the revised edition 2000 I wish to thank Jo Anne Geigner and Nancy Russell for typing the manuscript. Brian Braye and Joanne Long helped with the reproduction of the cartoons in chapter 7. Larry McBride invariably offered sound advice on everything from my intended audience to the cover of the book. It is my good fortune, once again, to have had Frank Oveis and his colleagues at Continuum handle the editing and production of my book.

How can I ever repay Andrew Greeley for taking an interest in the first edition of *Hair of the Dog* and in my subsequent career? He has never failed to read my manuscripts and offer advice. Without him my academic career would have been diminished.

Two former students, Claude Oberheim and Patricia Walsh, believed that *Hair of the Dog* should be back in print. Without their insistence—a kind of gentle nagging—this book would still be out of print. I am grateful to both.

I wish to thank my family—my father, my sister Ann, my sons Mark and Michael, and my daughter-in-law Rachelle—for their love and encouragement over the years.

My indebtedness begins and ends with my wife Janet, who is both my severest critic and my staunchest supporter. Not only did she assist in proofreading but offered many suggestions about content and style, always with sound judgment.

INDEX